# RACE AND UPWARD MOBILITY

*Stanford Studies in*
COMPARATIVE RACE AND ETHNICITY

# RACE AND
# UPWARD MOBILITY

*Seeking, Gatekeeping,*

*and Other Class Strategies*

*in Postwar America*

Elda María Román

Stanford University Press
Stanford, California

Stanford University Press
Stanford, California

This book has been partially underwritten by the Stanford Authors Fund. We are
grateful to the Fund for its support of scholarship by first-time authors. For more
information, please see www.sup.org/authors/authorsfund.

Printed in the United States of America on acid-free, archival-quality paper

Library of Congress Cataloging-in-Publication Data

Names: Román, Elda María, 1983– author.
Title: Race and upward mobility : seeking, gatekeeping, and other class strategies in
postwar America / Elda María Román.
Other titles: Stanford studies in comparative race and ethnicity.
Description: Stanford, California : Stanford University Press, 2017. |
Series: Stanford studies in comparative race and ethnicity | Includes bibliographical
references and index.
Identifiers: LCCN 2017004007 | ISBN 9781503602847 (cloth : alk. paper) |
ISBN 9781503603783 (pbk. : alk. paper) | ISBN 9781503603882 (epub)
Subjects: LCSH: American literature—Minority authors—History and criticism. |
African Americans in literature. | Mexican Americans in literature. | Social classes in
literature. | Social mobility in literature. | Ethnicity in literature. | Race in literature.
Classification: LCC PS153.M56 R66 2018 | DDC 810.9/920693—dc23
LC record available at https://lccn.loc.gov/2017004007

Typeset by Bruce Lundquist in 10.5/15 Adobe Garamond

*Dedicated to my parents, Elda and Miguel Román*

# CONTENTS

# ACKNOWLEDGMENTS

My book partly explores how much economic language informs the way we talk about identities, and the genre of acknowledgements is full of economic language; we credit the people and the support we value and the debts of gratitude we owe. We do so because there is so much labor involved. A lot of invisible labor goes into mentoring someone, and with heartfelt appreciation, I wish to recognize and thank those who helped me as I was conceptualizing and developing this project. Paula Moya has mentored me since I was a sophomore in college, modeling how to be a socially conscious and interdisciplinary scholar, and I can never thank her enough for coming into my life when she did, and for helping me ever since. I feel similarly fortunate to have learned from Ramón Saldívar, whose attention to form and politics shaped my scholarship and teaching in significant ways. At Stanford, I was also lucky to work with Michele Elam and Gavin Jones. Every draft with feedback from Michele felt like a gift, and I thank her for all her comments and for life advice that has made all the difference. Thank you to Gavin for also pushing my analyses further and for the many conversations about social class, including one that became central to this book's theoretical framework. Infinite thanks also to William "Sandy" Darity, for helping me see how I might produce scholarship combining literary analysis with the social sciences and for inspiring me through his commitment to economic and social change.

I am also so grateful for the intellectual engagement and support I have received as a faculty member in the English department at USC. John Carlos Rowe generously read the entire manuscript and provided invaluable advice. He, Tania Modleski, Viet Thanh Nguyen, David Román, and Karen Tongson deserve special thanks for all the help they have given me on book matters and more. I am also thankful for the feedback that Richard Berg, Hilary Schor, and Bruce Smith gave me on various chapters, which helped me strengthen the book's ideas and organization. I have also benefited from the collegiality and words of wisdom provided by Emily Anderson, Aimee Bender, Joseph Boone, Leo Braudy, Joseph Dane, Percival Everett, Kate Flint, Chris Freeman, Alice Gambrell, Larry Green, Devin Griffiths, Tim Gustafson, William Handley, Mark Irwin, Heather James, Dana Johnson, Rebecca Lemon, and Susan Segal. Thank you so much to department chairs Meg Russett and David St. John for helping me secure time and resources to complete this book. I thank Nellie Ayala-Reyes and Flora Ruiz for all their kindness toward me. I also thank colleagues in other departments who shared their time and advice: Alice Echols, Timothy Pinkston, Shana Redmond, Camille Gear Rich, Nayan Shah, and Jody Agius Vallejo. This project starts off with a discussion of two Georges, and I would be remiss if I did not thank two Georges who have helped me and whose mentoring of students and faculty at all levels I really admire: George Sánchez (at USC) and George Lipsitz (at UCSB). Thanks also to USC students Cecilia Caballero and Carrie Moore, for such excellent research assistance.

Thank you to Kate Wahl, Hazel Markus, Paula Moya, Jessica Ling, Bruce Lundquist, David Horne, Micah Siegel, and Stanford University Press for all their help in making the publication of this project possible. I am also indebted to those at other institutions who engaged with this work. As I was finishing up the book, Ralph Rodriguez served as my mentor through a Woodrow Wilson fellowship. I thank him for all his advice, for sharp insights, and for being a wonderful person all around. A *tremendous* thanks to John Alba Cutler, Marcial González, José Limón, Julie Avril Minich, and Randy Ontiveros for providing crucial commentary and suggestions. I also deeply appreciate all the feedback that Randy and my other anonymous reviewer gave me on the book manuscript; I thank them for taking the time to give comments that were clarifying as well as encouraging. I also wish to thank the anonymous reviewers of my *Aztlán* and *Contemporary Literature* articles for helping me develop early versions of this project. This book has also benefited from the engagement and insights of Ernest L. Gibson, Alma Granado, Monica Hannah, Molly Pulda, Cherene Sherrard-Johnson, and Katie Van-Heest—thank you all! Conversations with Herman Beavers, Gerry Cadava, Prudence Carter, Harry Elam, John Morán

González, Gordon Hutner, Tomás Jiménez, Douglas Jones, Lee Konstantinou, Anthony Macías, José David Saldívar, SOUL, and Salamishah Tillet were illuminating and influential, and I thank them for all their help. Thank you also to Rachel González-Martin, Sylvia Martínez, and the Latino Studies Program at Indiana University for inviting me to participate in the 2016 Politics of Social Class and Latino/a Identities symposium.

Thank you to the people and programs that helped me get to and through graduate school. When I was a high school student, the Pre-College Enrichment Program at Brown University paired me with Megan Lynch, a Brown undergraduate, and I thank the program and Megan for all the time she spent with me and for helping me through the college application process. At Brown, Stephanie Merrim and Josie Saldaña-Portillo taught such fantastic classes that my path toward literary criticism was set. I thank Stephanie for encouraging my interests in literary analysis and art, for teaching me the craft of academic writing, and for her continued friendship. Several of the texts I write about I first encountered in Josie's classes, and I thank her for exposing me to Chicana/o literature and forever changing my sense of self and life, and for serving as a role model to so many of us. Thank you to the Mellon Mays Undergraduate Fellowship Program, the Leadership Alliance, the Institute for the Recruitment of Teachers, Stanford's Center for Comparative Studies in Race and Ethnicity, and Stanford's El Centro Chicano for providing invaluable support, community, and learning opportunities. From these various programs I have been lucky to participate in, I thank Armando Bengochea, Joseph Brown, Joyce Foster, Evelyn Hu-Dehart, Frances Morales, Elvira Prieto, Besenia Rodriguez, Marisela Ramos, Laura Selznick, and Margaret Sena. I also thank the fellowship programs that have supported my graduate and postgraduate studies: the Beinecke Scholarship, the Ford Foundation, the Future of Minority Studies Research Project, and the Woodrow Wilson Early Career Enhancement Fellowship.

Thank you to the friends who have made academia more enjoyable: Lourdes Andrade, Magdalena Barrera, Brianne Bilsky, Maneka Brooks, Takkara Brunson, Agustin Cervantes, Tiq Chapa, Ernesto Chávez, Vanessa Díaz, Micaela Díaz-Sánchez, Joseph L. Tucker Edmonds, Justin Eichenlaub, James Estrella, Harris Feinsod, Chris Finley, Ed Finn, Lori Flores, Armando García, Marissa Gemma, Winston Groman, Laura Gutiérrez, Michael Hames-García, Heather Houser, Javier Huerta, Irvin Hunt, Tristan Ivory, Destin Jenkins, Cristina Jimenez,

Teresa Jimenez, Leora Johnson, Tiffany Joseph, Sarah Kessler, Ju Yon Kim, Long Le-Khac, Gustavo Licón, Marissa López, Shantal Marshall, Ernesto Martínez, Monica Martinez, Teresa Uyen Nguyen, Gabriela Nuñez, William Orchard, Steven Osuna, Mark Padoongpatt, Isabel Porras, Aneeta Rattan, Becky Richardson, John "Rio" Riofrio, Ricky Rodríguez, Ana Rosas, Adam Rosenblatt, Jayson Gonzales Sae-Saue, Maribel Santiago, Katerina Gonzalez Seligmann, Jeff Solomon, Alberto Varón, David Vázquez, James Wood, and Sylvia Zamora.

A loving thanks goes to my writing partner, Jennifer Harford Vargas. Her generosity has made producing first drafts less daunting, her warmth has soothed me when I have had doubts, and her brilliance has made discussing ideas so enjoyable. She has been there for every word, draft, and step of the way. Much love also to Lupe Carrillo, Jillian Hess, and Abigail Rosas; more than friends, they are my sisters. I thank them for being there for me in so many ways, and for their openness to sharing our minds, writing, and hearts so freely. Michelle Gordon has also become a cherished friend and intellectual interlocutor, and I thank her for all the emotional support and advice.

Thank you to those friends who provided community outside of academia: Jenny Beceren, Lily Benedict, Christine Orloff Fletcher, Kate Fratar, Kira Neel, and my dear friend from middle school, Oasis Sium. Thank you also to Oasis's parents, Sium Gebremariam and Alem Gebre, for being so kind and supportive. Marisa Hernández-Stern and her family also deserve special recognition; I treasure all the times I have spent with her and them. Thank you to Jenny Lederer for being my early reading buddy, for her sense of humor, and for the editing and photo-imaging help. Thank you to Jeff García and Zac Guevara for all the fun times and great conversations we have had about race and upward mobility.

Everyday I am thankful for my family. Carlos Garcia has enhanced my life in so many ways, and I thank him for giving me a family on the west coast, and for all his love, care, and making me laugh so much. I am grateful for the love from my grandparents, and all my aunts, uncles, and cousins, near and far. Most of all, I thank my parents, Elda and Miguel Román, and my brother, Miguel, for believing in me, and working so hard for our family and for others.

# RACE AND UPWARD MOBILITY

# INTRODUCTION

## A CASE OF TWO GEORGES

Starring in their own network sitcoms almost thirty years apart, two American fathers named George depicted Black and Mexican American upward mobility and made it palatable to mass audiences. Though their ascents were different, George Jefferson on *The Jeffersons* (CBS, 1975–1985) and George Lopez on the *George Lopez* show (ABC, 2002–2007) played out aspirational narratives with dreams attained and conflicts assuaged. Formerly a janitor, Jefferson invests money he received from an automobile accident into a chain of dry-cleaning stores; by the time of the pilot episode, he and his family have landed in an Upper East Side New York high-rise.[1] Also starting with the aftermath of ascension, Lopez's series begins when he has just been promoted to manager of an airplane parts factory after sixteen years on the assembly line—a promotion with strings attached. The first episode, "Prototype," features his dilemma as manager when his boss asks him to fire either his best friend or his own mother in order to cut costs.[2] Rather than a firing, the conflict in the *Jeffersons* pilot, "A Friend in Need," centers on a hiring, with Jefferson wanting a maid to help demonstrate his new wealth.[3] His wife, Louise, opposes it; she would prefer to befriend the Black woman who cleans the other apartments in their building instead of being her employer. Coming from manual-labor backgrounds, the Georges want to prove they belong—Lopez as manager and Jefferson as building resident. But their new positions also lead them to accept or desire hierarchical relationships with coethnics, with Lopez forced to fire someone close to him and Jefferson pressuring Louise to hire her friend.

As a genre that predominantly depicts middle-class families and aspirational values—a genre once aptly described as "The Great Middle American Dream Machine"—sitcoms implicitly endorse upward mobility, and in these two pilot episodes, resolutions to potentially contentious issues come easily.[4] It turns out Lopez's boss was just testing his loyalty to the company and never meant for him really to go through with the firing. Lopez manages to make it up to his mother by getting his boss to agree to more vacation days and back pay. And Louise's class angst at entering a hierarchical relationship gets reframed as helping a friend in need of a job. If these harmonious outcomes occur smoothly, it is only because these are not final solutions. Versions of these scenarios will be replayed over and over throughout both of these series, with the Georges striving for acceptance in work and social worlds that historically have treated them as inferior, and put in positions where their ethnic and working-class loyalties are continuously thrown into question.

The Georges' dilemma exemplifies the class conflicts and crises of affiliation that ethnic upward mobility narratives take on. That the shows revolve around two dark-skinned protagonists who are the first in their families to be upwardly mobile—and the first in their ethnic groups to centralize this ascent on television—makes these tensions even more salient. The Georges' economic rise does not entail assimilation into whiteness. Their racial otherness is conspicuously marked in majority-white middle- and upper-class contexts, while their class identity becomes marked around poorer coethnics. The two series consequently illustrate the dual negotiations that the Georges must make to achieve social mobility and mainstream appeal as part of racialized groups.[5] Genre conventions and the Georges' fresh entry into a field of power relations in which they are at the bottom of economic and social hierarchies dictate, to a large extent, their accommodation to the status quo. These are characters who are not rocking the boat to topple it. They are, however, navigating it off course to illustrate their ties to still-marginalized groups. When a childhood friend from Harlem surprises him with a visit, Jefferson worries about the dinner party he is hosting and making a poor impression on a business associate with class prejudices. He ultimately sides with his friend and kicks out the elitist associate.[6] And when a corporation wants to buy the factory where Lopez works and offers him a bigger salary to help shut down the factory and relocate, he refuses the offer and instead joins the workers in a protest. Both series depict upward mobility as potentially threatening for ethnic and working-class affiliation. More money and resources can beckon a person away from a community of origin, or make others question that person's commitment to the ethnic group. If the group in question is economically disadvantaged and socially marginalized, what prevents identification with one's economic interests over that of the group in need? And what does ethnicity mean in the context of middle- or upper-middle-class experiences?

To understand these defining tensions in the contemporary U.S. experience, *Race and Upward Mobility* examines a wide range of African American and Mexican American texts that portray racialized subjects' desires for financial solvency and social incorporation. Through cross-genre formal analyses, it identifies a typology of characters developed to stand in for competing visions of upward mobility, emblematic of a range of responses to the ideological and material effects of capitalism and white supremacy.[7] I argue that these character types can be understood as allegorical pathways of social incorporation reflecting actual strategies to negotiate membership within and between groups. I trace the historical circumstances giving rise to these narrative patterns and demonstrate how these figures manifest across genres and over time. In television, film, novels, and drama, these character types help us understand not only how race affects upward mobility but also how upward mobility informs interpretations of race.

## STAGGERED MOBILITY

Following World War II, the African American and Mexican American middle classes saw unprecedented growth rates due to economic development, civil rights legislation, and an expanded system of higher education.[8] Historically associated with impoverished urban and rural spaces, Mexican Americans and African Americans by the turn of the millennium owned homes in suburban neighborhoods across the United States. Once relegated onscreen to playing mammies and maids, chauffeurs and gardeners, Black and Latina/o actors began to reflect a wider set of vocations by portraying white-collar professionals and people in high-status positions. And, once seemingly impossible, the ascension of Barack Obama to the presidency signaled an audacious hope that barriers to achievement no longer capped the possibilities for people of color.

But these markers of racialized upward mobility belied the persistent inequities. All the manicured lawns, professional titles, and shows by Shonda Rhimes could not discount the fact that in 2011 the net worth of a Black or Latina/o household was equal to only 7 percent and 9 percent, respectively, of a white household.[9] Oprah's wealth could not counter the downward mobility that occurred in 2006 for millions of Black and Latina/o families whose only equity was tied up in their homes. When the housing bubble burst, so did their dreams for intergenerational savings.[10] All these trappings of apparent success also had little bearing on racial profiling policies such as "stop and frisk" in New York, "stand your ground" in Florida, and "show me your papers" in Arizona.[11]

With histories of ongoing racial profiling and criminalization, economic depression, and educational disparities, Blacks and Mexican Americans are two groups whose comparison offers a vital account of racialized class dynamics in the United States. They are the two largest racialized populations: in 2010, the Black population was 13.6 percent, while Latina/os were 16.3 percent of the population, with 63 percent of these identifying as Mexican or Mexican American.[12] Both groups have also significantly influenced U.S. social life, from the transformation of cities into minority-majority spaces to the food, dress, and music consumption patterns of the American population at large. Yet their numbers and influence have historically also been sources of fear, and these groups continue to be stigmatized as part of a perpetual underclass—ridden with crime, having too many kids, and seeking too many social services.

Historically, images of racial groups as threatening have maintained social and economic hierarchies, influencing whose lives, labor, and bodies of knowledge get valued and devalued. In the United States, the amalgamation of capitalist expansion and white supremacy produced particular racial formations characterized broadly as five main racial groups: white, Native American, Black, Latino, and Asian American. U.S. policies ensured that members of nonwhite groups, seen as threats to white landownership, labor, and purity, were systemically barred from becoming citizens or accessing the full rights that citizenship entailed. Throughout the nineteenth and early twentieth centuries, alarmist

discourse was directed at each racialized group. Native Americans were perceived in vacillating terms: admired and invoked for their "dignified nobility"
but rendered threatening and undeserving of lands because of their "inhuman
savagery," the latter image justifying their slaughter, forced removal, and relegation to reservations.[13] Expansion necessitated land and labor, and this equation
for growth often relied on the labor of racialized groups. Racism against Blacks
justified their designation as three-fifths of a person in the Constitution, and
their status as property and a labor pool that could be exploited to maximize
profit for an economically burgeoning America. In the post-emancipation period, images associated Blacks with rage and violence, suggesting Blacks needed
further regulation and control.[14] Seen as unassimilable foreigners, Asian Americans were ineligible for citizenship because they were designated as nonwhite
and were excluded from many job sectors.[15] Even those born in the United
States with birthright citizenship could be stripped of their rights, as occurred
during World War II with the internment of over a hundred thousand Japanese Americans out of political fears of possible disloyalty. Although Mexicans
were classified as white and eligible for citizenship through the 1848 Treaty of
Guadalupe Hidalgo that ended the U.S.-Mexican War, Mexicans' indigenous
backgrounds were referenced in racializing them as nonwhite threats to the
nation.[16] A profitable labor source but undesired as people, Mexicans were like
the other racialized groups, seen as inferior and expendable. All four groups
have been feared as cultural and genetic contaminants, and scapegoated during
times of economic and political crises.

By the late twentieth century, these alarmist narratives had undergone discursive shifts. Regarded as vanishing and outside of urban spaces and modernity,
Native Americans were predominantly associated with the past, seen as dying
out and nostalgically standing in for a preindustrial culture closer to nature and
more authentic. Consequently, as Philip Deloria observes, by the latter half of
the twentieth century, "Indian Others were imagined in almost exclusively positive terms—communitarianism, environmentally wise, spiritually insightful."[17]
Another group that had been described as "heathen"—Asian Americans—was
also viewed more favorably. Nineteenth-century images of Asians as heathens,
part of a "yellow peril," were replaced by a new stereotype—that of the "model
minority."[18] While Native Americans became perceived as nonvisible unless
imagined as part of a static, vanished culture, and Asian Americans became

associated with high achievement, African Americans and Mexican Americans continued to be highly visible in the media as part of a stigmatized underclass.[19] This book examines these two groups' narrative traditions stemming from their discursive and economic positions in the racial order.

At the turn of the century, news stories and popular culture still circulated images of Latina/os and Blacks as lawbreakers and social outsiders. In their contemporary, threatening incarnation, they were selling drugs through cartels and on the street, having anchor babies and living as welfare queens, stealing jobs and underperforming, and prone to violence and being oppositional. These images fed assessments of African Americans and Mexican Americans as not just poor, but culturally and criminally so. Political scientist Martin Gilens explains that until the late 1960s, the face of poverty was white. The racialization of poverty occurred in part through negative news stories of Black poverty.[20] Scholarship in the 1950s and 1960s also played a role in shaping perceptions of poverty and people of color. Works by Oscar Lewis and Daniel Patrick Moynihan helped propagate the idea that Latina/os and Blacks suffer from what Lewis called a "culture of poverty," and that their values and behavior kept them in a cycle of poverty.[21] Pundits continue to ascribe cultural (or genetic) reasons for poverty and underachievement, ignoring the historical factors that prevented Blacks and Latina/os from accumulating the intergenerational wealth and resources that white families have and the institutionalized mechanisms by which people of color are barred from accessing these resources in the present.[22] Further, the argument that poverty leads to dysfunctional communities, which leads to criminal behavior serves as ballast for policies targeting and further disenfranchising people of color, policies that entered a different phase in the post-1980s period, in the wake of the "war on drugs," the militarization of the border, and the "war on terror."[23] All have resulted in increased funding to militarize the police and border security forces, with intensified focus on, as criminologist Peter B. Kraska puts it, "social problems amenable to actual security strategies and tactics, such as urban violence, illegal drugs, and illegal immigration."[24] The effect has been increased criminalization and incarceration of Blacks and Latina/os.[25] Meanwhile, a history of dehumanizing language used to render Mexican immigrants into "wetbacks," "illegals," and "aliens" continues to make them into undeserving trespassers threatening the American way of life.[26]

In the context of a history of stigmatization and exclusion with lasting economic consequences, how one is identified and how one identifies became central concerns in African American and Mexican American cultural production. With disproportionate representation in institutions of power and uneven access to resources, these groups developed narrative traditions championing solidarity for social change. At the same time, the pressure to identify along racial-ethnic lines and within cultural boundaries has also prompted calls for more expansive understandings of identity and group composition. By examining portrayals of race and upward mobility together, we see how cultural producers have depicted socioeconomic realities along with shaping and questioning the phenomenon of racial and ethnic affiliation.

## ETHNIC UPWARD MOBILITY NARRATIVES

Reflecting the economic and ideological heterogeneity that exists, postwar African American and Mexican American upward mobility narratives interpret the effects that perceptions and treatment of racialized groups have had on self-identification and communal action. Upward mobility narratives play a didactic function and tend to be consumed as bootstrapping stories about self-reliance and individual success, but Bruce Robbins has shown in *Upward Mobility and the Common Good* that they are actually very much concerned with the collective.[27] Analyses of Black and Mexican American upward mobility narratives in particular allow us to see what kind of work these stories do in response to collective pressures and collective needs stemming from histories of racialization; how, for example, they deconflate race and class to acknowledge intragroup class disparities, or how they attempt to override class differences to reinforce a sense of group identity. We end up seeing continuous expansion and contraction—conceptualizations of the group expand to accommodate social mobility and group boundaries are policed for social and political purposes.

Upward mobility narratives are also interpreted as stories about super success, the rags-to-riches tales of high-profile people such as celebrities or CEOs. Those kinds of ascendant trajectories may make for television or box office hits, but usually upward mobility is portrayed with less glamour and in ways more representative of society at large. I analyze these latter kinds of representations—of class mobility achieved through various types of labor, such as factory or domestic work, or through law enforcement or artistic production, or small business ownership, or owning one's own home—to get at the broader patterns of incorporation characteristic of these two groups.

Examining Mexican American and African American representations together allows us to more accurately understand the discursive and material effects of racialization as part of a larger system that structures socioeconomic relations in the United States, insights that cannot be applied to one group solely. Comparing them together also enables us to see both more sharply. We profit from understanding their overlaps and misalignments, their shared narrative strategies and their historical differences. There is, for example, a longer history of scholarly writings on class variation within the Black population. In a 1903 essay, W. E. B. Du Bois encouraged members of the "Talented Tenth" to serve as leaders in the cause for racial uplift.[28] Several decades later another sociologist, E. Franklin Frazier, delivered a critical view of the Black middle class, arguing that the relationship its members had with whites led them to develop a deep inferiority complex and a pathological emulation of white bourgeois values.[29] Perceptions of the Black middle class and Black elites as leaders working toward social progress or as status hungry and removed from the general Black population were part of an early framing that informed subsequent critical discussions.

Literary representations of the Black middle class are even more plentiful than the scholarship. From the mid-nineteenth century on, Black creative writers documented and interpreted the lives of those striving for "respectability" and elevated class status along with those who had attained it, often expressing, as Andreá N. Williams has argued, "fears over downward mobility, misclassification, and estrangement."[30] Sometimes they illustrated the limits to class privilege when epistemic and physical violence could strip someone of their dignity and property, as demonstrated in Frank J. Webb's *The Garies and Their Friends* (1857).[31] Or they rendered the appeal of and fears associated with racial assimilation, as exemplified by the proliferation of nineteenth- and early twentieth-century passing novels. Portrayals of the Black middle class are integral to the upward mobility narrative tradition because they depict the social and economic disparities that can still exist even after class ascension has occurred.

In comparison, there are not only fewer scholarly engagements with and representations of the Mexican American middle class, there has been less published work from the Mexican American population in general. One contributing factor is that this is a more recent population. Consider that in 1870, the Black population in the United States was around five million.[32] The Mexican American population did not attain those numbers until a hundred years later, in the 1970s, after which it grew steadily. In 2010, the Mexican American population was almost thirty-two million and the Black population was around forty-two million.[33] Yet numbers alone do not explain the amount and content of writerly output. The two groups are now closer in numerical parity, but there is a significant historical difference regarding patterns of incorporation, which results in different narrative strategies and outcomes. For example, there is the issue of group identity. Among the group now labeled African American, the one-drop rule, virulent anti-Black racism, and segregation prompted the forging of group identity and affective bonds across classes. The group now labeled Mexican American has also comprised fractions negotiating identities in relation to the U.S. racial structure, but occupied positions within and external to whiteness; in addition, members negotiated their identities in relation to U.S. language and citizenship hierarchies. Until the 1940s, because of the scarcity and inequality of education, most Mexican American writers came from the upper classes, which informed the content and form of their writing.[34] With a smaller population and in the absence of publishing avenues and patronage, the overall number of Mexican American authors was bound to be smaller.[35] In factoring institutional history we can also take into account the contributions of historically Black colleges and universities (HBCUs) in serving Black communities and creating avenues of mobility. There are approximately one hundred HBCUs, all founded before 1964. Inspired by those institutions' success in creating Black professionals, a similar vision underwrote the 1981 founding of the National Hispanic University, a Latina/o-oriented educational institution which has already closed down and whose establishment cannot be compared to institutions that appeared during de jure segregation.[36]

There are social and historical reasons for why class variation among Mexican Americans has not garnered as much scholarly and literary attention, but there is also an ideological factor—most Mexican American scholars and writers came through the university system during and in the post-1960s period, helping institutionalize Chicana/o studies around working-class studies.[37] These generations rejected the writings of the 1930s–1940s generation, aspiring for collective upward mobility but doing so by distancing themselves ideologically from noncitizens and the Mexican poor. One effect of this is that there is a greater sense of betrayal linked with upward mobility in Chicana/o texts and scarce attention paid to intragroup class dynamics among Mexican Americans. Rather than treating Mexican Americans as a static population, which would obscure group heterogeneity, sociologists Tomás Jiménez, Jessica M. Vasquez, and Jody Agius Vallejo have asserted the importance of paying attention to a generational cohort, which indicates that Mexican Americans have achieved economic and social mobility over time.[38] Recent scholarship by José Limón also prompts us to see an activist Mexican American middle class, while John Alba Cutler asks that we reconsider our understanding of "assimilation" when analyzing Chicana/o literature.[39] My book joins the endeavor of reassessing the terms by which we understand Mexican American literature and puts them in conversation with analogous discursive changes in African American literature. Doing so furthers a comparative approach to ethnic literary studies, which in turn advances a more nuanced understanding of the class-based complexities of racial identity, and does so through one of the most ubiquitous of narrative arcs—the upward mobility narrative.

## SYMBOLIC WAGES, IDENTITY TAXES

To get at the heart of the theoretical framework of this book, I offer another example of ethnic upward mobility narratives representing class conflicts and crises of affiliation. Ayana Mathis's critically acclaimed and widely translated 2012 novel *The Twelve Tribes of Hattie* depicts the limits to a racialized middle-class identity under Jim Crow.[40] In one of the novel's chapters, set in 1954, Benny, a successful African American mortician, and his wife, Pearl, are making their way from Georgia to Philadelphia to pick up their niece from Pearl's sister, Hattie, to raise her as their own because they have more resources. They stop by a Virginia roadside to eat the lunch that Pearl has prepared. Pearl is the kind of genteel woman who wears face powder, presses her hair, and packs a picnic basket lunch with "white china plates" and "white cloth napkins" (142). Their peaceful repast is interrupted, however, when four white men start harassing them. The biggest of them "took in Benny's leather loafers and shining cuff links and his cotton shirt with the pressed collar" (144) and asks them if they are lost. He commands the couple to clear out, but forces them to leave their food behind, stating "Y'all done put yer stuff on white folks' table and now you gon' have to leave it here. It's a tax" (146). The charge is levied to make them pay for being Black and displaying markers of wealth, a reminder that no matter their class standing, they still have lower status.

Here, Mathis invokes the idea of the "Black tax," which refers, colloquially, to the "cost of being Black." It is a phrase that has been used in different contexts to evoke the history of racial discrimination toward African Americans in various forms, including the paying of higher mortgage and auto insurance interest rates, being denied housing or work opportunities, and having to work twice as hard as whites to get the same benefits.[41] Imani Perry has theorized Black taxes as part of a "social economy of race," in which the value of people, spaces, and practices are "shaped by the degree to which those things are associated with, come from, or are controlled by or proximate to a given racial group."[42] The scholarly conversation linking race with economics has roots in Du Bois's observation that whiteness grants a "public and psychological wage" and has been extended in David Roediger's *The Wages of Whiteness*, Cheryl Harris's "Whiteness as Property," and George Lipsitz's *The Possessive Investment in Whiteness*, all focusing on whiteness as a form of currency in a history of transactions that have historically enabled whites to own more property than people of color, acquire greater wealth, and assert an elevated social status.[43] The Black tax fits into this schema as a concept that conveys that while there are benefits associated with whiteness, there is a price to pay for one's nonwhite racial identity.

It becomes clear that paying a racial tax implies that there *is* a wage of some sort—otherwise the taxation metaphor would not obtain. Following Pierre Bourdieu's distinction between symbolic and economic capital, and emphasizing the aspect of continuous labor (social, discursive, and so on) involved in accruing these types of capital, we can shift metaphors to highlight the kinds of acts that earn material and symbolic wages. In Mathis's novel, for example, Pearl earns symbolic wages through her class performance, since her habits help her situate herself as part of a genteel Black society in Georgia. These symbolic wages are underwritten by the material earnings of her husband's profitable business. That image is forcefully disrupted during their picnic encounter. After the men leave, Pearl expresses her anger at Benny for furthering their denigration, for responding to the white man's questions with "Nossuh" and "Yessuh" even though she "had never heard Benny talk that way" (144). Pearl exclaims,

"You didn't have to stoop so low. You could have kept your dignity! I've never been so humiliated" (147). Benny stands by his actions, replying, "Oh, Yes you have. Yes, you have and you know it. You've been in the house with your afternoon teas and garden club so long you think you can pretend we're not who we are, but you know just as well as I do that my dignity, my goddamned dignity, would have had us swinging from a tree" (147). The difference between coping and surviving get played out through Pearl and Benny's distinct class identity performances. Pearl's way of coping—relying on the symbolic wages of class—is framed as a retreat from reality, which Benny suggests would have had dangerous repercussions for them both, had he followed suit. Ethnic upward mobility narratives often depict some form of this moment, dramatizing how the symbolic wages that come from racial and ethnic minorities' elevated class identity are enticing in that they enable cognitive and social distancing from others who remain marginalized. But this tends to be represented as deep naïveté and threatening to community solidarity.[44]

In short, if upward mobility grants wages, it also imposes a tax. This tax reveals the impossibility of straight-line assimilation into a white mainstream. It registers the factors that make racial identities salient and which have led to the social, political, and narrative strategies that individuals and groups have developed to work within and against the socioeconomic status quo. Ethnic upward mobility narratives participate in these endeavors, reflecting how the tax has also produced aesthetic translations of the contradictions inherent in a stratified society. The "sellout narrative" can be seen as one manifestation of this tax in discursive terms, another example of how economic language informs how we think about identity. Fears that individuals would identify with a privileged class group as opposed to a minority ethnic group find their literary expression in these kinds of narratives. "Selling out" conveys that an individual is hawking or exchanging his or her communal identity, or the community itself, for membership in the dominant group. In sellout narratives, characters may pass for white, act subservient to whites, Anglicize their names, define themselves in opposition to the racialized or immigrant working class, and deny their cultural heritage—all in an attempt to improve their socioeconomic status. These status seeking characters are vilified for leaving their communities behind or, even worse, for selling out "their people" for individual gain. Think of the eponymous protagonist in James Weldon Johnson's *The Autobiography of an Ex-Colored Man*, who passes as white to accrue the social and economic advantages of whiteness; George Washington Gómez in Américo Paredes's novel by the same name, who turns his back on his Mexican American community once he goes off to college and comes back as a border spy; and Dr. Bledsoe in Ralph Ellison's *Invisible Man*, who would rather see Blacks remain powerless than give up his own higher status, one that he maintains by catering to whites.[45] Sellout narratives expose how the symbolic wages accrued through assimilation can turn into material wages for racialized subjects striving to override racial and ethnic markers and/or who want to leave affiliation behind. In other words, they dramatize the profitability of normativity, of the social and financial value that one can earn when one is not stigmatized by difference. The twin economic metaphors of symbolic wages and identity taxes log the value and cost of identity resulting from relations of economic, social, and narrative exchange.

While symbolic wages come from class markers, they can also come from ethnic group membership. Individuals convey the cultural codes that mark them as group insiders, part of a community with shared cultural practices, linguistic codes, and values. This, in turn, can have personal and collective benefits, enabling an affirmative identity and serving as a way for a community to pool its resources for social action.[46] Black and Chicano cultural nationalism helped cohere a sense of group identities affirming racial and ethnic difference. Taking more oppositional stances toward the mainstream than had previous generations in the fight for civil rights, the 1960s and 1970s generations rallied around Black and Chicana/o identity, allied with the working class, and claimed roots in Africa and Aztlán—outside the current nation-state. The creation of these collective identities enabled disparate groups of people to fight for social equality under shared political visions. Part of the political legacy of nationalist movements, these identities are still used to mobilize social justice efforts in grassroots activism and in institutional arenas. This politicization also produced a rich body of cultural and academic work, though that community coherence necessitated some omissions, which feminists and queer critiques have sought to rectify. What still has not received enough attention is the mixed-class component of these movements. José Limón has argued, for example, that "productive as [the Chicano] movement was . . . it generated a less than comprehensive, less than complex view of Mexican-America as it largely overlooked the middle class."[47] Candice M. Jenkins similarly remarks that Black nationalism's "greatest misstep [was the way in which it] collapsed intraracial differences, particularly class differences, and represented all African Americans as essentially the same."[48]

In the postnationalist (1980s–present), multiculturalist era, we increasingly see attempts to reconcile the symbolic wages of class with those of ethnicity, to convey middle-class identity and ethnic affiliation. A precursor to this shift, Trey Ellis's 1989 essay "The New Black Aesthetic," announced the proliferation of Black artists and intellectuals—largely second-generation middle class—who, as "cultural mulattos," were moving between Black and white worlds to produce avant-garde art "that shamelessly borrows and reassembles across both race and class lines."[49] Continuing the project of describing expansive Black identities, the journalist Touré's *Who's Afraid of Post-Blackness? What It Means to Be Black Now* moves beyond the realm of aesthetics.[50] The coining of the term *post-Black* is attributed to Thelma Golden, curator of the 2001 Studio Museum in Harlem exhibit "Freestyle," along with artist Glenn Ligon, who used it to describe varied expressions of Blackness in a postnationalist era. Touré applies *post-Black* to describe artists, but also media celebrities, politicians, academics, and other elites like Oprah and Obama, who are not "leaving Blackness behind" but rather "leaving behind the vision of Blackness as something narrowly definable and [are] embracing every conception of Blackness as legitimate."[51] Touré's book wants to legitimize middle- and upper-class Black identity in particular. As he explains, post-Blackness accommodates markers of class and social mobility, so that a Black person who plays tennis, goes to an elite school, and has an interracial relationship would not be seen as inauthentic. Touré calls for an end to the assessment of Blackness according to a "hierarchy of authenticity" that is

based on proximity to the ghetto experience, as if that were the sun around which Blackness revolves. The further the planet you live on is from the ghetto the less authentically Black you are. I reject the idea that the 'hood is the center of Blackness and that Blackness is somehow lost the further you go up the class ladder, like milk moving toward spoilage as it sits longer and longer outside the fridge. To suggest that underclass Blackness is authentic and middle-class is not self-destructive thinking. It suggests that Blackness requires us to stay poor in order for it to survive and it dies as more of us become economically successful.[52]

In order to deconflate race and class, Touré flips the connotations of the ghetto and the middle class. The ghetto is not the site of marginalization but the sun around which Blackness revolves, and not a place where fresh food is hard to find but where Blackness is the freshest, and death is divorced from actual bodies and refers here to a loss of authenticity. Touré rewrites the relationship between the ghetto and the middle class as one of inverse privilege. But these metaphorical turns can only be intelligible in an era when the authenticity of ethnicity has high symbolic value, when there is a desire to assert not only middle-classness but also ethnic affiliation.

Ultimately, Touré wants an end to a policing of Black identity in order to expand the boundaries of Black community. Legal scholars Randall Kennedy and Brando Simeo Starkey assert, however, that in order to have Black solidarity, policing rhetoric is unavoidable.[53] Starkey distinguishes between the policing of constructive and destructive norms. Constructive norms "help build black solidarity by penalizing individuals for consciously promoting the interests of antiblack entities, for exhibiting inexcusable meekness in the face of racism, or for lacking concern for the race."[54] The use of destructive norms, in contrast, are attempts to police cultural Blackness, which Starkey argues is unproductive and creates divisions instead of solidarity.[55] Policing markers of class would fall under destructive norms, since doing so can exclude and limit allies and strategies for collective action.

Terms like *post-Black* and the similar *post-Chicano* represent attempts to capture the varied sense of ethnic identity resulting from increased understandings of heterogeneity in both groups. Like the concept of *post-Black*, *post-Chicano* originated in the arts world and designates a historical marker. Implying "post-Chicano movement," it can refer to artists completely disidentifying with Chicana/o ideology and themes—artists who eschew identity labels, for example. But it has also been used to refer to artists who identify as Chicana/o but who, like many post-Black artists, display playful irreverence toward the cultural nationalist era. Or to those who extend Chicano movement themes and imagery by mixing "high" and "low" culture or by incorporating global references. First used in 1990 by Max Benavidez and Liz Lerma Bowerman, curators of the *Post-Chicano Generation in Art: Breaking Boundaries* exhibit at the Phoenix art cooperative Movimiento Artístico del Río Salado, the term was meant to describe artists like the conceptual and public performance group

ASCO, who were not following, according to Benavidez, the path of cultural glorification characteristic of Chicano movement art but were instead drawing from mixed-cultural contexts and reveling in contradiction and ambiguity.[56] In marking the mixed cultural influence visible in post-Chicano art, Benavidez parallels Trey Ellis's announcement of a new generation of Black artists. All identity movements have their developments, and the *posts* signify ethnic traditions undergoing redefinition.

Representing ethnic identities with mixed-cultural influences and less oppositional relationships to the mainstream is one way connotations of the group expand. But this is occurring even while cultural producers reinforce a sense of ethnic identity with continuities from the past. The *post-* identity prefixes are ambiguous enough that they can designate a distancing not just from a homogeneous sense of identity but also from the politics that led to a communal identity in the first place. Taking issue with this latter interpretation, Chicana artist Melanie Cervantes, one half of the Bay Area printmaking duo Dignidad Rebelde, declared that the term *post-Chicano*

eclipses the art that's still happening that's within the tradition. . . . It's not the dominant art for arts sake. . . . we fit into that trajectory of artists that were seen as Chicana/ Chicano movement artists in that we believe in being artists connected to a community and that there's this emancipatory space that's built out of the work we're creating. And creating the art and marching in the streets and doing civil disobedience like all of that works toward the same goals. . . . post-Chicano triggers me to think, wow that totally negates the reality that I live. . . . we're marching in the rain May 1st, 2009, every year folks are coming out and determined because there's still police checkpoints happening. And there's still raids happening and people are having their doors knocked on and being asked about whether they're documented or not. Those issues are still relevant to young Chicanos . . .[57]

The label is relevant to Cervantes because it still describes her community-based organizing and art production. Her critique aligns with Greg Thomas's assessment of "posts": "The 'post' is never meant for 'some'; it's supposed to be for 'all.' It is never a questionable desire; it is a supposedly unquestionable reality. It is class elite-led yet presented as a supposed cure for the masses."[58] With a Berkeley degree, Cervantes is one example of many who marshal their educational capital on behalf of ethnic communities, see their ethnic identities as still salient, and participate in mediating efforts that help reinforce a sense of ethnic community for political purposes. My analysis of ethnic upward mobility narratives draws out what is implied in these identity and aesthetic debates: that cultural producers are grappling with the simultaneous expansion and contraction of group boundaries, and a relationship to the mainstream and class identity are often sources of tension around which this fluctuation occurs.[59]

## THE IDENTITY TAX AND
## THE MINORITY CULTURE OF MOBILITY

The identity tax encompasses how individuals navigate their cultural economies when there is both a need to acculturate and also a desire to maintain ties to the ethnic community. In fleshing out these dual negotiations, this book analyzes the aesthetic strategies used to capture what sociologists have called the "minority culture of mobility." The idea of cultural producers maintaining ethnic affiliation even after achieving social mobility correlates with more recent assimilation theories, with the Black and Mexican American middle classes countering older theoretical models. Previous studies by sociologists Alejandro Portes and Min Zhou explained that immigrants and their children could follow three assimilation pathways: into the white middle class (the concern of the sellout narrative), into a racialized underclass, or into a middle class that preserves elements from the immigrant community.[60] Sociologists Kathryn M. Neckerman, Prudence Carter, and Jennifer Lee expand on this latter path to propose that African Americans might offer immigrants a model of how to gain access to resources while retaining ethnic affiliation through the development of a "minority culture of mobility."[61] Defining the minority culture of mobility as the "cultural elements provid[ing] strategies for economic mobility in the context of discrimination and group disadvantage," they argue that it arises out of contact with whites and also from the interclass distinctions within the minority community.[62] The minority culture of mobility encompasses speech patterns and interactional styles to communicate with the white middle class and with other coethnics: ways of dealing with loneliness, isolation, and discrimination in white-dominant spaces, and managing relations with poor family and community members.[63]

Perhaps Barack Obama is the most visible example of the deployment of the minority culture of mobility. Linguists H. Samy Alim and Geneva Smitherman found through survey research that because Obama demonstrated a facility with cultural codes from both the mainstream and his ethnic community, he drew the kind of mass appeal needed to win a national election.[64] Testing whether the minority culture of mobility applies to Mexican Americans, Jody Agius Vallejo found that, in contrast to beliefs that Mexican Americans continue to live in poverty generations after they have immigrated to the United States, or to the belief that they assimilate into the white middle class, a sizable contingent is entering the middle class while retaining their ethnic identity.[65] What needs more elaboration, however, is the role cultural texts play in representing and mediating inter- and intra-ethnic class differences. Neckerman and colleagues state that the minority culture of mobility includes knowledge and behavioral strategies, but it also "draws on available symbols, idioms and practices to respond to distinctive problems of being middle class and minority."[66] Building on this work, my book analyzes the symbolic elements of ethnic-affiliated upward mobility narratives, showing how they illustrate a minority culture of mobility and also contribute to it. The minority culture of mobility stems from tensions that lead to narrative and behavioral strategies. In similar terms, the metaphorical wages of upward mobility (material and symbolic) are mitigated by the need to develop a culture to deal with marginality and inequality. Portraying class and racial conflict, ethnic cultural production serves both as a product of this tax and as payment of the social and aesthetic dues given to both the mainstream and the ethnic community.

The consequences of paying that tax are still in question. If we think of the social function that taxes serve, they can be seen as impositions (because there's no choice involved), but they can also be seen as contributions (because they address collective social need). If the group purpose to which the taxes are put maintains the status quo and its accompanying social hierarchies, the tax is decidedly not in the interest of the racialized ethnic group. But the history of Blacks and Latina/os in the United States shows us that oppressive and alienating conditions have also manifested cultural responses contributing to a sense of distinct collective identities constructed for social action. In these terms, an identity tax has cross-ethnic applicability. It marks the social and economic impositions that make racial and ethnic identity salient *and* the interpretive response to those impositions. It is, therefore, analogous to the process by which ethnic literature is produced.

One way of interpreting ethnic literature is that it is a positive made out of a negative, a reaction to racism and marginalization that leads to the creation of literary difference. Writing about Sandra Cisneros's alienating experience as an ethnic and economic outsider in the prestigious University of Iowa Writing Workshop, Mark McGurl characterizes those experiences as an "enabling disablement" that led to the writing of *The House on Mango Street*.[67] Kenneth Warren gives the equivalent assessment about African American literature as a whole when he argues for its periodization under Jim Crow:

One cannot treat African American literature as a literature apart from the necessary conditions that made it a literature. Absent white suspicions of, or commitment to imposing, black inferiority, African American literature would not have existed as a literature. Writers of African descent would have certainly emerged and written novels, plays, and poems that merited critical attention, but the imperative to produce and to consider their literature as a corporate enterprise would not have obtained.[68]

But seeing ethnic literature as just a reaction to white racism leads to an inevitable question that Warren poses in *What Was African American Literature?*: What happens when the external conditions that led to its fruition are no longer there? Jim Crow treated all Blacks the same regardless of class; with its end, argues Warren, African American literature lost its justification as a collective enterprise.

Consequently, Warren argues that in the post–Jim Crow era, we have narratives about middle-class Blacks that try to convince us that the bourgeois concerns of protagonists matter to Blacks as a whole. In his reading of Michael Thomas's novel *Man Gone Down* (2009), Warren demonstrates the means by which the narrative correlates the protagonist's dilemma—how to raise thousands of dollars in four days so he can send his kids to private school—with the fate of the race. It occurs through a scene on a country club golf course; the protagonist is participating in a tournament and is about to swing when he conjures up the voices of Black people rooting for him. As Warren puts it,

He needs to believe, perhaps despite himself, that what he does matters to someone other than him and his immediate family. To put the matter in broader terms, the idea that sustains the possibility of an African American literature is a belief that the welfare of the race as a whole depends on the success of black writers and those who are depicted in their texts.[69]

His analysis cautions us to avoid ignoring class dynamics under the umbrella of race. Walter Benn Michaels has advanced this argument as well, agreeing with Warren that literature expresses "nostalgia for racism. What we like about racism is precisely the fact that its victims are the victims of discrimination rather than [economic] exploitation."[70] By focusing on racism as the dominant issue, in other words, texts and critics can rally around wanting racial identities affirmed rather than addressing class inequities.

But this interpretation of ethnic literature assumes that texts do not portray the compounded effects of inequality and exclusion. William Darity's work in stratification economics offers empirically based accounts of how racial hierarchies have perpetuated material advantages over generations.[71] In a similar vein, legal scholar Daria Roithmayr has analogized white supremacy to a monopoly that got rid of its nonwhite economic competitors during Jim Crow, resulting in white advantage becoming "institutionally locked in" and vast economic racial disparities persisting to this day.[72] These effects we see in ethnic literature along with characters who exhibit a range of strategies for dealing with socioeconomic realities. We see, for example, characters who strive for status symbols to show signs of worth, or who have internalized the value system that sees poor racialized subjects as lesser and do their most to distance themselves from that group, while other characters in similar positions attempt to address inequities through legal channels, anarchy, institutional reform, or artistic means. As Lawrence Buell puts it, "the ethnic turn in American up-from stories of aspirant youth, far from giving acquisitive individualism a free pass, has tended—with exceptions of course—to bring issues of social justice more robustly to the fore than in earlier novels of aspiration. At least in part, that's because the condition of marked ethnicity conduces to even greater like-it-or-not self-consciousness of the (un)fairness of social arrangements across the board."[73] In contrast to interpretations of ethnic literature that subsume class concerns, or see the work as endorsing a politics of recognition while not challenging economic inequality, I demonstrate that ethnic upward mobility narratives are cultural sites showing the tactics—manifesting as allegorical pathways of social incorporation—developed to deal with economic and social stratification.

By giving us a window into a fictional character's interiority, cultural production shows us how class is experienced on a day-to-day basis. It captures interpretations of class by representing status. The characters parsed in this book are either socially and economically mobile or middle class, identified as such by their position in the middle of rather than at the bottom of economic and social hierarchies. Max Weber famously distinguished class as one's position in an economic hierarchy, and status as how one is perceived in that hierarchy.[74] An attention to status illuminates how a class position acquires meaning through social relations and also provides an explanation for why members of the minority middle class would still identify with the minority group as opposed to their class group. Weber argued that individuals were more likely to form communities as a result of sharing similar social statuses than they would with those sharing the same class positioning. Seeing ethnic groups as status groups, as Weber does, helps clarify why individuals would work across class lines for collective social action to improve the opportunities for and perception of their status group as a whole. It also explicates why some characters would want to improve their social status by distancing themselves from the racialized poor. The inclusion of a Black or Mexican lower class and an elite class (white or ethnic) against which fictional figures define themselves or are defined allows their in-between status to become a key component of their characterization.

## FOUR FACES OF UPWARD MOBILITY NARRATIVES

Despite temporal and generational differences, Mexican American and African American cultural productions now pose common questions: What does group identity mean today? And how do you represent and analyze its diversity? The traditional ethnic studies method has been to locate signs of resistance in texts and to focus on particular figures: Elizabeth McHenry argues that this has led to seeing slaves and the African American working class as the sole and most authentic sites of resistance, which then "artificially diminishes the complexity of the black community and advances the notion of a monolithic black culture that is unsupported by historical fact."[75] Ralph Rodriguez has also urged Chicana/o studies to move beyond the familiar; he provocatively asks, "could it now be time to move away from the propensity to analyze the oppositional quality of Mexican-American cultural production? If this model is inadequate, it is not because the warrior hero has disappeared from Mexican-American culture, but precisely the opposite. When a figure of opposition is well represented and firmly entrenched in contemporary novels, films, music, do we really need an act of exegesis to explain its presence, or even its necessity?"[76] Since African American and Chicana/o literature is often read as resistant, working class, and about the disenfranchised, how do we read character types that do not entirely fit these expectations? What do we make of the figures whose class movement is a key feature of their relationship to other coethnics and to a broader U.S. population? Since upwardly mobile characters are in the middle of social and economic hierarchies, I argue that authors can employ them to theorize the fluctuation of group boundaries. Their in-between status also offers us the opportunity to reflect on the pressures that inform the way characters deal with class and race, which cannot always be reduced to assessments of resistance or selling out if we understand that texts exhibit a range of strategies to respond to social and economic inequalities. What Viet Thanh Nguyen has argued about Asian American texts applies cross-ethnically: "resistance and accommodation are actually limited, polarizing options that do not sufficiently demonstrate the *flexible strategies* often chosen by authors and characters to navigate their political and ethical situations."[77] Looking beyond the trope of the resistant or sellout figure so that we can parse out the flexible strategies employed in ethnic upward mobility narratives, this book focuses on African American and Mexican American texts developed to depict a central contradiction understood in theorizations of intersectionality—that racialized minorities can be simultaneously inside and outside positions of privilege. In doing so, we see that there are *other* figural types common to both groups' narrative traditions, and that they open windows onto other strategies for negotiating race, ethnicity, and class.

I find that there are four reoccurring character types, symbolic of actual social and vocational positions, that appear in ethnic upward mobility narratives to model competing strategies for negotiating race and class. *Status seekers* are characters who desire increased status; they may buy into the correlation between material worth and social worth and/or strive for mainstream approval. As a result, they may distance themselves from poorer coethnics and markers of difference. *Conflicted artists* are often juxtaposed with status seekers; these characters channel the ethical critique and offer an alternative to material accumulation and status seeking. They may be conflicted because they come from poor communities where being an artist is not seen as a viable path or a profitable one, their communities need immediate representation in forms other than art, or they chafe against representing for a group.[78] *Mediators* are characters who use their new class positions to work on behalf of poorer coethnics. They represent a desire to see upward mobility routed into a politically conscious path. Antithetical to mediators, *gatekeepers* use their class positions to keep other coethnics from accessing resources they themselves enjoy. Gatekeepers can also be characters that police ethnic allegiances through markers that designate those inside and outside the group. To appreciate these figures, we must apprehend them in the representational worlds they inhabit and the narratives in which they are entwined. We must also understand that there can be movement between figures, with texts transforming gatekeepers and status seekers into mediators or artists, or illustrating how individuals can embody multiple types. In *Hunger of Memory*, for example, Richard Rodriguez narrates both his aspirational drive toward mainstream approval and the pain that comes with it, rendering him a status seeker who is also a conflicted artist. I am not arguing that these figures do not appear in non-African American or non-Mexican American cultural production. In this book, I am demonstrating how they function in these particular traditions to work through social and political issues inflected by both race and class. As heuristics, these figures reveal how a text concretizes sociopolitical strategies and help us chart continuities and changes over time.

In selecting sites—cultural productions—for analysis, I sought representations that exemplify how these figures appear in a variety of genres. Literary works such as Paule Marshall's novel *Brown Girl, Brownstones* (1959), for example, can be more critical about upward mobility than can a mass-market pitched sitcom like the show *George Lopez*. Yet they both advance arguments about hierarchies of power and economic pressures, and revolve around crises of self-identification and communal membership. And while the sincere portrayals of migrant suffering depicted in the films *The Gatekeeper* (2002) and *Sleep Dealer* (2008) might bear little resemblance to the ironic and comic portrayal of a public relation rep's identity crisis in Lynn Nottage's play *Fabulation* (2004), they are all about middle-class ethnic characters who end up realigning with the working poor. The novels, television programs, films, and dramas I analyze reveal patterns across genres—helping us understand the overarching genre of the ethnic upward mobility narrative—as recurring figural types and plot trajectories appear to unfold inter- and intra-ethnic class tensions. The spectrum of Mexican American and African American upward mobility nar-

ratives showcases complementary and conflicting responses to social and economic pressures ranging from the self-interested to the collectively oriented,
but all giving us a fuller scope of their sociopolitical qualities in depicting race
and class under capitalism.

OUTLINE OF THE BOOK

This book is organized conceptually and loosely chronologically in spanning
from the 1940s to the 2000s to demonstrate how texts employ the figural types
to engage with histories of exclusion and inequality. In most chapters I discuss
patterns in both African American and Mexican American texts to illuminate the
narrative strategies they employ to treat shared concerns, while in two chapters
(Chapters 3 and 5) I focus on a single group to attune to the particularities of
that group's narrative traditions while still contextualizing within a comparative
framework. An engagement with these two groups necessitates that we look
at them together and also separately to account for their distinct patterns of
incorporation and institutional histories.

   Chapter 1 analyzes representations of home ownership. Desires to own a
home are not bound to any one racial or ethnic group, and property attainment
is tied to the "American Dream" and ideas about "making it." However, racist housing policies have historically affected African Americans the most, and
Black writers have represented this history to explore its effects on individuals
and communities. Dorothy West's *The Living Is Easy*, Paule Marshall's *Brown
Girl, Brownstones*, and Gloria Naylor's *Linden Hills*[79] are novels working out
ways to be sympathetic to and critical of the pursuit of status symbols, which
gets concretized in these novels in the form of houses in certain neighborhoods.
These novels create status seeking characters who desire houses to differentiate
themselves from others who are racialized and hope subsequent generations will
keep up the monetary, cognitive, and social payments required to maintain or
increase their status, which include keeping poorer coethnics at a distance and
pursuing only profitable professions. Status seekers thus act as the initial investors
in a hierarchical and ownership-oriented value system, and latter generations can
either accept or refuse this ideological inheritance and reinterpret the end goal
of mobility. The artist figures in these novels reject materialist pursuits for more
creative paths, but do so at the cost of communal support. Demonstrating the

means by which these novels represent the ideological effects of racial capitalism manifesting in consumption habits and communal identification, this chapter draws out narrative patterns integral to the subsequent texts under discussion.

As the chapters will illustrate, sometimes the figural types emerge out of compromise: they question and express dissatisfaction with a system that creates social and economic hierarchies, but they still work within it. Then there are the characters who as mediators between disenfranchised people and oppressive institutions want to tear the system down altogether. In Chapter 2, I analyze Sam Greenlee's *The Spook Who Sat by the Door*, John A. Williams's *Sons of Darkness, Sons of Light*, and Oscar Zeta Acosta's *The Autobiography of a Brown Buffalo* and *The Revolt of the Cockroach People* to discuss how they imagined characters willing to give up middle-class jobs and commit what Amílcar Cabral called "class suicide," in order to implement radical politics informed by Black Power and Chicano movement ideology.[80] These texts grapple with the question of what kind of relationship middle-class minority activists could or *should* have with historically exclusionary institutions such as the government or academia. Written in the nationalist era—when liberation movements were closely linked with working-class politics—these novels construct characters wholeheartedly embracing the revolutionary route or wavering between revolution and institutional reform to envision ways to work for cross-class social change.

One of the outcomes of the Black Power and Chicano movements was the affirmation of markers of difference as the basis of identities formed for collective social action. In addition to enabling empowered subjectivities, this discourse also contributed to the essentialization of racialized groups as having particular cultures. While scholarship has engaged with sellout discourse and portrayals of the middle class in African American culture, these phenomena have been sparsely examined in Chicana/o cultural production. Chapter 3 focuses on how Chicana/o texts responded to the threat of ideological divisions stemming from economic heterogeneity. Since upward mobility is associated with assimilation, individualism, and materialism, ideals that Chicano nationalism labored to counter, upward mobility and middle-class status have been largely maligned or overlooked in Chicana/o studies even as desires to get out of poverty resonate across texts. After demonstrating how Chicana/o class politics informs texts even in the postnationalist period through a reading of the film *My Family/ Mi Familia* (1995), I segue into an analysis of Helena María Viramontes's novel

*Under the Feet of Jesus* as another text produced in the mid-1990s that reinforces Chicana/o working-class collectivity.[81] The novel, however, is imbued with figurative language expressing an ethos of class mobility and ends with a scene of a mediator's ascension through physical and mental labor. It does not represent changes in class but encodes a desire for it that would result in a politically conscious upward path. By depicting upward mobility allegorically, the novel reconciles Chicano movement concerns in a postnationalist context, when the Mexican American population was becoming more economically heterogeneous.

Viramontes's novel depicts the potential for and outcome of upward mobility obliquely, but the next two chapters analyze texts representing it explicitly. In Chapter 4, I analyze mass-market depictions of a racialized ethnic middle class.[82] Countering perceptions of Mexican Americans and Blacks as poor and the middle class as white, Richard Rodriguez's *Hunger of Memory*, the sitcom *George Lopez*, Michele Serros's *Honey Blonde Chica*, and the sitcom *black-ish* depict the social tensions that accompany this dual endeavor.[83] In the process, these works centralize racial, ethnic, and class conflicts and expand upon what C. Wright Mills termed "status panic." I argue that mainstream depictions of ethnic status panic since the 1980s correlate with the visibility of people of color in white-collar occupations and in mainstream representations, the effects of and backlash toward affirmative action, and the use of authenticity discourse in reinforcing and policing ethnic identity.

Critiques of the conflation of race with class also inform two satiric texts analyzed in Chapter 5 that offer contrasting perspectives on the association of Blackness with poverty. Percival Everett's novel *Erasure* and Lynn Nottage's play *Fabulation, or the Re-Education of Undine* are works featuring characters striving to be seen as individuals rather than part of an overdetermined racial group.[84] The class performances depicted in *Erasure* and *Fabulation* suggest that the conflation of race and class, in which whiteness is associated with wealth and Blackness with poverty, is so strong a frame of reference that their protagonists cannot disrupt it with their individual performative acts. *Erasure* ends in cynicism over an artist's inability to contest, to modify George Lipsitz's phrase, *the possessive investment in blackness*, through which individuals and industries profit from representing Blackness as poverty-stricken and pathological. *Fabulation*, meanwhile, depicts a protagonist who has bought into the possessive investment in blackness and has denied her working-class origins in order to gain status, but by the end of the play is realigned with her working-class community, a realignment representative of texts trying to counter intra-ethnic class divisions.

Attempts to imagine working-class unity as occurs in *Fabulation* can be seen as nostalgic in the sense they gesture back to a previous state of group identity associated with wholeness and authenticity. Such imaginings can also emerge in response to pressing political issues in the present. Chapter 6 focuses on three immigration films that take up this task to counter anti-immigrant sentiment. *The Gatekeeper*, *Sleep Dealer*, and *Machete* are films that initially thematize ethnic betrayal through Mexican American Border Patrol agents who have distanced themselves professionally and ideologically from Mexican migrants in order to accrue the advantages of assimilation.[85] These films disrupt the fantasy that upward mobility is solely a domestic issue by tying the border agents' class mobility to U.S. power and privilege maintained through military efforts and class exploitation transnationally. By depicting gatekeepers becoming mediators, they also imagine scenarios whereby threatening outliers gain awareness of the exploitive effects of neoliberal economic policies and get reintegrated into an affective community for political purposes. This chapter concludes by demonstrating that while Mexican American law enforcement figures can get redeemed in Latina/o films, if we look at correlating Black characters in film—Black police officers depicted as sellouts—the option of redemption gets foreclosed.

These dramas, while fictional, develop the very real tensions inherent in a racially and economically stratified society. Representing intragroup class differences is no easy task, and ethnic cultural producers have addressed the formal and ideological challenges of doing so through a range of strategies. These aesthetic choices reveal how these narratives work to expand ethnic identity to include socially mobile or middle-class experiences or how they work to strengthen group cohesiveness by countering class divisions. *Race and Upward Mobility* delineates those strategies and theorizes the signification of race and ethnicity once assumptions about class homogeneity break down, foregrounding the social and aesthetic dues integral to the processes of self- and communal identification.

# MORTGAGED STATUS

And that lie that success was a rising *upward*. What a crummy
lie they kept us dominated by. Not only could you travel upward
toward success but you could travel downward as well; up *and* down,
in retreat as well as in advance, crabways and crossways and around
in a circle, meeting your old selves coming and going and perhaps all
at the same time.

Ralph Ellison, *Invisible Man*[1]

An absurd vice, this wicked wanton
writer's life.

Sandra Cisneros, *My Wicked Wicked Ways*[2]

## SYMBOLIZING STRATIFICATION

In *The Housing Status of Black Americans*, economist Wilhelmina A. Leigh observes that the percentage of Black home ownership in the 1980s equaled that of
whites in the 1940s.[3] With a forty-year lag, federal policy came closer to catching
up with needs in 1988, when the Fair Housing Amendments Act gave the U.S.
Department of Housing and Urban Development power to enforce the anti-
discriminatory legislation passed in 1968.[4] Leigh's study allows us to understand
this historical period in terms of a time lag between the government and the
people it served. In this chapter, I analyze novels concerned with this contradictory time in the postwar period—a time when more African Americans were
entering the middle class than ever before, but when home ownership was still
circumscribed due to the ideological climate. It was a time, as sociologist Bart
Landry notes in his 1988 study of the Black middle class, when a house could

be seen as the "symbol of success in a society that allowed [Blacks] precious few opportunities for conspicuous achievement,"[5] yet Black authors were also questioning that very symbol of success. It was out of these contradictions, in the wavering between the enticement of class ascension and a disillusionment with its fruition, that novels such as Dorothy West's *The Living Is Easy* (1948), Paule Marshall's *Brown Girl, Brownstones* (1959), and Gloria Naylor's *Linden Hills* (1985) emerged. By symbolizing upward mobility through the acquisition of houses in neighborhoods associated with social and economic success, these novels historicize communal consumption patterns and reflect how status symbols function as part of an ideological inheritance. Characters who pass down and characters who are bequeathed this inheritance enact a conceptual framework, what I am calling mortgaged status, that lays bare the process and interpretation of social mobility over generations.

Given the existence of economic and social hierarchies upheld through histories of white violence, these novelists portray how hierarchies can also be internalized and reinforced by racialized peoples seeking ascension through prevailing value systems, while also developing characters trying to imagine alternatives to intragroup stratification and material accumulation. Amy Schrager Lang has argued that in the mid-nineteenth century, American writers endeavored to construct a "syntax of class" in order to describe and order class differences.[6] Similarly, these novels produced from the 1940s to the 1980s were developing figures and symbols to narrate the struggle for social incorporation during a period of simultaneous growth and limitation for the Black middle class; for even though economic advancements and civil rights gains did much to alter the field of possibilities, there still existed a disparity in the actual attainment of equal housing and employment opportunities as well as a lag in the realm of possibilities imagined for a minority middle class.

I argue that one prominent figure in these novels is the status seeker, who strives for social elevation on material grounds. As a financial asset, a house offers the possibility of intergenerational wealth and a sense of stability. But in these novels, the symbolic significance of houses as markers of wealth and inclusion—conveying who gets to own and live in certain areas—becomes a way for authors to critique hegemonic standards of incorporation and assessment. More than just a place to raise one's family, a house can stand for investments in self- and communal worth in that it necessitates continuous psychic, social, and monetary payments over time. So while the status seeker acts as the original investor, this status is mortgaged, borrowed in the hopes of uninterrupted upward mobility and dependent on subsequent generations to keep up payments. But later generations can have different interpretations of upward mobility's end goal, and in portraying this disconnect, these novels nuance the trajectory of upward mobility and depict status as an accruement of a kind of debt, one that cannot or will not be paid off by subsequent generations.

In this generational disconnect of aspirational values at odds with the changing environment, there is a critique of ideologies associated with previous historical moments that are no longer viable in the present. The portrayal of temporal incongruity in *The Living Is Easy*; *Brown Girl, Brownstones*; and *Linden Hills* illustrates how artistic production can intervene and make sense of historically situated social contradictions. I thus end with readings of artist figures trying to interpret the contradictions around them, endeavors that render them conflicted about their role in and relationship to their communities. Situated in opposition to status seekers and orienting the ethical perspective, these conflicted artists serve as the primary vehicles by which the later novels offer an understanding of the ways in which conceptions of home, community, and the slipperiness of status intersect. The artist figures in Marshall and Naylor's novels eschew the idealization of property accumulation and are instead, as a character in *Linden Hills* states, searching for "a middle ground somewhere," somewhere in between poverty and material striving.

## STATUS SEEKING AND HYSTERESIS IN *THE LIVING IS EASY*

Set in the Boston of the 1930s and 1940s, Dorothy West's *The Living Is Easy*[7] centers on the Judsons, a middle-class Black family supported by the earnings of Bart Judson, a prosperous fruit vendor known as "The Black Banana King" who is the son of a former slave. Bart's story is one of upward mobility achieved through individual entrepreneurship. He also models the virtues of hard work and thrift, vested as he is with the traditional traits found in narratives of the self-made man. Tracing the history of the self-made man as a literary construct, Jeffrey Louis Decker points out that in its early manifestations, such as in Benjamin Franklin's autobiography and Horatio Alger novels, the cultivation of moral character was coded as white, male, and middle class. This construct, however, gets destabilized over the twentieth century with the emergence of socially mobile women, immigrants, and ethnic minorities who "expose[d] morality as a discourse traditionally placed in the service of normative power."[8] That Bart Judson eventually fails in his self-making endeavor aligns with Decker's argument; it turns out that no amount of hard work or thrift can prevent the onset of capitalistic changes that leaves small businessmen like Bart vulnerable. And since Bart does not have access to the kinds of networks and capital that could enable him to enter big business, West's novel shows how the traditional self-made-man narrative can only temporarily and uneasily accommodate the story of racialized upward mobility. But the rise and fall of the Black self-made man is only part of the story that West tells, since she instead spotlights the woman who has to marry the self-made man because her own options for self-making are limited.

Cleo Judson starts out with desires for independence and financial prosperity, unrealizable as they are, given her employment options and subsequent marriage, but her aspirations are rechanneled and ultimately end up contributing to her family's downward mobility. The eldest daughter of a Southern fieldworker, Cleo originally moved northward seeking adventure, wanting to attend night school, and dreaming of a career on the stage. However, as historian Jacqueline Jones and sociologist Enobong Hannah Branch have found, prior to 1960, agrarian work and domestic service were the sectors in which most Black women worked,[9] and Cleo finds herself employed in the latter, tending to the households of first one and then another white employer. Considered a ward yet having the duties of a servant, Cleo works for "protectresses [who] felt that Cleo was better off without money" (28) and who sent her wages back home. She marries Bart not out of love but because "she wanted to get away" (34), and once wed she is still limited in what she can strive for. Having no opportunities beyond her role as a wife and mother, she directs her ambitions toward the domestic sphere. As Cleo seeks elevated status within her family and society, the house starts to represent the site of those demands. Over the course of the novel, Cleo coerces her husband into renting a house on the edge of Brookline (away from other Blacks) and dislodges her sisters from their homes so that they and their children end up living with her. Once they are in her home, she can make decisions on their behalf about the best way to live, which in her estimation is according to the status-conscious values of the Black Boston elite. A history of blocked financial gains and the limitations of domesticity consequently turn a fledgling narrative of self-making, which has traditionally had attached to it a positive moral valence, into one about immoral status seeking.

While the narrative is anchored through Cleo, she is only one status seeker among many. Like West's other novel, *The Wedding* (1995), *The Living Is Easy* presents a condemnatory portrayal of well-to-do Black families fated to ascend financially while declining morally due to intraracial and class prejudices. In *The Living Is Easy*, the downfall occurs both within the family, with the Judsons losing their fortune when wartime brings about changes in the marketplace, and throughout the Black bourgeoisie, whose members are dwindling in number and creating conditions that make their existence tenuous and self-destructive. Since Cleo is such a compelling character, most literary criticism on the novel has focused on her or the other female characters in the novel.[10] While my readings build on this work, I analyze the community of status seekers around Cleo and offer a temporal analysis to show how the novel stages setbacks in what I call mortgaged status.

In order to understand the dynamics among the Black Bostonians, the novel makes clear that one must interpret the house as a desirable symbol of status only if it is near whites. Narrative development begins with Cleo's pursuit of a house that would take the family out of Boston's South End, with its "influx of black cotton-belters," and establish them, enviously, within the Black elite, with a house touching "the arteries of sacred Brookline" (5). Believing it "better to give your child a good foundation than to save for his future" (148), Cleo literally interprets this desire as a house in a neighborhood that would enable her to send her daughter, Judy, to a better school, one where she would be among other Bostonians. In effect, Cleo and the other Bostonians see houses as "positional goods." As theorized by economist Fred Hirsch, positional goods can be explained by social scarcity, which influences the desirability of goods that are limited by social forces rather than physical ones, resulting in a scarcity of consumption. In other words, houses in desired neighborhoods—like titled jobs and tropical vacations—garner value not because the production of them is scarce but because the attainment of them is. They serve as positional goods in that the satisfaction felt as a result of consuming them arises from how they help position a person in relation to others: satisfaction "is derived from relative position alone, of being in front, or from others being behind."[11] In *The Living Is Easy*, as in the other two novels analyzed in this chapter, who lives where and next to whom becomes indicative of social worth and also of position in a social hierarchy.

Part of the value of a house near whites is that it enables the inhabitant to claim the title of "proper Bostonian" (39), which comes with the luxury of negating minority status, a luxury Cleo aims for when she succeeds in renting a house at the edge of Brookline. The third-person narration tells us that the Black Bostonians

acknowledged no more than a hundred best families in Boston, New York, Philadelphia, and Washington. Their lives were narrowly confined to a daily desperate effort to ignore their racial heritage. They did not consider themselves a minority group. The Irish were a minority group, the Jews, the Italians, the Greeks, who were barred from belonging by old country memories, accents, and mores. . . . Though they scorned the Jew, they were secretly pleased when they could pass for one. . . . There was nothing that disturbed them more than knowing that no one would take them for anything but colored. (105)

Part of a larger sprawl of middle-class Black communities, the Bostonians assert their nonminority status by claiming class and cultural superiority over ethnic whites. By appropriating aspects of whiteness that are valuable (such as appearance) and denigrating those that are not (such as being a recent arrival), they can increase their social status while also disidentifying as natives looking down upon immigrant newcomers. Furthermore, they have three reference groups against whom they can compare themselves, which is how they determine their social belonging: being economically above ethnic whites, living proximate to whites, and being definitely socially and economically above poor Blacks. Sociologist Vilna Bashi Treitler has defined these types of maneuvers as characteristic of "ethnic projects," through which ethnic groups strive to "foster a perception of themselves as 'different' from the bottom and 'similar' to the top of that racial hierarchy."[12] We can see that the Black Bostonians are depicted as attempting to make themselves into more of an ethnic group—recognized as such by cultural characteristics marked by class—so they are not perceived as solely part of a racial group, which would lump them with poorer Blacks and relegate them to the bottom of the social hierarchy.

In trying to maintain this triangular differentiation, these "nicer colored people" (5) show glaring contempt for poor Southern Blacks. They "viewed their southern brothers with alarm, and scattered all over the city and its suburbs to escape this plague of their own locusts" (5), creating not only spatial but also social distance by adhering to internalized belief in their own superiority by breeding and culture. Where they live and the kinds of homes they have become markers of how they perceive themselves in relation to the class and racial hierarchies of their day, and this self-perception obfuscates any collective racial or class consciousness. This is most evident in the scene at Cleo's holiday party when her guests, selected from the best of the Black Bostonians, dismiss a visiting dean's plea for monetary support on behalf of a destitute Southern Black man accused of killing a white man. Cleo declares, "when one colored man commits a crime, the whole race is condemned" (263), and her guests echo her in agreement, refusing both to identify with the accused man and to help in his cause.

The novel vilifies the Black middle class's distancing from and disidentifying with the Black poor, while situating this maneuvering in a particular historical era. Historian Benjamin P. Bowser periodizes three eras of emergence of the Black middle class, categorizing them by their rise during Reconstruction, Jim Crow, and the post-civil-rights era. He recounts the acts of violence toward and the disenfranchisement of Blacks during Reconstruction and Jim Crow that prevented the Black middle class from achieving equal footing with whites, arguing that without the racial barriers and continued European immigration, their sizable population and skills would have put them in a "position to be one of the most successful and well-off ethnic groups in the United States by the time of World War II."[13] However, since under Jim Crow the Black middle class faced such systemic opposition, "The result was that blacks formed a middle class unto itself that was more about image, aspiration, values, and moral pretense than it was about economics."[14]

In West's rendition of this historical moment, the Black middle class's pursuit of image-making goes hand in hand with classism and colorism and is leading to a state of self-decay. Born into relative privilege, the progeny of the original class of upwardly mobile Blacks in the United States had internalized these dual psychic strategies, which at this point were preventing them from acknowledging that the social environment had changed. While the Black elite that arose after Reconstruction garnered status by providing services to whites, by 1915 the economic landscape had changed, and a new Black elite was emerging that understood the value of aligning with and catering to the Black community.

Consequently, Landry notes, a "position at the top of the Black community could now be secured through economic achievement rather than through family background, skin color, or white approval."[15] Yet the Black Bostonians in *The Living Is Easy* have been raised to think of themselves as gentlemen and gentlewomen, even though the scarcity of jobs available to Blacks during the Jim Crow era makes it nearly impossible for them to live up to the aspirations and lifestyles established by their forebears. Thus many live near impoverishment but rich in pride. Diagnosing their affliction, Simeon Binney, the son of one of the most esteemed old Black Bostonians, astutely declares that he and his sister are of a kind "who have bloomed and will die in one generation," in recognition that their fathers not only started family businesses but "built a social class" and did so "out of tailor shops and barbershops and stables and caterers' coats" (139), all profitable services but ones that do not carry enough status currency for subsequent generations. "We cannot afford its upkeep because they have taught us to think above their profitable occupations" (139), Simeon states, revealing that theirs is a mortgaged status, borrowed on the promise of uninterrupted upward mobility.

Mortgaged status captures how the maintenance of social hierarchies becomes part of a process of transactions necessitating continual payments, in the form of both cognitive tasks, including the distancing and negation of other minority groups, and material accumulation, which includes houses that serve as visualizations of geographical distancing and social elitism. Acknowledging the actual price of their standing would take much cognitive work, involving a rearrangement in how the Black Bostonians perceive themselves in relation to their reference groups. They would, for instance, have to confront how similarly they and poor Blacks are treated and how whites base their interactions with them not on class but on perceptions of race. The primacy of race over class is made painfully clear to Simeon through the encounter he has with several Harvard classmates who physically assault him for walking with his white-appearing sister. The novel dramatizes how attempts are made to ignore this blatant act of racial discrimination through the conversation Simeon has with his father, one of those founders of the social class that would rather see this encounter as a "mistake" made by "Harvard gentlemen" who "forgot themselves" (133). When Simeon presses the issue, his father continues to avoid blaming his son's attackers and instead names the source of the problem as the "riffraff [that] has come up from the South" and the "colored men walking with low-type white women" (133). And despite Simeon's attempts to correlate the attack with a larger race issue, he himself quickly states that he and his sister, Thea, "are hardly comparable" to the latter group (133). Thus even as he tries to express indignation about racial discrimination, Simeon cannot avoid making a classed moral judgment about Southern Black men and lower-class white women because "his pride could not let that observation pass." Both father and son exhibit the kind of backtracking typical of those confronted with information that might force them into new ideological territory.

This scene is reflective of how much psychic work the Black Bostonians undertake to maintain their conception of themselves as superior. The novel implicitly suggests that if they became aware of and acknowledged how taxing their status seeking and status maintenance are, they might be more willing to participate in a large-scale racial and class movement. They have an opportunity to do so, even if only by supporting Simeon's newspaper, *The Clarion*, which reports on the plight of all Blacks. However, they see themselves as being above the troubles recounted within its pages. As Cherene Sherrard-Johnson has noted, "without a coalition of pooled resources or the recognition of a shared black kinship crossing class, color, and regional boundaries, the exclusionary practices of the black middle class precipitate its own self-destruction."[16] Its members remain blind to how they are complicit in perpetuating ideologies that keep them denigrated and are leading to their decaying lifestyles. To become aware is unimaginable for them, according to the logic of the novel, which equates character action with temporal disconnection.

*The Living Is Easy* provides three examples of temporal disconnection, all in the realm of business. The first centers on the aforementioned Binney family, founded on the earnings of Carter Burrows Binney, "the awe-inspiring owner of a tailoring establishment in a downtown shopping center" whose "rent had been several thousand dollars a year, and his income had been triple that figure" (93). With this income he is able to send his children to Harvard and give them the upbringing of gentlefolk—that is, until

the readymade suit grew in favor, and a well-dressed man was not ashamed of his appearance when he wore one. Where Mr. Binney's store had once stood, a great department store soared seven stories and sold readymades at a price that would have sent Mr. Binney spinning into bankruptcy sooner than he did.

Mr. Binney, forced to vacate his premises, had moved across the street to continue his business, against the advice of his lawyer, who was of the opinion that he should sell out while his chances of breaking even were good. But Mr. Binney couldn't believe that a man above a laborer's station would wear a readymade suit on Sunday. (93)

Conditioned to think of himself as a gentleman providing a necessity to other gentlemen, Binney cannot fathom that manufacturing developments would change the tastes of his clientele, effectively making his business obsolete and his status uncertain. He is not attuned to the needs of the middle class, which was changing during this time from a population of predominately small property owners to salaried employees, many of whom wore the ready-made suits. His identity is too invested in his role as a status provider, a role from which he garners an elevated status himself.

The way the novel narrates the fate of the elder Binney parallels his misstep. By the middle of the passage, we have already learned that Binney goes bankrupt. The passage restructures the chronology of events to impart information so that the reader is aware of the effect before its cause, paralleling how Binney himself sets in motion an outcome he was advised was a possibility. The end of his business comes before he grasps its cause, and even then he refuses to believe that the status market has changed. His unwavering faith in the status quo leads to an unwillingness to change his business, revealing the disconnect between his values and those required by his changing social environment.

The novel offers two more representations of families experiencing reversals of fortune to render this outcome into a communal phenomenon. The second occurs with the Hartnetts, a family that began its upward mobility story on the earnings of a coachman whose great-grandson was eventually able to run his own "livery stable covering half a city block" (111). Indicative of their prominent social presence, the stable emblematizes the movement of the family from workers to owners, the latter "able to live like lords" (112). This phrase references a process of upward mobility possible in a capitalistic society yet describes the family in anachronistically feudal terms. The incongruence is, however, similar to the temporal incongruity of the values that lead to their ruin, since the Hartnetts

did not save. For were not horses the delight of kings, and what could supplant them in the hearts of civilized men? The automobile, the dirty sputtering automobile. The rich, who should have had more taste, began to buy them. Mr. Hartnett failed in business, and blew his brains out just like a white man. Everybody was a little proud of his suicide. (112)

From a service man to a man who can pay for services: what could have been a successful class-mobility story fails and is attributed to overconfidence and business myopia. The emulation of whites is noted ironically, in referring both to how Hartnett commits suicide and to how the community's collective self-esteem rises from this self-destructive act.

The third example is perhaps the most poignant, since it involves a character who by all accounts is not interested in his social status. He is, rather, concerned only about his savings so that he may leave his family financially secure. Taught by his formerly enslaved mother that "money was the measure of independence" (57), Bart Judson accumulates wealth as part of a continuing familial project to assess the extent of freedom. How much money he can make is therefore directly tied to his self-worth. Yet, even though he is an independent entrepreneur, he is dependent on market forces, to which he turns a blind eye. Dismissing rumors of a second world war and then dwindling contracts, Bart is confident that his fruit store can withstand the test of time and even contrasts himself to the other two noted failed businessmen:

An automobile can get you places same as a horse, only faster. A readymade suit can cover a man same as a tailor-made suit, only cheaper. But nothing man is apt to think of can substitute for fruit and vegetables. That's what I sell, and I sell the choicest. Man thinks a lot of his stomach, and he wants the best that money can buy. (149)

What he does not take into account is that the rise of chain stores and the power of collectives can put independents out of business, and in his case, can end his enterprise of assessing his independence. From his vantage point, Bart cannot see how modern capitalism is fostering new forms of economic activity, what economic theorist Lewis Corey identified as the "great change from individualism to collectivism" that resulted from trustification, monopolies, and collectives and led to a decrease in small business ownership.[17] The novel thus provides a palimpsest of economic models, with characters caught between the old and new, unable to see how capitalism is the driving force behind these temporal incongruities. Inevitably, Bart is forced into bankruptcy, and his failed business venture makes it impossible for him to remain in the house that Cleo has attained as a status symbol for the family, with the final scene of the novel staging his exit.

The novel correlates these business failings with moral failings, with the values keeping the Bostonians in a state in which they are holding on to past successes and past means of maintaining social rank. To represent the ideological and structural tensions that reveal a community at odds with itself, the novel thematizes what Pierre Bourdieu would decades later term "hysteresis." In *Outline of a Theory of Practice*, Bourdieu explains that hysteresis characterizes the "lag between opportunities and the dispositions to grasp them which is the cause of missed opportunities and, in particular, of the frequently observed incapacity to think historical crises in categories of perception and thought other than those of the past."[18] Pinpointing a time lag, the term refers to when the *habitus* (internalized dispositions) and *field* (the social environment) are out of sync, leading to missed opportunities. The Black Bostonians' habitus in the novel emerges out of their upbringing, education, and environment and consists of an internalization of classism and colorism. At one point, this habitus allowed them to maintain a degree of superiority over poorer and darker Blacks; at that time, their evaluations of self-worth were bolstered by net worth. However, since the social field has changed and their habitus has not, the Black Bostonians are missing opportunities to change the social and structural conditions that keep them in an inferior position. They instead continue to live beyond their means to prove their worth and maintain their status. Because the novel shows that they live in denial and keep trying to distance themselves from the wider Black population, it is easy to read them as victims of their own elitism. However, we can also read their behavior through Bourdieu's understanding that it is those from privileged backgrounds in dominant cultural positions who can more readily see the advantages of changing their habitus to keep up with a changing field and thus do so more easily. Those in dominated positions, meanwhile—such as those in the working class or, in the case of *The Living Is Easy*, a newly established and fragile Black middle class—do so at a slower pace and only after it is less advantageous. As Cheryl Hardy puts it, the hysteresis effect "provides opportunities for the already successful to succeed further, while the less successful continue to misrecognize the strengths and weaknesses of relative field positions."[19] So, on one hand, by ignoring the signs of change, the Black Bostonians fall prey to their own foreclosed opportunities. The novel suggests that if the Black Bostonians, with their antiquated habitus, could only adapt to the changing social environment and work for collective uplift, they could become a more secure Black middle class. On the other hand, the novel also contextualizes their status seeking behavior as the only kind that makes sense, given the limited options for proving one's worth during the Jim Crow era. Because the Black Bostonians lack the social and cultural capital that comes with being part of the dominant group and because they lack an extensive network or intergenerational wealth to help them ride out economic downturns and changes in industry, they are unable to prevent their downward mobility.

The insecurity of class status depicted in *The Living Is Easy* shares similarities with William Dean Howells's *The Rise of Silas Lapham* (1885). In Howells's novel, the paint-selling entrepreneur Silas Lapham embarks on a quest to expand his business and amass wealth. Whereas his provincial family previously "had not a conceit of themselves, but a sort of content in their own ways,"[20] their increasing prosperity exposes them to Boston's social elite, which leads them to alter their habits and dress in order to gain social acceptance. Just as Cleo aspires to live in a house near Boston's best, so does Silas attempt to build a house in fashionable Boston's Beacon Hill neighborhood to prove his family's social worth. And similar to Silas's inability to realize his dream of living in a home ensuring intergenerational status, since he loses a significant part of his wealth by the end of the novel, the Black bourgeoisie finds its class status precarious and its net worth declining. What makes *The Living Is Easy* different, however, is that this is not just a novel about a self-made man. It is a novel that warns about racial gatekeeping—the strategies that the Black bourgeoisie use to designate who is inside or outside of their group that emerged in response to gatekeeping by whites, providing a critique of those who go into social debt in order to accrue status at the expense of others who are also racialized. While Silas is tempted at various times to go against his ethics in conducting his business dealings and suffers a reversal of fortune, at the end of the novel he is still fortuitous even if he has downsized. Having evaded an ultimate fall from status through luck and a marriage plot, Howells's protagonist ultimately emerges tested but unscathed, holding on to his virtues and the promise of continued, if compromised, economic success. There is no such optimism in *The Living Is Easy*, not in its critical depiction of a racialized community unable to afford its mortgaged status due to classism and colorism.

## *BROWN GIRL, BROWNSTONES*
## AND THE VALUE OF ARTISTS

Like *The Living Is Easy*, Paule Marshall's *Brown Girl, Brownstones* sets its story at the end of a migration tale. The trajectories of Bart and Cleo reference the Southern-to-Northern migration of millions of African Americans in the post-Reconstruction era and early twentieth century. The experiences of the Boyce family in *Brown Girl*, in contrast, register migration into a new country. Evoking the history of West Indians who immigrated to the United States before the civil rights movement and settled largely in New York, the Boyces have left Barbados and reside in Brooklyn.[21] Like Cleo, who wants to attain a home that will enable her daughter to grow up an esteemed Bostonian, Silla Boyce above all wants to "buy house" as the starting point for her family, so that they may follow in the success of other enterprising Barbadians in Brooklyn who eventually make it to the suburbs after first buying brownstones.[22] *Brown Girl* reminds us, however, through its heteroglossic nature, that there are different imaginings of the home and different voices competing to express and enact visions of the ideal home.

Though a family of four, the Boyces are represented by three central characters—Silla, Deighton, and Selina, with the novel's first section centering on the conflict between husband and wife and the second on their daughter Selina. The older daughter, Ina, for the most part follows the path set out for her by her community: at the end of the novel she is about to marry a hard-working Barbadian boy and will establish a home of her own. Though it would have been interesting if Ina had had her own section, the novel relegates her to a minor character, to be combined with the other Barbadian youth who, for Selina, represent a path not taken and not desired. Following traditional routes, they stand in for a status esteemed and secure within their communities. With its exploration of ideological and temporal contradictions, the novel is more interested in depicting those with insecure status, those who do not make sense according to the logic that informs their communities.

The portrayal of insecure status is enacted in the pursuit of home ownership and also in the articulation of aesthetic inclination. Scholars have made a strong case for considering the trope of the house in the novel. Kimberly Benston argues that the architectural imagery acts as the unifying symbol of the novel, apparent not only in descriptions of the environment but also in the organization of the plot, formation of character interiority, and creation of metaphors.[23] Building on Benston's work, Vanessa D. Dickerson focuses more specifically on the relationship between the female characters and the brownstones, playing on the phrase "property of being" to refer to how the brownstones are directly tied to characters' senses of self in the novel. As she puts it, Silla understands what the ownership of the brownstones means "economically and politically, while her daughter realizes how spirit is invested in the brownstones."[24] Properties used to describe the brownstones, then, not only reveal how the characters perceive the buildings, they also reflect how the characters see themselves. I argue that the metaphorization of the house also participates in the aestheticization of insecure status, which in turn is how the novel expresses its interest in the role of the ethnic artist.

In the first few pages of the novel, we learn that the brownstones are witnesses to demographic shifts, ones alluded to through imagistic language. As depicted in the novel, the brownstones can signify either a transitional moment for ethnic immigrants—the state before they indeed reach the middle class and mainstream success and move out of ethnic enclaves—or the final stop for them. The novel tells us that the brownstones were built and first inhabited by the "Dutch-English" and "Scotch-Irish," and that there was "tea in the afternoon then and skirts rustling across the parquet floors and mild voices" (4). Yet the novel's action begins in 1939, in the period after "it had been only the whites, each generation unraveling in a quiet skein of years behind the green shades." In the present moment, "the last of them were discreetly dying behind those shades or selling the houses and moving away," and with their exit, "the West Indians slowly edged their way in" (4). Setting up the West Indians' class ascension as one contingent on the decline of white gentility, the description of this process contrasts the "mild" presence of the original tenants and their discreet ways to what is to come, what in the following sentences is described as "a dark sea nudging its way onto a white beach and staining the sand" (4), referring to the community of Barbadians who introduce into the previously "hushed rooms" an "odd speech" (4). In describing how an earlier group leaves and another takes its place, the narrative voice alludes to the factors slowing down the process of mobility rather than explicitly stating them. These forces require the Barbadians to slowly edge into previously all-white neighborhoods rather than allowing them to flow there smoothly.

Hinting at these factors is the narrativized perspective itself, which sees this historical and geographical movement as decline and decay rather than rein-vigoration and opportunity. By focalizing from this judgmental perspective, one that sees these new tenants as "odd" and their presence as a "stain," the narrative ventriloquizes an anti-immigrant stance. The passage not only sets up a model for reading the West Indians' relationship to the brownstones as one that is part of an immigrant enclave cycle, it also indirectly conveys what kind of prejudice they might face in their attempts to integrate, enabling a more contextualized reading of this process without being didactic in tone. Gavin Jones has argued that the sea imagery in the novel personifies the fluidity and multidimensionality of the Black diasporic community, and here we can see how the passage creates a cyclical and wave-like process for the immigrant home-ownership experience, one that flows and ebbs just like the sea to which the community is compared.[25] The question remains whether the Barbadians will keep on moving, continuing a journey to the suburbs and to professions that will supposedly guarantee them secure economic and, by extension, social status in the United States, or whether they will stay in the area like some of the inhabitants before them.

Struggles for inclusion and acceptance are explored within the brownstones as well, through the marital battle between Deighton and Silla, whose ongoing conflict over where and how to live emerges from distinct class backgrounds and desires for status in different locales. Deighton wants to return to Barba-dos and build an estate in the country of his upbringing. The son of a seamstress who instilled in him a confidence at odds with his actual realm of possibilities, Deighton expresses a yearning for his "land home" (12), where he can build a house on inherited property and live in a style impossible in the United States, where he cannot find a job, is undocumented, and has failed as the head of a household. His feeling of not belonging is evident in how he sleeps in the mar-gins of their rented brownstone, seeking solace in the sunroom and avoiding

the kitchen door, shaken as always by the stark light there, the antiseptic white furni-ture and enameled white walls. The room seemed a strange unfeeling world which con-tinually challenged him to deal with it, to impose himself somehow on its whiteness.

His wife stood easily amid the whiteness. (22)

Whiteness, sterility, and insensitivity here become associated with a feminine space and Silla, who has seemingly adapted more easily to life in the United

States. Not only does Deighton feel like an outsider in his own home, but else-where it is revealed that he even questions his manhood and how to express it outside of sanctioned gender norms like drinking, violence, and promiscuity. Deighton passes by "dim lit bars with the little islands of men" exhibiting "vio-lence in their coarse play" who could easily prove they were men "by flashing a knife or smashing out with their fists or tumbling one of the whores in the bar into a bed," and the narrator wonders, "But what of those, then, to whom these proofs of manhood were alien? Who must find other, more sanctioned, ways? It was harder, that was all . . ." (37–38). We are then told that "None of this ever crystallized for Deighton as he stood watching them, and he would turn away thinking only that they were somehow more fortunate" (38). The novel portrays Deighton as a man insecure in his worth because of limitations on the expression of masculinity and on the possibilities for Black men, and as suggested by the language in the novel, which contrasts the bright white do-mestic space with the dimly lit bars—the lack of opportunities open to dark-skinned immigrant men. The narrative also makes a point of communicating that Deighton has not yet made nor will he ever make the connections that would allow him to "crystallize" his observations so as to come up with an-swers to his questions. Thus the narrative voice subtly makes known its own contribution in articulating Deighton's uncertainty about his masculinity and outsider status.

Although Deighton's homesickness is a product of his outsider status in the United States, Silla reveals to Selina that he had confrontations with whiteness back in Barbados, too: "He was always putting himself up in the face of the big white people in town asking for some big job—and they would chuck him out fast enough. He was always dressing up like white people" (33). In the United States, Deighton continues to maintain that he is entitled to high-paying jobs and faces repeated rejection from white employers who will not hire him. If hysteresis occurred in *The Living Is Easy* due to the time lag between the habi-tus of the characters and the social field, where the latter had changed but the former had not, this novel illustrates that Deighton's habitus is out of sync with his social field because he is, in effect, *too far ahead*. While his confidence and ambition might have secured him a desirable job in the post-civil-rights era, during 1940s Jim Crow it gets him booted out of offices for thinking too highly of himself. Again, character action is depicted as misaligned with the environment, but in contrast to *The Living Is Easy*, the novel does not place the fault for this disconnection solely on the character. By focalizing the narrative through Selina, who adores and sympathizes with her father, Marshall offers a critique of an environment that will not allow a man like Deighton to realize his full potential.

Deighton's attempts at realizing his ambitions fail, and the only avenue for upward mobility that seems viable to many of the Barbadians is home ownership. Whereas a return migration would establish Deighton's sense of worth, only an upward trajectory in the U.S. class system would satisfy Silla's. "How else a man your color gon get ahead?" she asks her husband, and when he refuses to work menial jobs to build up savings, she endeavors to buy the brownstone alone, joining the other Barbadian women in scrubbing floors and renting out rooms. In contrast to Deighton's privileged upbringing, her memories of Barbados are of living "down some gully or up on some hill behind God back" (10), while working and being lashed in the fields as a young girl. Coming from and immigrating into societies where she is disadvantaged because of her gender, race, and laboring background, Silla's status seeking is an effort to counter marginality. Engaged in a relationship that is more a competition than a partnership, Deighton and Silla cannot reconcile their different conceptualizations of home and status. After Silla machinates to sell his plot of land behind his back to secure funds for a down payment on the brownstone, Deighton enacts his own plan of vengeance and spends the nine hundred dollars Silla has received for the land in one full-blown shopping spree. As a result, he gives up on the American dream and begins living in a dream world altogether.

What happens to Deighton at the end of the novel is actually a modification of an old narrative convention. Critics have noted that nineteenth-century authors depicted what Nina Baym calls "the melodrama of beset manhood," in which "the role of entrapper and impediment . . . is reserved for women"[26] and which, as Lora Romero has put it, features "flight[s] of male characters into the wilderness or out to sea (and thus away from the rule of women)."[27] In a similar way, Deighton makes an escape after his symbolic emasculation by Silla, albeit to a frontier in his own mind. There, in his madness it is possible to renounce all responsibility to himself and his family, which he does once he joins the religious cult and starts worshiping its leader, Father Peace. He abnegates his role as a father and husband when he sinks mentally into an infantile state. This mental descent ends only when he jumps off the ship that is about to deport him back to Barbados and drowns.

With men leaving home and with houses ruled by tyrannical women, the similarities between *The Living Is Easy* and *Brown Girl, Brownstones* are striking. Why correlate women with the quest to secure a house and bestow on them qualities that end in the ruin of a home? This question is especially interesting considering that the autobiographical elements of *Brown Girl* appear reversed in Marshall's novel. In an interview, Marshall stated that in actuality it was her mother who had inherited money and her father who wanted to invest it in a brownstone.[28] "That whole thing of money works into *Brown Girl*, although it is developed very differently," she notes, with no further explanation as to why she reversed the scenario of who wanted the brownstone.[29] That she has done so, however, foregrounds how status seeking is tied to the constrained possibilities that women had outside of the home and why Black women in particular would be trying to improve their status. In *Opportunity Denied*, sociologist Enobong Hannah Branch illustrates that despite changes in the labor market broadly and expanding opportunities for women, Black women have historically been relegated to devalued and low-status jobs because

Race and gender shaped the occupational placement of Black women. More than Blacks or women generally, Black women experienced severe restrictions that limited them to jobs where they did the same work they had done during slavery. The opening of new jobs in the early to mid-twentieth century had little to no effect on their employment picture. . . . White women entered feminizing occupations that privileged Whiteness. Black men entered traditionally male occupations. Black women, however, stood outside the gates of occupational and economic change. They were neither White nor men. They lacked something that was essential in the pre-1960 labor market—a privileged status that would facilitate their uplift.[30]

While the novels are certainly critical of Cleo and Silla for their status seeking, they provide details that enable us to read them in relation to Black women's labor history, a history that explains why the desire for improved self- and communal status would be so intense. Like Cleo, Silla comes from an agricultural background and spent her upbringing working in the fields. Even though she has escaped that life, Silla later works in an industry in which, even during the wartime economic boom, "labor-hungry employers hired either white women

or black men first, depending upon the industry, but black women always last,"
according to historian Jacqueline Jones.[31] When Black women were hired, points
out Branch, they "perform[ed] the most undesirable work, often under hazard-
ous conditions with no possibility of advancement. Yet even the lowest- paying
jobs in the factory represented significant progress from the farm and domestic
labor sectors in which the majority of Black women toiled."[32] Seeing Silla (and
Cleo) against this economic background reveals why the marital battle is over
not just who controls the domestic space but also why the idealization of the
home would be so tied up with a desire to be an agent of change.

Their desires for status symbols signal endeavors to assert agency in a hostile society. In 2013, sociologist Tressie McMillan Cottom broached this topic
through an opinion piece addressing criticisms launched at the seemingly para-
doxical actions of the Black poor: "If you are poor, why do you spend money
on useless status symbols like handbags and belts and clothes and shoes and
televisions and cars?" She answers by sharing a lesson she learned as a child,
watching her mother model strategies for bolstering her value in the eyes of
people with the power to devalue her and deny her resources:

I remember my mother taking a next door neighbor down to the social service agency.
The elderly woman had been denied benefits to care for the granddaughter she was
raising. The woman had been denied in the genteel bureaucratic way—lots of waiting,
forms, and deadlines she could not quite navigate. I watched my mother put on her
best Diana Ross "Mahogany" outfit: a camel colored cape with matching slacks and
knee high boots. . . . It took half a day but something about my mother's performance
of respectable black person—her Queen's English, her Mahogany outfit, her straight
bob and pearl earrings—got done what the elderly lady next door had not been able to
get done in over a year. I learned, watching my mother, that there was a price we had
to pay to signal to gatekeepers that we were worthy of engaging.[33]

Learning from her mother that there was a payoff to adopting status-bolstering
strategies, Cottom heightens the value of the lesson by referring to a story in
which the strategies are employed to help a neighbor in need, so that signaling higher status is not only a "survival skill," as she puts it, but also a means
to help others. She shares anecdotes in which her mother's and her own uses
of status symbols are strategic and successful, delivering a critique of systemic
racism while also showing what sociologists have called the "minority culture

of mobility" might look like in an institutional setting. The "price [she and her mother] had to pay" is costly in that it requires conformity to a value system that demands the performance of certain habits of speech and dress in order to be found "worthy of engaging." But it also enables access to resources. Ultimately, it is a tax given charge because of the power of white supremacy and classism.

Marshall's narrative, in contrast, depicts not momentary acts of status nego-tiation but the permanent internalization of status seeking. In Marshall's novel, the price is too high. Silla's actions are unwavering and self-serving, and social mobility comes at the cost of her family. Her daughter Selina consequently has a more critical take on status strategies. While Silla willingly accedes to a mortgaged status, her daughter is unwilling to accept it and pay off the sym-bolic promissory note. In *Brown Girl*, the narrative shifts to a focus on the sec-ond generation, the generation that will inherit middle-class status, continue to work toward it, or reinterpret its end goals. Selina does not want to be like her mother, the social Darwinist who believes that one must exploit others in order to avoid someone else's getting ahead instead. Silla joins the Barbadian Association with other like-minded community members and wants Selina to participate, hoping that she will win their youth scholarship and start on her way to becoming a success in business, law, or medicine. Selina, however, is a nonconformist, has a poetic quality to her, and is critical of her Barbadian com-munity's drive toward accumulation as embodied by her mother. Martin Japtok has described the conflict in the novel as one of ethnicity versus individualism, arguing that the novel "explores the potential of coercion behind the notion of ethnic solidarity."[34] The novel also poses a question that ties the two realms together, one that has to do with the status of the arts in an ethnic immigrant community. In other words, it raises a concern about how individual artistic endeavors can fit within or emerge from collective struggles and highlights the value of having a divergent perspective and being able to represent it.

While Selina is not an outright artist, she has an aesthetic sensibility and functions as the protagonist of this *Künstlerroman*; she is the means by which the novel offers hope for a reconciliation between aesthetic desires and the will to bring them to fruition. While the women in the novel are headstrong and follow up on their goals, the men are portrayed as artistically minded but debilitated by their inability to achieve their dreams. After her father loses his mind and will to live, Selina finds another companion with artistic inclinations, engaging in her first romantic relationship, with Clive, a fellow second-generation Barbadian. Like her father, Clive cannot find his footing in the community, having unappreciated aesthetic aspirations. After his mother burns all his paintings, he is wracked with guilt—aware of how hard his mother has worked and sacrificed in order to invest in his status as a professional and yet unwilling to proceed on the path dictated for him. Instead, Clive spends his days in a mental existential limbo, staring at his unfinished paintings and unable to commit to either the business trajectory or the artist's way. He is, however, aware of the reasons why their community does not support individualistic endeavors: "Take the Barbadian Association. They've got plans, haven't they? . . . [W]hat can they do with aesthetes with paintbrushes in this kind of plan? They simply cannot afford us" (263). In "Criteria of Negro Art," W. E. B. Du Bois considers such an opposition to artistic endeavors in his opening, where he rhetorically asks, "[W]hat have we who are slaves and black to do with Art?"[35] Unlike Du Bois, who goes on to argue on behalf of the value of Black self-representation, Clive does not take an affirmative stance. He tells Selina that people like the two of them are liabilities for a community that has a set business plan, that knows only one way in which to rise up in a hostile country; he does not see an alternative to either communal ostracism or communal material achievement.

The novel's portrayal of the ethnic artist's plight has echoes of what Andrew Hoberek, extending William H. Whyte's work, terms the "organization-man narrative," which characterizes white-collar conformity stories in 1950s fiction.[36] But in *Brown Girl, Brownstones*, the ethnic artist is both sympathetic and antagonistic to the community's demand that members share the quest for home ownership and material success. The West Indian immigrants in the novel have adopted the American dream of upward mobility and are working for collective success, as Japtok has argued: "*Brown Girl* indicates what one might call the 'ethnicization of materialism,' in that acquisition is a *communal* goal rather than exclusively an individual one."[37] This communal goal, however, rests on a strict definition of what constitutes community, and here the novel likens the status of the artist with the status of African Americans. In order to guard and ensure the progress of specifically West Indians, the Barbadian Association at first discriminates against African Americans, seeing them as far too denigrated by U.S. society to include in their own quest for social acceptance,

a stance which leads them to miss out on opportunities to increase membership in their organization.

Yet by including descriptions in the novel of discrimination by whites,
Marshall renders the Barbadians' goals sympathetically, if ambivalently. She
even stated that certain characters were included in the novel to help her work
out her conflicting feelings about her community's values. Asked if Selina's best
friend, Beryl (who like Ina conforms to her community's expectations), was
based on a real character, Marshall explained,

She's based on a number of friends over the years with a large dose of imagination.
She was interesting to me because Beryl represented something I had to work out for
myself and using her as a character helped me to deal with this, to deal with the fact
that my family did not follow the pattern of the typical Barbadian West Indian immigrant family. They never succeeded in purchasing the Brownstone house, you see. . . .
My father, after I was about age thirteen, became so involved with Father Divine that
he was no longer part of our household. . . . So the set patterns for families that was
so true for most of the West Indians that I knew in Brooklyn was disrupted for me.
Beryl represents the child of those families who went the so-called established route
. . . whose families have been successful, have realized the immigrant dream. A part of
me always longed for that. At the same time a part questioned it and in a sense even
rejected it because it seemed so narrow to my mind.[38]

I venture into Marshall's biography not to argue that literature acts as a form
of personal therapy but to show how it can bring to the surface embedded tensions about the cultural producer's lived experience. In this novel, the tensions
are expressed in the form of antinomies, with acquisition pitted against aesthetic
expression, and these tensions speak to the subjective experiences of both the
protagonist and the author. If one of the questions implicitly posed by the novel
is, What is the value of the ethnic artist arising from a community trying to
rise up into the middle class?, the novel does not deliver an answer on the level
of plot, since the explicitly artistic figures are men who cannot reconcile their
community's values with their own. Moreover, the depiction of bohemianism,
which historically has been the avenue of antimaterialist rebellion, is embodied in
Clive, who cannot help himself or his community and therefore represents a dead
end. The answer offered by the novel emerges through the text itself, in its rich
and complex images gradating the insecurity of social and communal status.

Recall that in *Brown Girl*, personal and communal status is correlated to the status of the brownstones. They first appear as "an army massed at attention" (3) in their uniform coloring and formidable appearance but by the novel's end are depicted in a ruined state. Invested with subjectivity, the brownstones are described in the first passages of the novel as if in "mourning," "indifferent," confus[ed]," and "aloof" (3–4), putting forth affective and cognitive states that will be shared by the Barbadian characters throughout the novel. The last paragraphs reveal the brownstones reduced to "a vast waste—an area where blocks of brownstones had been blasted to make way for a city project" (309). After Selina turns away, "For it was like seeing the bodies of all the people she had ever known broken" (310), she desires, "suddenly, to leave something with them" and gives the only token she has with her, one of the two silver bangles that she, like other Barbadian girls, has always worn on her wrist. A moment of reconciliation and identification, the ending nevertheless renders the immigrant community in a state of wreckage, with Selina as its "sole survivor" (310). Her aesthetic sensibility has fueled her distrust of acquisition and now allows her to be the one to give something to her community. By insinuating that the immigrant community is living without permanent security, this last scene underscores the threat of dispossession immanent in every desire for possession. To own things is also to be owned by the ideologies and structures that make that ownership possible. By investing Selina with an outsider's perspective, Marshall can bring to the fore an alternative viewpoint that values the insights articulated through imaginative works. As a product of her own immigrant community, one of Marshall's most valuable aesthetic contributions has been in rendering the complexities of home ownership.

Moreover, by juxtaposing the tensions between monetary and aesthetic value and leaving open the possible achievement of an alternative, nonbohemian but creative lifestyle, Marshall's novel anticipates something like the rise of what urban studies scholar Richard Florida has termed the "creative class." Arguing that the percentage of workers "who add economic value through their creativity" increased over the twentieth century from 10 to 30 percent at the century's end,[39] Florida includes in the creative class members of the labor force "whose economic function is to create new ideas, new technology and/or new creative content."[40] The creative class, part of the "creative economy" that has emerged as people have come to value individuality, meritocracy, diversity, flexible schedules, and work-lives with inherent incentives, is a shift from the old business model of organizational industry, with its emphasis on high financial reward over personal fulfillment, its stifling of individuality, and its expectations of conformity and routine. Set in the middle of the twentieth century, *Brown Girl* fits within the constellation of texts that criticized the prevailing business ethos of organizational industry, themes represented in novels such as Sloan Wilson's *The Man in the Gray Flannel Suit* (1955) and Richard Yates's *Revolutionary Road* (1961) and discussed in scholarship by William Whyte, C. Wright Mills, and Robert L. Heilbroner.[41] Its dismissal of property as the ultimate marker of worth accords with Florida's claim about a different value system at play in the new economy: "Most members of the Creative Class do not own and control any significant property in the physical sense. Their property—which stems from their creative capacity—is intangible because it is literally in their heads."[42] The suggestion at the end of the novel is that Selina, imbued with both an aesthetic appreciation bequeathed by her father and an independent streak and work ethic inherited from her mother, would desire to pursue some form of gainful creative work. The novel does not venture into her future to show us how she would reconcile those desires. Instead, it captures a moment when the possibility of being both middle class and engaged in independent creative work, especially for a member of a newly arrived immigrant population, may have seemed impossible, on the one hand, and not worth the social costs, on the other.

The fear toward and uncertainty about becoming an artist that Marshall's novel tapped into in the 1950s makes logical sense, since half a century later, the "creative class" continues to be predominantly white. As with the Black bourgeoisie depicted in *The Living Is Easy*, the actions of the Barbadian community in *Brown Girl* are not irrational. Rather, they make logical sense given the proven viable options for achieving social incorporation and financial solvency in a country stratified by race and class. Over fifty years after the publication of *Brown Girl*, a national study of data collected from the Census Bureau's 2012 American Community Survey found that Blacks' and Latina/os' chances of being a working artist are still slim: 77.6 percent of working artists are white, with only 7.5 percent of working artists being Black and 8.3 percent Latina/o.[43] Arguably, largely contributing to this disparity is family net worth—which differs significantly along racial lines—since working artists are more likely to come from families that do not rely on their income contributions and/or who could support them in the lean times. As NPR's *Planet Money* found, artists were more likely to come from higher-income households.[44]

These historic realities explain the narrative negotiations Marshall makes in representing a character conflicted about aesthetic inclinations and her relationship to her community. In how she offers ethical arguments at odds with dominant values, Marshall shares some similarities with the group of writers and intellectuals that Stephen Schryer examines in his book *Fantasies of the New Class*. Analyzing writers and sociologists from the 1940s to the 1980s, Schryer argues that in the postwar period, with the rise of a professional-managerial class (the new class), intellectuals saw themselves as "cultural educators and national therapists"[45] who, as a result of their education and cultural capital, could serve as models for society at large, disseminating cultural values that "would mitigate the self-interest and acquisitiveness of American society."[46] Unlike some of the writers Schryer examines, however, who range from Lionel Trilling to C. Wright Mills to Ursula K. Le Guin, Marshall does not read as unequivocal about adopting and disseminating a new class fantasy since she provides empathetic understanding of why her community is driven toward material acquisition and also portrays the costs of challenging the group. She therefore has more in common with Ralph Ellison, whom Schryer sees as more ambivalent about a new class fantasy since *Invisible Man* "imagines the black artist as an inventor of new rites and rituals that can synthesize black and white experiences in order to give voice to egalitarian principles at odds with the prevalent materialism of American social life. . . . At the same time, through its anatomization of black intellectuals' dependence on white economic capital, the novel calls this cultural idealism into question."[47] In the novel, Marshall, in turn, expresses the new class fantasy and shows its limits by documenting a community that understandably feels like it "simply cannot afford" (263) to diverge from proven paths for social incorporation. She constructs a conflicted artist who registers the challenges and compromises of addressing both intra- and inter-ethnic class tensions.

## TOWARD A CREATIVE MIDDLE PATH IN *LINDEN HILLS*

By focusing on the instability of the home against the backdrop of the 1930s and 1940s, *The Living Is Easy* and *Brown Girl, Brownstones* explore horizons of possibilities within the Jim Crow and World War II eras. Their pessimistic portrayals of houses as status symbols and positional goods read as logical, given that the nation was not equitably habitable for all its residents and that the political upheavals and xenophobia of wartime made the longing for stability and social belonging that much more urgent. In the 1980s, this pessimism about upward mobility as a constrained means of enfranchisement was explored in the publication of Gloria Naylor's novel *Linden Hills*, with its depiction of the effects of desiring and attaining upward mobility according to prevailing value systems.

As a critical depiction of race and upward mobility, Naylor's novel contrasts with mainstream representations of the Black middle class in the 1980s. Writing about the conservative political climate and the representations of African Americans in film, Donald Bogle has called the 1980s "the Era of Tan." He cites the 1980s as a decade of more mainstream integration of African Americans, with Michael Jackson, Whitney Houston, Bill Cosby, as well as Jesse Jackson's run for president all evidence of a turning point in African American participation in entertainment and in politics. However, he points out that films in the 1980s "did all they could to make audiences forget the blackness of a star." He explains,

Often when a black performer appeared in a general release, he or she had no cultural identity. All ethnic edges had been sanded down, so that while they *looked* black, everything about them seemed expressed in a white cultural context; and in the long run, characters were neither black nor white but a tan blend. Even so, tan, like black, was often kept in the background.[48]

Bogle is discussing film representations such as interracial buddy movies, but similar criticism was launched at the most successful television show in the 1980s—*The Cosby Show*. Running on NBC for eight seasons from 1984 to 1992, and starring Bill Cosby as Dr. Heathcliff Huxtable and Phylicia Rashad as his attorney wife, Clair, who together head a five-child household, the show was both praised and critiqued for its depiction of an upper-middle-class Black family. Offering portraits of successful, professional African Americans that countered negative stereotypes, the show was lauded for using the sitcom genre to portray African Americans as just a "normal" family. But part of this semblance of normality meant that the show did not delve into explicitly racial or class conflicts, which scholars have argued promoted the message that structural barriers were no longer a problem for African Americans and that upward mobility was possible for anyone who worked hard.[49] Along these lines, it was critiqued for not being a realistic representation of what life was like for the Black middle class, as one middle-class Black viewer expressed in an interview:

I have a problem with the fact *The Cosby Show* will build a 30-minute episode around Heathcliff Huxtable building a hero sandwich. Why aren't we dealing with, and I'm not saying do this every week, but every now and then why aren't we dealing with some real issues that are confronting the Black middle class . . . what happened to me in the courtroom, if I'm an attorney, or what racist thing happened to me in the hospital, if I'm a surgeon. That's what they come home talking about . . .[50]

If the tax Bill Cosby paid in order to win mainstream appeal was circumventing issues such as those raised by the interviewee, the outcome was a show that suggested it could not afford to explore controversial scenarios in a world outside of the home. Even though Gloria Naylor's *Linden Hills*, like the other two novels I have discussed, is subject to market pressures, none of these books are pitched to a mass market in the same way that a network sitcom or mainstream feature films would be. As a result, the novels offer more trenchant critiques of the effects of capitalism and white supremacy in creating pressures and values internalized by individuals and communities trying to counter economic exclusion and social marginality.

Set in a fictitious elite Black suburb, *Linden Hills* literalizes mortgaged status, the outcome of a community established on leased land. Structured into four parts for the four days before Christmas, the novel begins with a prologue that describes the transformation of Linden Hills from a worthless plot of land with a two-room cabin into an enviable community with showcase homes for the Black upwardly mobile. Founded during Reconstruction by the monomaniacal Luther Nedeed and developed by his heirs (four more generations of Luthers who resemble him in looks and disposition), Linden Hills is a community meant to fulfill a revenge plot. Wanting to spite neighboring whites who had laughed at his seemingly unprofitable land, consisting of tough soil and bordering a cemetery, Nedeed sets out to prove that "This wedge of earth was his—he couldn't rule but he sure as hell could ruin. He could be a fly in that ointment, a spot on that bleached sheet, and Linden Hills would prove it."[51] He establishes a mortuary business, and since the only tenants who would tolerate living near his cemetery are rumored to be "murderers, root doctors, carpetbaggers, and bootleg preachers" (5), to these he gives a lease of a thousand years and a day.

The lease, with its longevity, gives a semblance of ownership, but Nedeed is careful to keep ultimate possession, foreseeing a future of white supremacy and unwilling to cede control to people he sees as unfit and out of sync with the social milieu:

These people, his people, were always out of step, a step behind or a step ahead, still griping and crying about slavery, hanging up portraits of Abraham Lincoln in those lousy shacks. They couldn't do nothing because they *were* slaves or because they *will be* in heaven. (8)

In other words, Nedeed is claiming hysteresis, convinced that other Blacks are not aware enough of the present to catalyze effective action. Rather than try to help them, he wants to exploit them, taking money for their dead and using them in his project of creating a demographic blight. As a character who is given insight into a possible fissure between prevailing values and the changing social environment, the founder of Linden Hills could have been given heroic qualities; instead, his foresight is turned toward personal profit and status seeking, beginning a pattern detrimental to subsequent inhabitants of Linden Hills.

Future inhabitants start to pay a costly price when the leased land turns into a tract of mortgaged homes under the third Luther: "Watching America's nervous breakdown during the thirties, he realized that nothing was closer to the spleen and guts of the country than success" (9). He modifies his grandfather's dream, taking into account that the land has increased in value: "the fact that they had this land was a blister to the community, but to make that sore fester and pus over, Linden Hills had to be a showcase" (9). He is the one who starts Tupelo Realty Corporation, a real-estate agency with the mission of filling the homes of Linden Hills with only a "certain" kind of people, since "making it into Linden Hills meant 'making it'" (15). We learn that the Tupelo Realty Corporation is highly selective about the types of families who can receive its mortgages, and that the "certain" something turns out to be a drive for material success. Tupelo Realty does not discriminate against a person's or a family's origins; in the Linden Hills gated community, the only gate is an ideological barrier having to do with who is deemed worthy enough, and those who are worthy are willing to

buy into a value system of mortgaged status. Thus in a perverse upward mobility narrative, the goal is to get to the bottom of Linden Hills, closer to Luther
Nedeed and his circle of hell, where accumulated status costs one's soul.

Catherine C. Ward has compared Linden Hills to Dante's hell because it
"represents not so much a place as a state: the consequences of man's choices."[52]
Indeed, those accepted into Linden Hills compose a diverse group of the seemingly condemned:

Applications from any future Baptist ministers, political activists, and Ivy League
graduates were now given first priority, since their kind seemed to reach the bottom
faster than the others, leaving more room at the top. And whenever anyone reached
the Tupelo area, they eventually disappeared. Finally, devoured by their own drives,
there just wasn't enough humanity left to fill the rooms of a real home, and the property went up for sale. (17–18)

No matter their moral and political convictions or educational backgrounds,
the residents of Linden Hills are all status seekers, hungering for something that
they believe they can find in an elite neighborhood. As an allegory about filled
homes serving as symbols of empty worth, the novel speaks to the argument
made by Esther Milner in *The Failure of Success*, that the belief that "the achievement of high occupational and consumer status will convert us into happy,
psychologically whole human beings" is a modern fallacy.[53] Milner adds that
middle-class individuals, in their quest for status, have forgotten that they are
ends in themselves. A portrayal of this effect on the Black middle class, Naylor's
novel delivers the message that what is driving and ultimately self-negating
about this endeavor is that Linden Hills residents are basing their worth on
how whites perceive them. To underscore this point, the novel delves into the
lives of several minor characters who exemplify material gain and self-loss.

In a novel in which one of the main characters is hinted to engage in necro-
philia, minor character Maxwell Smyth rivals Nedeed in a depiction of the
unnatural. A rising executive at General Motors, Maxwell sees his Blackness
as a professional liability and engages in methodical efforts to "minimize his
handicap to nothing more than a nervous tic" (103). He puts in twenty-one-
hour workdays, adheres to asexuality, regulates room temperatures so as not
to sweat, and even monitors his diet so as not to defecate any odorous solids.
Calculating his every move to appear in the most advantageous and nonracial-

ized light, "He weighed the decision of whether or not to smile at his secretary with the same gravity as that with which he considered the advisability of a new line of sedans" (104). An extreme portrayal of attempts to deny the body in response to racist stereotyping, Maxwell shares similarities with Lawrence Otis Graham's "colorless dreamer," one of the nine roles in his classification of Blacks in corporate America included in his book *Member of the Club*. According to Graham, the colorless dreamer believes "that I'm the kind of person who can make others forget I'm black. When I walk into a room, people see a professional. It's much later that they think about my race. Since I don't focus on color, neither do they."[54] Naylor's depiction of Maxwell also evokes E. Franklin Frazier's criticism in 1957 of the Black bourgeoisie as living in a world of make-believe in pursuit of white acceptance. Describing the emulative behavior of the Black bourgeoisie, Frazier remarks, "Since they have no status in the larger American society, the intense struggle for status among middle-class Negroes is, as we have seen, an attempt to compensate for the contempt and low esteem of the whites."[55] Naylor is clearly aware of Frazier's work, since one character has his book, *Black Bourgeoisie*, in his bookcase (255). In a cynical portrayal of the knowing yet complicit academic, the book belongs to the historian who lives in Linden Hills, who is recording its history but is doing nothing to change its course. Furthermore, through Maxwell the novel presents the extreme version of the status seeker, demonstrating how one of the ways art can contribute to social analysis is by passing ethical judgments, which the novel does while depicting the taxing nature of status negotiation.

Naylor's updated version of the status seeker (in the tradition of Frazier) reflects a broader interest in the psychic costs of Black upward mobility in the 1980s. Political scientist T. Alexander Smith and economic policy scholar Lenahan O'Connell argue that this era saw the increasing visibility of the "paradox of progress," which they explain as the growing political involvement, social advancement, and material accumulation by Blacks after the civil rights movement and affirmative action, coupled with the mounting frustration and alienation they might experience while striving to be treated as social equals.[56] Naylor's novel gestures to the pressures of white corporate America and resonates with the "paradox of progress" assessment but also refocuses attention on a minority middle-class community itself, depicting how it might contribute to and support attempts at social striving even at the expense of the individual.

A self-consciously literary text, the novel passes its ethical judgment through its conflicted artist figure, making explicit the need for an aestheticization of mortgaged status that in *Brown Girl, Brownstones* was only suggested. The artist in the novel is Willie K. Mason, a street poet and a resident of the neighboring ghetto, Putney Wayne. He is at first in awe of Linden Hills and receives insider access when he works odd jobs for the upscale neighborhood's residents in the days leading up to Christmas. During this time he is privy to the oddities, immorality, and sadness that pervade the community. In addition to meeting Maxwell Smyth, Willie learns of Laurel Dumont. While Maxwell's story appears in the middle of the novel, Laurel Dumont's appears at the end, serving as the impetus for the novel's closure, which depends on Willie's reassessment of Linden Hills. In her portrait of Laurel, Naylor shows the psychic crisis that may befall the status seeker who, in pursuit of possessions, loses possession of herself. Even though she has made it to the top of the corporate ladder at IBM and married a district attorney with a covetable house in Linden Hills, Laurel suffers from depression and an uncertainty about where her "home" really is. After weeks spent living in a state of inertia and fear, avoiding work, family, and friends, she is still unable to pinpoint what she really wants amid a house that has everything. Self-reflection comes too late, and Laurel commits suicide, joining others who have contributed to Linden Hills's high turnover rate.

The compounded effect of bearing witness to Laurel's death, Maxwell's affectations, and the acts of other Linden Hill residents (which include a man denying his love for a woman just because she is darker and a man denying his love for another man) weigh on Willie to the point at which the only possible way for him to make sense of it all is through aestheticization. After a week of working in Linden Hills for Christmas-gift money,

he was tired of thinking about it, tired of trying to put all those pieces together as if it were some great big puzzle whose solution was just beyond his fingers. . . . [W]here was he going? . . . He wasn't going to stay in Putney Wayne, that much he knew. And he wasn't going to keep bagging groceries until he was fifty years old. There was better for him than that. (274–75)

The question Willie struggles with is tied to understanding the realm of possibilities open to him once he acknowledges that he even has possibilities. He recognizes his worth but does not yet know how that may translate into living.

Distraught, his solution for the time being is "to put Linden Hills into a poem" (275), which allows him to order his thoughts and begin the process of imagining answers. The novel provides the beginning lines of his poem: "There is a man in a house at the bottom of a hill. And his wife has no name" (277). By including a couple of lines from the poem, *Linden Hills* emphasizes the power of organizing thought through aesthetic form. However, Naylor still privileges the novel as the form that can, like the other novels discussed in this chapter, more richly capture "All the fissures and rents which are inherent in the historical situation," as Georg Lukács argues.[57]

It is during a conversation with Willie's best friend, Lester, that the novel offers a possible answer of how to live with increased resources. Lester suggests, "maybe there's a middle ground somewhere. . . . I don't know why it must be one or the other—ya know, ditchdigger or duke. But people always think that way: it's Linden Hills or nothing" (283). Accordingly, the novel is itself an aestheticization of the yearning for a third option, one by which it is possible to refuse status seeking while at the same time understanding the social and economic pressures driving it, both of which give birth to the socially conscious and conflicted ethnic artist depicted in *Linden Hills* and *Brown Girl, Brownstones*. If, presumably, that middle path is gainful creative work, it would probably provide a livelihood that is no duke's, but no ditchdigger's either. In Mark McGurl's assessment, "[e]xplicitly or not, every work of serious fiction in this [postwar] period is, on one level, a portrait of the artist."[58] Novels about the need for and the process of artistic self-fashioning consequently "stage the autobiographical drama of heroic self-authorization that accounts for their own existence."[59] Rendering the social contexts in which the artist can provide a privileged perspective, these narratives express a desire to reconcile social pressures by avoiding the social immobility that the status seeker fears while also contributing to a communal enterprise through the representation of that community. In *Upward Mobility and the Common Good*, Bruce Robbins has argued that upward mobility narratives, while traditionally interpreted as stories about individual success, actually demonstrate ways of giving back to a collective and theorizes the role of the artist as a way these narratives do so: "The life of the writer or artist serves the genre of upward mobility because it is itself a metaphorical compromise between individual social climbing and commitment to some version of the common good."[60]

These novels work toward a creative middle path that in economically vulnerable communities is not an easy one to take, given the riskiness of the move when one lacks generational financial and social capital. Communities with materialistic values are portrayed as more precariously situated, however, and their ruin is represented as both loss and opportunity. In order to move forward, a movement underwriting the optimism of their alternative viewpoints, Willie and Selina must first gaze backward and mourn their relationships to the people and places occasioning their emergence as artists. Before leaving Brooklyn to board a ship to Barbados, Selina grieves the ruined brownstones that were status symbols for her community. As Willie leaves the fiery ruins of Luther Nedeed's house, his insights coalesce in the staggering recognition that the residents of Linden Hills did nothing to stop the fire, complicit as they are in the evils of Linden Hills. Mourning the ruin of once-grandiose dreams figured through houses, Selina and Willie express the novels' ambivalent relationship to the aspirations behind those homes: sympathetic as they are to the reasons why those who have been historically disenfranchised would strive for social mobility through status symbols, they do distance themselves from those strivers. The novels illustrate how as "artifacts of the imagination, literary works are by their very nature engaged in imagining other ways of being" and posit the conflicted artist as the one who can start to make sense of the factors that would lead individuals and communities to agree to or disavow mortgaged status.[61]

Granted, these latter two novels are more optimistic than West's about the possibility of creating alternatives to the status seeking they represent, and arguably are so because their artist figures are at the cusp of self-realization. One might ask why there is no artist figure in *The Living Is Easy*. In fact, *The Living Is Easy* presents a disillusioned version of the artist in the form of Simeon Binney, who starts his own newspaper to make "colored people . . . face the facts of their second-class citizenship" (134). Simeon is himself compromised by the values he upholds in regarding himself and his sister as superior because of their class upbringing. Furthermore, his newspaper has financial difficulties stemming from the fact that many who have the means to subscribe either are not doing so out of apathy or are forcing him to compromise on the content because, as genteel Black Bostonians, they see it as "thoughtless cruelty to call attention to the dregs of the colored race" (135). The difficulties of securing a readership along with funding would have been frustrations that West herself was well acquainted with, so it is understandable that she would not idealize the writer-editor's life.[62] But even as she represents the practical hardships of trying to produce social commentary dependent on a market to sustain it, West offers through her novel a case for how artistic production can deliver that commentary in a way that is rich, moving, and multilayered.

As texts engaged in a discourse about individual and group worth, *The Living Is Easy*, *Brown Girl, Brownstone*, and *Linden Hills* illustrate how the search for status can prove costly for the individual psyche and community alike. And they theorize Black social mobility in ways that would later be echoed by major sociological works.[63] By aggregating the disconnects between time and place, self and community, acquisition and aesthetic expression, these novels enact destabilizations that within their pages signal reversals of fortune but which can prompt and even model critical reevaluations of status. The pursuit of a house—metaphor for the process of buying into a value system—illustrates mortgaged status and its effects on the initial investors and on subsequent generations. Passed down this ideological inheritance, the younger generation questions this value system upholding consumption habits as markers of social mobility and yearns for nonmaterialistic, creative paths. Together, status seekers and conflicted artists serve as types to portray generational mobility, with social mobility measured not through material achievement but in the ability to critique materialism.[64] Ultimately, these novels show characters paying an identity tax in contexts in which status is denigrated and status symbols provide a strategy for signaling worth. That is the tax paid within the narrative. On the level of narrative production, the status seeker–conflicted artist dyad is both marker and product of that tax. Whether the pair is portrayed in the novels (Silla and Selina, the Linden Hills residents and Willie) or exists as a relationship between character and author (Cleo Judson and Dorothy West), the tax drives the ethical critique. By vilifying the status seekers, the novels express a refusal to endorse a capitalistic value system. But at the same time, they contextualize status seeking as a response to historical circumstances, as an understandable recourse in a society that racializes and assigns worth.

While there is a discernable pattern of African American novels centralizing the desire for home ownership, this is not a dominant theme in Mexican American literature. I speculate that this is due to several factors: even though both groups experienced housing discrimination due to racially restrictive covenants, African Americans migrated northward to majority white areas much earlier; the majority of Mexican American novels were written and published in the post-1960s period, after racially restrictive covenants were deemed unconstitutional; and the large influence of immigration on Chicana/o literature has driven a concern with remembering and defining a symbolic homespace, whether that is imagined as Mexico, Greater Mexico, Aztlán, or the borderlands, rather than owning property. However, an intense desire to own a house does drive one of the most widely read Mexican American texts of all time: Sandra Cisneros's *The House on Mango Street*.[65] At the beginning of the text, the young protagonist, Esperanza, expresses her yearning for "A real house. One I could point to" (5). Her working-class family has moved frequently and finally owns a home on Mango Street in a working-class ethnic neighborhood in Chicago, but it is a house that Esperanza can only claim with shame. When a teacher finds her playing in front of the house and asks if she lives there, she narrates that she "had to look to where she pointed—the third floor, the paint peeling, wooden bars Papa had nailed on the windows so we wouldn't fall out. You live *there*? The way she said it made me feel like nothing. *There*. I lived there. I nodded. . . . I knew then I had to have a house" (5).

The trajectory of wanting a house to valuing an aesthetic sensibility that occurs across generations in the novels discussed in this chapter occurs within Esparanza's sole character arc. Having started out wanting a material house because her family's experience has been one of poverty and instability, she is the one seeking status through a house that would symbolize social acceptance, stability, and worth. Her desires change, however, in the course of relating her day-to-day experiences and those of her neighbors. She comes to value instead, like Selina Boyd of *Brown Girl, Brownstones* and Willie Mason of *Linden Hills*, an aesthetic imagination that can interpret and give structure to stories that are personal and communal. In this sense, the desire for a physical house gets easily rechanneled toward authorial aspirations. However, like Selina and Willie, Esperanza must mourn a parting with her community as well: "I put it down on paper then the ghost does not ache so much. I write down and Mango says goodbye sometimes. She does not hold me with both arms. She sets me free" (110). Entering and leaving Mango Street metaphorically through narration, Esperanza projects a future in which she would literally leave Mango Street when she achieves class mobility through education and becomes a writer. She attempts to deflect possible accusations of betrayal while asserting a communal consciousness through the assurance that although her neighbors will wonder where she went, "They will not know I have gone away to come back. For the ones I left behind. For the ones who cannot out" (110).

The texts discussed in this and subsequent chapters reveal how much intragroup as well as intergroup class stratification shapes narrative choices in Chicana/o and African American literature. Here I have analyzed texts featuring protagonists with aesthetic sensibilities who relate stories about class aspirations, conveying faith in the role of art as social mediation, in its ability to document social phenomena, and its capacity to critique economic and social inequalities and their accompanying value systems. In doing so, these texts end up valuing the status of the artist. But history shows us that art alone cannot be credited with social change. In the next chapter, I examine novels that portray characters working for "those who cannot out," in and out of institutional settings such as the government, academia, or the judicial system. Written during the Black Power and Chicano movement era, these novels about upward mobility and middle-class characters reflect the political experimentation of the period through characters testing out strategies for enacting revolutionary or reformist politics.

# CHAPTER 2

# CLASS SUICIDE

> The petty bourgeoisie has only one choice: to strengthen its
> revolutionary consciousness, to reject the temptations of becoming
> more bourgeois and the natural concerns of its class mentality,
> to identify itself with the working classes and not to oppose the
> normal development of the process of revolution. This means that
> in order to truly fulfill the role in the national liberation struggle,
> the revolutionary petty bourgeoisie must be capable of committing
> suicide as a class in order to be reborn as revolutionary workers,
> completely identified with the deepest aspirations of the people to
> which they belong.
>
> Amílcar Cabral, "The Weapon of Theory," 1966

## MIDDLE-CLASS REVOLUTIONARIES

In his address to the 1966 first Tricontinental Conference of the Peoples of
Asia, Africa, and Latin America, which took place in Havana, Cuba, Amílcar
Cabral outlined his theory for revolutionary action.[1] Born in 1924 in Guinea,
which was still under Portuguese rule, Cabral was a leader in the national
liberation movement that helped Guinea-Bissau achieve its independence in
1973. Arguing that national liberation movements needed a socialist theoretical framework to understand the historical progression of colonialism and class
struggle, "The Weapon of Theory" speech also discussed the factors by which
they would succeed, namely, through armed struggle and the help of a petite
bourgeoisie that would have to work against its own material interests. Cabral
asserted that those in the middle stratum would be pivotal to the movement

because their access to education and positions of power would make them the most influential class to potentially undermine imperial powers. Involved in the practical implementation of revolutionary ideals in disseminating ideology and providing leadership, they would also have a role to play in the post-liberated state since they would be the ones "directing the state apparatus inherited from this domination."[2] But in order for nations to make the transition into socialist states, the petite bourgeoisie would have to "reject the temptations of becoming more bourgeois"[3] and not settle for the material comforts and privileges that come with positions of power. They would, Cabral argues, have to commit "class suicide," and identify with the working masses rather than with their own class interests.

Cabral offered a paradigm for liberation and state transformation dependent on a cross-class coalition. Historian Basil Davidson observes that Cabral's theory of class suicide emerged from his direct experiences working with the PAIGC, the party founded to secure independence for Guinea and Cape Verde and composed of a petite bourgeoisie.[4] One of the challenges facing the PAIGC was that Guinea did not have a working class; it had a large peasantry, one without a revolutionary consciousness. Noting that Socialist revolutions have occurred most often in less-industrialized countries, sociologist Thomas Meisenhelder points out that Cabral's "theory of revolution set in the periphery of global capitalism" helps us understand how revolutions occur in areas without a large working class.[5] Coming out of a particular socioeconomic imperialist context, Cabral's framework has to be understood in this light. His theory of class suicide nevertheless has broad significance in its identification of a politicized renunciation of materialist aspirations by a middle class with revolutionary aims. In the mid-1960s when Cabral gave his speech, the spirit of revolution was felt throughout the world, and in the United States, activists of color identified with anticolonial struggles in Africa, Asia, and Latin America, seeing minority groups in the U.S. as internal colonies that needed to be liberated from a white supremacist state. It is in this context that Sam Greenlee, John A. Williams, and Oscar Zeta Acosta wrote novels that dramatized scenarios along the lines of Cabral's call to action, in which middle-class minorities renounced stability and material comforts in the service of revolutionary action.

. . .

In the previous chapter, I discussed novels that featured upwardly mobile ethnic characters coming into consciousness about the value of artistic mediation,
interpreting and making sense of their community's internalization of racism
and materialism. This chapter turns to representations of social mediators in
Greenlee's *The Spook Who Sat by the Door* (1969); Williams's *Sons of Darkness,
Sons of Light* (1969); and Acosta's *The Autobiography of a Brown Buffalo* (1972)
and *The Revolt of the Cockroach People* (1973). The protagonists in these novels
come from working-class backgrounds and work for nonprofit or civil rights
organizations during a historically volatile moment. By the mid-1960s, the
Black Power movement had departed from the integrationist goals of the civil
rights movement and had embraced more militant strategies for the radical
transformation of U.S. society, a move that inspired Chicano movement activists as well. These novels feature characters who similarly feel that working
within the system will not bring about racial equality. Tired of being social
mediators who help maintain the status quo, and expressing Black Power and
Chicano movement aims, these protagonists aspire to be revolutionary agents.
By portraying characters who either wholeheartedly embrace the revolutionary
route or waver between revolutionary change and institutional reform, these
novels capture the impetuses for and also the challenges standing in the way
of cross-class politics.

Expanding the scope of how these texts have been analyzed, this chapter
highlights some of the cross-ethnic similarities and differences in these authors'
approaches to portraying political activism. There is a dearth of scholarship on
*The Spook Who Sat by the Door* and *Sons of Darkness, Sons of Light*, and when
they have been analyzed, it has been with a focus on their portrayal of a war
between the races. Charles D. Peavy and Kali Tal include them in their discussions of Black novels featuring revolutionary characters, calling them "black
revolutionary novels" and "black militant near-future fiction," respectively.[6]
Both see the roots of this genre in Sutton Griggs's *Imperium in Imperio* (1899),
which lays out plans for a Black revolt against the United States. Peavy notes
that while "[t]he possibility of a black insurrection or revolt in America has
been the fantasy of many blacks, and the phobia of many whites, for more
than a century," the 1960s and 1970s Black revolutionary novels illustrate a
shift in how probable authors imagined a "final confrontation between the
races" to be,[7] with novels such as Greenlee's *The Spook Who Sat by the Door*

and Williams's *Sons of Darkness, Sons of Light* indicating that a violent outcome seemed inevitable. Arguing for the inclusion of these types of novels in the sci-fi genre, Tal identifies features of Black militant near-future fiction to include a "contest between violence and nonviolence . . . the theme of male friendship . . . the marginalization of women . . . [and an] act of betrayal."[8] Looking at an expanded set of texts, Mark Bould has also examined the sci-fi elements of Black revolutionary novels, while Julie A. Fiorelli continues this endeavor to categorize *Sons of Darkness* and *The Spook* as "apocalyptic race-war novels" that reveal the limitations of a race-based political platform.[9] I propose another categorization—novels of class suicide—novels that dramatize a renouncing of materialist rewards as part of attempts at cross-class revolutionary politics. Under this category we can include Acosta's autobiographical novels. All these novels depict circumstances that would motivate the middle-class minority professional to commit or consider committing class suicide. In the process, they reinterpret the upward mobility narrative to foreground a rejection of its materialist rewards, centralize a tension between individual and collective uplift, and test tactics for achieving systemic change through temporary or transformative institutional participation.

With the benefit of historical distance, critical assessments of the 1960s and 1970s social movements have stressed the failure of these movements in accomplishing the more radical goal of redistributing resources. Pointing to the success of Richard Nixon's strategy of promoting "Black Capitalism," which aimed to diffuse oppositional elements by supporting and encouraging Black participation in business through government and private-sector programs, scholars have argued that we can understand the persistence of racialized class inequalities by recognizing how this strategy enabled gains for a small segment of the Black population while leaving intact the economic social order. Political scientist Adolph Reed locates the successful incorporation of this elite strata and the derailment of radical reform in an organizational framework "built on the assumption of a homogeneity of black political interests embodied in community leadership."[10] By conceptualizing the Black population as a homogeneous community, Black leaders were able to speak on behalf of the masses, which Reed argues resulted in a "mystification of the social structure of the black community," which "was largely the result of a failure to come to terms with [this strata's] own privileged relation to the corporate elite's program of social reconstruction.[11] In a similar vein, Cornel West has assessed that "beneath the rhetoric of Black Power, black control and black self-determination was a budding 'new' black middle class hungry for power and status."[12] But he also sees the formation of a Black middle-class leadership during and in the aftermath of the 1960s and 1970s as an unavoidable paradox:

Despite the historical limitations of the "new" black petite bourgeoisie, the Afro-American predicament dictates that this group play a crucial role in carrying out these tasks. This is because the black middle class—preachers, teachers, lawyers, doctors and politicians—possess the requisite skills and legitimacy in the eyes of the majority of Afro-Americans for the articulation of the needs and interests of Afro-America. This unfortunate but inescapable situation requires that the politicized progressive wing of the black petite bourgeoisie and stable working class incessantly push beyond the self-serving liberalism of major black leaders and raise issues of fundamental concern to the black working poor and underclass.[13]

Scholars have vitally challenged the idea that middle-class leadership politics are the most legitimate and central to Black social movements, and have highlighted the contributions of the working class, the oppression inflicted by the Black middle class, and the patriarchal nature of leadership paradigms.[14] What is interesting about Greenlee, Williams, and Acosta's novels is that they too are critical of forms of middle-class leadership even as they focus on middle-class characters searching for ways to enact alternative forms of activism. The question of what role the middle class or petite bourgeoisie can play in leftist movements has a long history, with roots in nineteenth-century Marxist political theory. We can think of it as a two-part question, as West does above and Cabral does in his "Weapon of Theory" speech. If the first question is, What role can the middle class play in leftist movements?, the second is, What must this class do in order to work for true social and economic transformation? As relayed in Reed and West's analyses, many activists did not "reject the temptations of becoming more bourgeois,"[15] contrary to what Cabral encouraged. What we find in Greenlee, Williams, and Acosta's novels is a recognition of this temptation as opposed to a denial of it, along with attempts to imagine ways to confront and work against it, self-aware as these authors were that they were writing in a time of political experimentation.

## BETWEEN JOY AND FREEDOM IN
## *THE SPOOK WHO SAT BY THE DOOR*

In a 2004 *New York Times* article about the re-release of the film version of *The Spook Who Sat by the Door,* Henry Louis Gates is quoted on the novel's appeal for his generation, remarking that the novel "was a cult book for us because we all wanted to be spooks who sat by the door. . . . We all wanted to be inside the system, integrated into the historically elite white institutions of America, transforming them from inside."[16] The novel's endorsement of Black subversion of white institutions is why, perhaps not unsurprisingly, it had a rocky institutional history. Rejected by U.S. publishers over thirty times, Sam Greenlee's *The Spook Who Sat by the Door* was first published in London in 1969 and became a bestseller.[17] Not until 1973 was it published in the United States—the same year Sam Greenlee and director Ivan Dixon released it as a film.[18] Like the book, the film had difficulty getting disseminated in the U.S. and disappeared from movie theaters soon after its release. Greenlee reports, "When the film first got out there, we noticed that it would open on a Friday and be closed the following Sunday. . . . Then we found out that moviehouses had been visited by the FBI. United Artists agreed to stop distribution of the film."[19] The book and film's controversial subject matter stemmed from its portrayal of a 1960s nationwide, armed Black uprising as the inevitable outcome of an unjust system: an uprising facilitated by a Black former CIA agent named Dan Freeman.

In depicting a Black government agent, Greenlee drew from firsthand knowledge, and his writing reflects a historical pattern and contradiction—that education and empowerment have come from institutions that have also played a role in countering both. As with Williams and Acosta, Greenlee's relationship with the government and government-subsidized institutions played a significant role in his social mobility, but it also incited rather than placated a critical perspective toward these institutions.[20] All three authors participated in the armed forces. Williams went to college on the GI Bill and Greenlee honed his propaganda-writing skills while working for the U.S. Foreign Services after college and graduate study. Not only are they representative of how military involvement historically has contributed to class mobility, they are part of an era in which U.S. student social movements such as the Black Power and Chicano movements benefited from an expanding system of higher education that allowed for greater inclusion of diverse populations but depended on monies from militarization, such as funds from the GI Bill and the National Defense Education Act.[21] They also reveal how experiences in the military and in higher education can prompt a globalized perspective of racism and class exploitation. These experiences shaped the way the three authors understood and translated racial and class conflicts in their writing.

A specific consideration of Greenlee's academic and military career illuminates this point. After getting his undergraduate degree at the University of Wisconsin, he served as an Army ROTC commissioned Lieutenant in the 31st Infantry Dixie Division National Guard in Mississippi, where his experiences with Southern racism even within the military camp made him want to quit the military altogether.[22] After serving out his term, he was honorably discharged. He pursued studies in international relations at the University of Chicago, and there he was recruited by the United States Information Agency and became a member of the U.S. Foreign Service stationed in Baghdad.[23] He was in Iraq prior to and during the 1958 revolution, which is an experience that informed both *The Spook Who Sat by the Door* and his other novel, *Baghdad Blues* (1976). It was in Iraq that he became aware of global anticolonial movements and saw connections to the struggle of Blacks in the United States.[24] Christine Acham reports that after his military service, Greenlee returned to his hometown, Chicago, in the mid-1960s and was inspired by Black nationalism and the Black Power movement. As a result of witnessing the buildup of revolutionary sentiment in Iraq, Greenlee sensed that violent outbreaks like the 1965 Watts riots were only a sign of more to come. According to Greenlee, he wrote *The Spook Who Sat by the Door* as a revolutionary manual, "so that people who would do it, would do it right." He explained that "*The Spook Who Sat by the Door* . . . is a handbook on urban guerrilla warfare, organization, supply and propaganda. All of it's in there and that's what made it so threatening."[25] As a handbook, the novel plots out the way in which one could initiate and carry out an armed uprising. The novel also models how to translate middle-class cultural capital into radical politics, endorsing an instrumental approach to middle-class status.

Even though the protagonist, Dan Freeman, has ascended from the working class into the middle class through education and vocation, he embodies the novel's hostility toward the middle class. The novel's interpretation of the middle class echoes Marx and Engels's assessment in the *Communist Manifesto* that individuals fight "to save from extinction their existence as fractions of the middle class. They are therefore not revolutionary but conservative. Nay more, they are reactionary, for they try to roll back the wheel of history."[26] To express its working-class affiliation, the novel portrays the Black middle class as opportunistic and self-serving. At the beginning of the novel, the CIA holds a trial period to find its first Black agent, a move prompted by a senator hoping to win over Black votes by endorsing integration. The narrative tells us that the trial,

was a black middle-class reunion. . . . Only Freeman was not middle class, and the others knew it. Even if he had not dressed as he did, not used the speech patterns and mannerisms of the Chicago ghetto slums, they would have known. His presence made them uneasy and insecure; they were members of the black elite, and a product of the ghetto streets did not belong among them. (12)

Here, class is rendered as something sensed, and not through speech or dress but as some kind of essence, as if fixed and dictated by one's origins. But we see later through another character, Freeman's ex-girlfriend, Joy (who comes from similar circumstances), that class is also understood as an ideological outlook that is not determined by one's original class position. However, Freeman's political outlook is unwavering. Even though he is professionally middle class (his job before he becomes an agent is that of a social worker), he maintains a working-class ideology, which apparently members of the Black middle class can perceive. He is threatening to them because he does not share the same values. While observing this "middle-class reunion," Freeman's consciousness rails on those he sees around him: "You have a ceiling on you and yours, your ambitions; but the others are in the basement and you will help Mr. Charlie keep them there. If they get out and move up to your level, then what will you have?" (13). By metaphorizing status seeking through architectural imagery, Freeman reiterates the critique posed by the novels discussed in the previous chapter, that status is mortgaged due to the social and psychic payments necessary to maintain status. This status seeking leads members of the Black middle class to act as gatekeepers, preventing others from accessing resources because resources are understood to be scarce.

Freeman, in contrast, is represented as someone who pretends to be a status seeker only to get access to resources that he can then distribute. During the trial period, in which he has to prove his analytical and fighting skills and compete against the other Black males, Freeman begins his dissimulation. It entails hiding his educationally acquired cultural capital, which is a feat easily done because his working-class background makes people accept his performance: "No one at the training camp, white or colored, thought it strange that Freeman . . . although he had attended two first-rate educational institutions, he should speak with so limited a vocabulary, so pronounced an accent and such Uncle Tom humor" (18). His plan is to play to stereotypes in order to fly beneath the radar and outlast the others. He continues his feigned deference once he survives the trial period and is brought into the CIA. He comes to be known as "the CIA Tom in Washington" (31) and poses as nonthreatening to white authority. While his first position is no more than that of a copy clerk with a title, he is promoted to be the director's assistant and "given a glass enclosed office in the director's suite" (47). There his "job was to be black and conspicuous as the integrated Negro of the Central Intelligence Agency" (47). Freeman allows himself to be a visible token and to be perceived as an Uncle Tom, acting similar to how others of the Black middle class are portrayed in the novel, particularly in their willingness to accept token honors that give some individuals perks while the majority remain disenfranchised.

In offering a model of how one can participate in institutions for strategic purposes, the novel's implicit mandate is that one must develop the skill to juggle multiple identities for an extended amount of time. After five years at the agency, Freeman leaves his position to run a social services outreach program for urban youth gangs in Chicago funded by white-owned corporations, but this, too, is part of his ruse. This new job is a return to his hometown and to the kind of work he had done prior to becoming an agent for the CIA but with a prestigious title and a higher salary. Freeman keeps on pretending to care more about his new elite lifestyle than contesting the status quo, taking care to dress and live with material excess: "Freeman continued to contribute to his playboy image . . . those of his committed friends who were now in the 'movement' and who remembered Freeman as a tireless firebrand in the struggle for civil rights now regarded him with contempt as a hopeless sellout" (136). Understanding that the sellout rhetoric helps reinforce his cover to white authorities, Freeman keeps his real plans to himself, until he establishes trust and begins working with one of the most powerful gangs in Chicago, the Cobras. Freeman then begins sharing his counterintelligence and combat training with the youths in order to organize them and other gangs across the country to be ready to participate in guerilla warfare. Only briefly does the novel offer moments in which Freeman reveals that maintaining control of his various masks is causing him psychic stress or doubt, but these he is able to counteract quickly. Seeing militant tactics as the only way to truly shake up the system, Freeman has the ability to lay low like a sleeper agent until he can use his training in the service of advancing the cause for civil rights. His orders come not from any government, but from his vision for an egalitarian society.

As a spy novel, *The Spook Who Sat by the Door* joins other novels of its time in critiquing U.S. politics. According to Katy Fletcher, British and American spy novels written before and after World War II featured spies upholding the political status quo, but after the Cold War it became harder to see the United States as a moral agent. Fletcher adds that spy novel authors in the 1960s and 1970s were "no longer content to use the spy novel to reaffirm popular political attitudes . . . [and began] to educate [their] readers on controversial issues, instead of fuelling their prejudices and paranoias."[27] As noted, a large part of the novel's educational mission focuses on how to perceive members of the middle class, how to *act* middle class, and also how to prepare for class suicide, because Freeman is willing to give up all the gains he has made professionally and materially in order to fight back against an unjust government and later is in the process of recruiting other members of the Black middle class to do the same.

One may argue that Freeman does not actually commit class suicide because he was never invested in middle-class status in the first place and just used it as a ruse to attain his revolutionary ends. Sandra Hollin Flowers has argued that this ruse is contradicted in "ludicrous ways" because of the novel's emphasis on describing Freeman's middle-class lifestyle.[28] Flowers suggests that "of his three personae—the CIA agent who appears as gold-toothed bumpkin in pointy shoes, the Negro Playboy of the Western World, and the avenging black revolutionary—[Freeman] relishes most that of the Negro Playboy."[29] She takes issue with how often Greenlee mentions Freeman's worldly artistic artifacts and expensive furnishings, such as Freeman's

"Javanese Buddha head of black volcanic stone" (187), his "Saarinen womb chair next to the teak floor lamp" (240), and the "Saito woodblock he has purchased in Tokyo" (241), arguing that these are "simply instances of the 'thing dropping'—Greenlee's equivalent of name-dropping—that occurs needlessly throughout the novel."[30] Thus, rather than taking the stance that the novel does not demonstrate class suicide because Freeman was never invested in middle-class membership in the first place, she argues that the novel is actually overinvested in his middle-class lifestyle, creating too glaring a contradiction. For Flowers, to read Freeman as an example of class suicide "would be a generous interpretation . . . since the flaunting of Freeman's middle-class trappings never has a political context."[31]

I contend, however, that the portrayal of Freeman's leisure and consumption habits demonstrates the novel's wrestling with the effects of institutionally acquired cultural capital. Freeman's consumption habits reveal, for example, that despite his affiliation with the working class, he is a product of socialization in middle-class cultural institutions. Along with his cultural awareness, his leisure funds and time enable him to appreciate a wide range of art and music:

He saw Thelonious Monk at the Five Spot, the band with Johnny Griffin, Charlie Mingus at the Village Gate. He saw *Threepenny Opera* in the Village and *Five-Finger Exercise, The Night of the Iguana* and *I Can Get It for You Wholesale* on Broadway. He visited the newly-opened Guggenheim and decided that Wright had goofed, but he enjoyed the Kandinskys. He visited the galleries on Fifty-seventh Street and Museum of Modern Art (31).

In this passage we learn that Freeman is someone who knows about and values artistic expression of various forms, whether jazz or architecture, Brecht, or Barbra Streisand. It also supports a portrait of Freeman as an educated and politically aware member of the middle class—the kind of person who would most likely have come across the teachings of Mao (from which he draws inspiration) and the kind of person Cabral envisioned as being integral to revolutionary change. The novel does, however, acknowledge the temptation to identify with the material goals of the middle class, how it "would be so easy to sink into the softness of this scene. Let's face it, [Freeman] thought, I like this shit. I drive a beautiful piece of machinery, drink good whiskey, wear good clothes and have more chicks than I can really handle. It would only take a little lying to myself to think I was really into something; tell myself I'd earned it all in the best Horatio Alger tradition" (190). But Freeman rejects being content with his individual ascension, and the novel ultimately reconciles his character contradictions by positing that one can be culturally middle class but not ideologically middle class in the sense that one is invested in the social order as it is. If this seems too easy a reconciliation, we have to take into account that even the indisputable icon of the Black Power movement embodied contradictions that did not lessen the significance of his trenchant cultural critique, as historian Robin Kelley observes:

As often as Malcolm invoked the "house slave/field slave" dichotomy in numerous speeches and debates, his relationship to the black middle class was a complicated matter. He hated and emulated them; he ridiculed and admired them; he was part of a movement that tried to turn the most lumpen Negroes into respectable (by bourgeois standards, at least), well-mannered, "civilized" black men and women. . . . However imperfect and contradictory, he did offer a critique of the black bourgeoisie at a time when such a critique was unpopular.[32]

Instead of portraying Freeman as an outsider to institutions of power, whether government, academic, philanthropic, or artistic, the novel envisions a character who can traffic in them and learn from them, without losing the core sense of self and firm commitment to an ideological mission that the novel conveys one must have in order to be in spheres of power and not beholden to them.

The novel invests Freeman with a psychic arsenal so strong that he is never at risk of wavering from his revolutionary path, but what he cannot combat are the betrayals by those close to him who are unwilling to give up material comforts or individual social status. His former girlfriend, Joy, and he both "had been born during the bleak depression years. . . . But poverty had done different things to them. Joy had become determined she would never be poor again; Freeman that one day to be black and poor would no longer be synonymous" (54–55). While Freeman was still working for the CIA, Joy urged him to try for a more lucrative position as a lawyer. When it becomes clear to Joy that he would not give up his political commitment to the working class, she reveals that she is marrying a wealthy doctor and tells Freeman, "I'm sorry, but I can't sacrifice my life for a cause. I admire the way you feel, but I fought too hard to get out of the slums and you continue to identify with the slum people you left behind" (51). Freeman responds by stating simply that he "never left them behind" (51). Their romantic breakup illustrates competing visions for upward mobility: one that is individualist and another collectivist. Their names also signal their politics, with Joy referencing a feeling and Freeman referencing a state of existence—one a temporary high, the other permanent liberation. Desires for temporary happiness threaten the goal of liberation, as allegorized through Joy's betrayal of Freeman. Even though he never discloses to her that he is the one behind the nationwide riots, she senses his involvement and tells the police about his identity out of fear that the mass social instability will threaten her and her husband's comfortable social positions.

Freeman's first betrayal comes from a status seeker and his second comes from a gatekeeper. Freeman leaves the CIA to serve as a social worker with gangs yet does not see mediation through social work as doing enough, hence his turn to militant tactics. To further endorse his path, the novel contrasts him with Dawson, a childhood friend who grew up in the same neighborhood and became a police officer. Since he has been able to recruit other members of the law enforcement, Freeman hopes to recruit Dawson as his second-in-command. But it is Dawson, acting on Joy's tip, who comes to arrest Freeman in his apartment. Unlike Freeman, Dawson is convinced that working as a government functionary is the best means of serving one's community. In the midst of the nationwide riots, he cannot understand why other Blacks see him as the enemy and why they have rioted in the first place. He tells Freeman, "It's not enough to say they had it tough; they didn't have it any tougher than we did. Without respect for law and order, we might as well be back in the jungle." Freeman's response urges him to consider their role in helping to contain the conflict rather than in helping to address its root cause: "Shit, Daws, the ghetto's always been a jungle. You really think you can treat people like animals and not have them act like animals? You really believe you're just a cop and I'm just a social worker? Man, we're keepers of the zoo" (175). The novel strips government jobs of any virtue since Dawson sees law and order as a way out of dehumanizing conditions while Freeman sees them as contributing to them. As mediators in that system, Freeman argues, they are zookeeping; in other words, they are gatekeeping, preventing others from accessing resources

and keeping the gate closed on conflict that could transform social and economic conditions. Since Dawson ends up shooting Freeman, the novel ends on
two notes: with hope that Freeman's preparation for class suicide has sparked
a movement that will continue beyond his death, but also with a cautionary
scenario to warn against individuals like Joy and Dawson willing to commit
counterrevolutionary homicide.[33]

## BETWEEN INSTITUTIONS AND BLACK POWER
## IN *SONS OF DARKNESS, SONS OF LIGHT*

Freeman is described as a man with a plan, who never wavers in the path he
chooses to implement his ideological beliefs. Eugene Browning in John A.
Williams's *Sons of Darkness, Sons of Light* has no such certainty. Browning is a
former political science professor trying to address social inequities through his
vocational choices. He gives up teaching political science because he feels complicit in upholding a system of higher education that inculcates students into a
narrative of nationalist and racial supremacy: "My God, you started lying with
the Pilgrims and you kept right on lying . . ." (10). His disillusionment with
academia leads him to leave his teaching position and assume a job at a civil
rights organization called the Institute for Racial Justice, so that he could work
in the "Movement." This is a shift to another institution that, like academia,
is initially envisioned as a way for the Black middle class to participate in the
civil rights cause. The novel's plot then builds around Browning's anonymous
hiring of a hitman to kill a white police officer who has gotten away with fatally
shooting a Black teen, an act that sets off a chain of attacks by both whites and
Blacks and inspires various Black militants to organize for armed conflict. In
the course of these events, Browning wavers back and forth between participating in institutions or engaging in Black Power politics, a shifting that indicates
his view that these spheres are irreconcilable.

Browning's disillusionment with civil rights organizations reaches its peak
when he hears about the shooting of a sixteen-year-old Black male by a white
police officer. That the police officer shot the Black teen with impunity convinces him that nonviolent resistance has been futile:

You could work in a famous and vigorous civil rights organization in charge of the
college program as the number two man; you could work with all your heart and what

was left of your soul, but you also had to know, finally, that none of that was going to do any good; that you had to obtain your goals by almost the same means Chuck obtained his, remained the only obvious conclusion, and Chuck did not get his with Freedom Now or Love Your Brother marches. (11–12)

Williams has stated that he created the character of Browning to "somehow tell people that it doesn't matter how much education you've got if you're black. There's no such thing as removing one's self from it. You're always to some degree involved."[34] At this point, Browning increases his degree of involvement by abandoning a stance of nonviolence. When the Institute for Racial Justice cannot stop the violence that ensues after the hit on the officer that Browning set in motion, since whites start raiding Black neighborhoods in revenge and Black militants execute counterattacks, it loses white donor support. Browning's boss, Billy Barton, is thrown into a panic, revealing that he cares more about his own job than in the status of Blacks as a whole. We are told that Browning had

always been cynical about the guys who'd given all their lives to running Negro advancement organizations. At what point did idealism give way and the hard realities close in? At what point did one start thinking of raises and suburban living and tailored suits and vacations in Europe? And why not, after all? It was almost impossible to live in this society without being tainted by what it was made up of. (159–60)

In contrast to his boss, Browning is seemingly willing to commit class suicide when he decides that armed resistance is the only route to go. He decides that "One didn't go about shouting from the podiums. The years proved that didn't work. Secrecy, apparent noninvolvement, selected acts. That was the answer the only answer, a wee bit of Mao" (22). Like Freeman in *The Spook Who Sat by the Door*, Browning is inspired by global revolutionary leaders. He engages in secrecy and duplicity by hiring a hitman to enact his plan of revenge, but the fact that he thinks he can act the revolutionary a "wee bit" here hints at his naïveté and a limitation to his radical commitment. Furthermore, as Richard Yarborough observes, it is ironic that Browning uses monies he's collected for the Institute to fund this act.[35] Even his radical act depends on institutional support.

In spanning beyond Browning's story, *Sons of Darkness* depicts middle-class Blacks like Barton as status seekers complicit in upholding systemic inequalities. However, it does not condemn the Black middle class as a whole, as Greenlee's novel does. It portrays several members of the Black middle class engaging in militant efforts, such as Herb Dixon, who has a PhD in sociology but who "had run out of non-violence" (58) after white supremacists bombed his house and injured his daughter. The novel also describes the efforts of Dr. Millard Jessup, a wealthy doctor who regularly donated to the Institute but who turns his attention and funds to more militant efforts, telling Browning that "[t]he black middle class, if I'm a member, is returning to grass roots and the knuckle-to-knuckle" (76). Jessup is the character most similar to Freeman in that he is preparing for a national uprising by training people in guerrilla warfare and the one who most definitively articulates a commitment to class suicide. That the novel is not focused on him suggests that it is primarily invested in exploring both the circumstances that could motivate a middle-class minority to partici-pate in armed conflict and the challenges of remaining steadfast to that decision.

In narrating the efforts of these middle-class Blacks in leadership positions, the novel envisions a catalyzing incident that could lead to the breakdown of divided class interests under Black Power politics, even as Browning's actions reveal the limits to cross-class identification. At the end of the novel, Brown-ing and his family are staying in Sag Harbor, "the old whaling port with its black middle-class summer community" (129). Browning thinks to himself of the "[t]eachers, doctors, lawyers, social workers, and more recently, upper-level business executives—what were their concerns now with the brothers and sisters living in chicken coops? A few years ago, nothing. Today, a lot; they were coming together; had to come together" (129). Ironically, he thinks this to himself even as he has removed his own middle-class family from the urban conflict. Williams's minor characters, however, provide alternative ex-amples of Black revolutionaries who do not retreat from the intensified vio-lence. Morris Green, another militant, has a guerilla coalition and organizes across classes. In order to communicate the urgency of their social demands, he coordinates bombings of bridges leading into New York City and employs the help of civil servants:

Early the morning after the first raid, Green had called his teams together—the black guards and toll collectors, the engineers with their various specialties; they had been brought together by the violent force of the American policeman during a decade of rebellions that had gone nowhere; the cops hadn't looked at status symbols, only black faces, and therefore, pounding down the streets clubbing anything black, murdering anything black, had welded together the ghetto and middle-class Negro. (236)

As conveyed in this passage, the symbolic wages of class—the "status symbols"—are futile bulwarks against racism. The tightening of racial bonds invoked here as a welding of two separate classes potentially offers a stronger oppositional force, albeit a cross-class coalition that is the result of white violence.

Imagining a coalition across classes, the novel also illustrates a cross-racial alliance. Browning has four white allies. The first is an old friend with ties to the mob who brings Browning's interest in hiring a hitman to the attention of his uncle, an elderly retired Sicilian mobster named Carlo who develops a personal interest in Browning's cause. He never reveals to Browning that he is helping him, even though he meets him on two occasions. The other white ally that Browning does not know personally is the immigrant Jew Itzhak Hod, whom Carlo has hired on Browning's behalf to kill the police officer. After his deed, Hod has a conversation with his fiancée that convinces him that like Jews, Blacks are an oppressed group who have just motive in using more militant tactics to enact social change.[36] He decides to help them by pursuing a hit on another white supremacist, who bombed a church that led to the deaths of three Black female college students. Browning's fourth white ally turns out to be his daughter's boyfriend, whom his wife was adamantly against. But at the end of the novel when the violence has reached its peak, the boyfriend comes to their summer home with two guns that he gives to Browning for protection after overhearing some of his neighbors talking about shooting at Black neighborhoods. Matthew Calihman argues that the cross-racial unity in Williams's novels reflects his nostalgic support for Popular Front cultural pluralism. Calihman surmises that "[w]riting at a time when most American intellectuals could not envision a multi-ethnic coalition that would include both people of color and white ethnics," Williams "searched for a Black Power beyond black nationalism."[37] The novel's vision for a revolutionary politics underscores these interracial alliances that will continue to work for racial equality even if Browning himself is no longer part of the action.

Readers may find the end of the novel disappointing, with Browning and his family hiding out in their beach house in Sag Harbor, away from the chaotic city and the fomenting violence. The ending, however, helps foreground a crucial difference between Browning and Freeman: Freeman is a bachelor with no represented family ties, while Browning has a wife and two daughters. Browning was seemingly ready to commit class suicide by instigating violence that would lead to the loss of his job and the life he had known, but by the end of the novel the violence has gotten too out of hand for him and he views it as a never-ending cycle, which along with the concern for his family's safety provides an explanation for why he retreats from overt political involvement. Gilbert Muller reads this as a limitation Williams places on his character, observing that "like a figure in a futuristic fairy tale, [Browning] is able to walk away from the destruction that he has spawned."[38] Just as Browning has distanced himself from the violence at the end of the novel, so has Williams distanced himself from his novel and protagonist, stating in an interview that *Sons of Darkness* is his least favorite novel because of its potboiler element. Furthermore, he has said of Browning that he "thinks in revolutionary terms out of the boredom and frustration of middle-class existence."[39] And yet, asked whether the novel endorses Browning's actions more than Jessup's more radical approach to social change, Williams answered, "Yes, because [Browning is] the kind of guy who's around today," explaining that Jessup "believes that he can make deals with the devil and come away unscorched. And Browning just never had that spirit. Browning is the kind of activist-nonactivist that all of us would like to be, so that we can press a button and set things in motion without paying the consequences. In this sense, his thing is really a big daydream."[40] As a writer and an academic, Williams might have been reflecting on the role that these two occupations serve in relation to social change, and the criticism that both have received for staying in the sphere of the imagination or for being removed from praxis. Since Browning was driven to imagine some form of resistance that would send a message, but in the end cannot continue to participate in militant politics, his relegation to the private domestic sphere and back to academia at the end of the novel may read as a letdown. But if we assess the novel's political vision in terms of Browning's plot outcome, we are reading for success or failure measured in terms of individual achievement. The novel devotes significant narrative space to other characters who have their own vision of how to enact social change, from Hod, who allies with the ideal of retributive justice, to the other Black militants who are continuing the fight, to the interracial relationship between Browning's daughter and her boyfriend.

Browning ultimately decides that militant politics are not for him and resumes the institutional route. When asked by his boss at the Institute how things went so wrong, Browning answers, "Maybe working from within in-

stead of outside the system. Can't be done, just can't be done; if you're working inside the system then you're not working at all" (258). Asked whether
he is going back to teaching, Browning responds, "It's all I know, that and
this, but I won't teach the way I taught before. I'm going to teach down this
system, if I can, but I know teaching's a part of it" (258). Even though he
tells Barton that working within the system is not "working at all," Browning starts seeing academia as a site that could be reformed from within and
where one's labor could translate into systemic overhaul. If Browning wavers
back and forth between institutional participation and militant politics, it is
because he has seen these as incongruent spheres. The novel's depiction of
radical politics parallels the periodization of the Black liberation movement,
in which the years associated with the Black Power movement, the late 1960s
and early 1970s, are viewed as its tail end, due to the escalation of violence and
counterattacks from the government.[41] However, scholars have demonstrated
that Black Power, along with Chicano movement ideology, lived on in institutional arenas. This is evident in the creation of Black and Chicana/o studies
departments and programs across the country.[42] Furthermore, Joyce M. Bell's
scholarship shows a correlation between Black Power ideology and the rise of
Black professional organizations, which led to lasting changes in interracial
workplace dynamics and practices to help the wider Black population.[43] If
Browning's plot plays out the difficulties of following through with class suicide, it depicts the birth of Browning's reinforced belief in "civil institutionalization, or the implementation of movement goals, ideas and practices in the
institutions of the civil sphere—that exist between the level of the household
and the exercise of state power."[44] As a character, Browning stands between
two seemingly disparate poles—middle-class stability and revolutionary upheaval. Rather than give up one or the other, Browning registers a desire to
reconcile the two.

Searching for a way to be a politically conscious mediator within an institution, Browning shares the yearning expressed by Selina in *Brown Girl, Brownstones*
and Willie in *Linden Hills* for a middle path. In this way, all three fit within an
American liberal literary tradition, in which liberal individualism stands for a
middle ground between extremes and literary works trace, as John Carlos Rowe
puts it, "the development of such a distinctively American individual out of his
diverse, often contradictory backgrounds."[45] Many of the ethnic upward mobility

narratives I examine in this book forge characters who are highly aware of so-cial and economic inequalities or come into awareness of them as part of their socialization as American individuals. Not discounting the conservative uses to which liberal individualism can be put, Rowe has demonstrated the ways in which liberal values in American literature have also expressed a commitment on the part of authors "to reach a better understanding of how social justice might be achieved."[46] Vested with characteristics and restrictions that cause them to respond to socioeconomic pressures in certain ways, individuals can serve as filters for ethical critiques, composites that synthesize competing value systems, and testers of strategies for navigating hierarchies of power. They can also serve as axes around which the text shows how characters diverge in their responses to similar pressures, as *Sons of Darkness* shows through Browning's pursuit of a middle path while the others pursue more radical ones.

## BETWEEN ART AND ACTIVISM IN *THE REVOLT OF THE COCKROACH PEOPLE*

In offering their interpretations of strategies to counter the effects of socio-economic stratification, *The Spook* and *Sons of Darkness* center on social me-diators, while the narratives themselves attest to the contributions of artistic mediators. That artistic mediators are not depicted can be explained by the concern these novels share in portraying strategies for mobilization after con-sciousness has been raised and in response to immediate political needs.

Browning's story takes us in the direction of considering characters who struggle with translating their politics in institutional realms. This uncertainty is magnified in Oscar Zeta Acosta's two autobiographical novels, *The Autobiog-raphy of a Brown Buffalo* and *The Revolt of the Cockroach People*. Like Browning, the character Oscar struggles over whether to work in or out of the system, while adding another layer to this quandary by contemplating the value of the act of writing.

Although being a writer can have admirable connotations, as a profession it can seem impractical or too costly for those coming from working-class backgrounds. In the previous chapter I discussed the moment in *Brown Girl, Brownstones* when Clive tells Selina that their community "cannot afford" them as artists, since as a community seeking upward mobility, the Barbadian immigrants need their members to pursue profitable occupations. John A. Williams was asked about any challenges he experienced as a writer, and his response echoes that of Clive's assessment of his community:

The problem with writing for me personally lay outside writing itself. It was considered an illness to be involved in the arts, since in the black community there were no artists to speak of. One did not earn his keep by writing poetry or novels. That was out there in never-never-never land. What I really wanted to do was get a good job, work from nine-to-five, or ten-to-four, and live in that fashion.[47]

Due to the financial risk involved, Williams understands why his community saw pursuing art as an "illness." In poor communities of color, this aversion to the idea of making art production one's vocation arises from histories of exclusion and economic vulnerability. The pathology, however, can be misinterpreted as located in the artist, a diagnosis made to prevent poverty and further social marginality. Speaking of his own family's antipathy to his desire to be a writer, author Junot Díaz has shared, "When I started to float the concept that I might want to be an artist, my family, had I said I wanted to be a cannibal, they probably would have received that better."[48]

Acosta's novels layer this issue by portraying a community that needs representation in other forms besides art. In *The Autobiography*, Oscar states that he became a lawyer "[n]ot to practice law. But just to get a job so I could write my life history without having to put up with scags who thought only they knew what literature was all about" (155). Oscar then strives to reconcile his individual desires to write with communal desires for uplift by writing about and helping Chicano militants as their lawyer, which he documents in *The Revolt*. Overwhelmed with the responsibility, he confesses to Cesar Chavez at one point that he does not want to be a lawyer. Chavez answers him, "So? . . . Who in his right mind would *want* to be a lawyer, eh?" (46). Urged to subsume his own desires for the greater good, he resolves to do so since he has committed to the political cause. Nevertheless, Acosta depicts himself as a social mediator who wants to be an artist, but who has a responsibility to his community as someone with a law degree, which results in his representation as a conflicted artist. The desire to write never leaves him, and in the midst of major Chicano movement legal battles he laments, "in two years now, I still had not written one single word for myself" (77).

Acosta ended up representing Chicana/os legally and artistically, writing two memoirs that provide moving portrayals of the ideological and economic circumstances that ignited the necessity of the Chicano movement in the first place. As a lawyer, he represented the East L.A. 13, the activists arrested for organizing the 1968 East L.A. Walkouts, the series of protests by thousands of high school students in East Los Angeles schools to contest an unequal educational system, and the Biltmore 6, accused of starting a fire during Ronald Reagan's visit to the Biltmore Hotel. Fighting to free these activists, he also fought against institutionalized racism in the judicial system, bringing attention to the under-representation of people of color on juries and as judges.

In his novels, however, Acosta never reconciles his profession with his politics or his artistic desires. Documenting what life was like prior to and during the Chicano movement, Acosta offers us a portrayal of what it was like to be Chicano and middle class at a time when these terms were completely in tension, and which arguably continue to be so. In discussing the lack of representations of a Mexican American middle class and the Chicano studies tradition of critiquing the middle class, José Limón has pointed out that these trends are part of a "broader Western intellectual legacy of maligning the middle class," with origins in writings by Matthew Arnold and Karl Marx, who viewed the middle class in culturally or politically negative terms.[49] This critical stance stands in the face of the fact that many Chicana/o activists and academics are actually middle class. The irony is, as Gordon Hutner has put it, "that too often, because it is the culture so many academics know best, middle-class life is the life that is studied least."[50] Acosta's writings might also not be recognized as about a minority middle-class subject since they differ so drastically from portrayals of the middle class more readily understood as such, for example, the writings of John Cheever and Richard Yates about the white suburbs. Acosta's life and art are so exemplary of the countercultural ethos of the 1960s that even if his structural position is middle class, his novels, narrated in a "Gonzo" journalistic style more famously associated with his friend Hunter S. Thompson and filled with stream of consciousness, scenes of drug inducement, violence, and sex, are in clear opposition to ideas about middle-class conformity and morality. What Acosta's novels show us is how one can be structurally middle class but not ideologically middle class, or wedded to class hierarchies.

Chicano ideology was heavily informed by anti-capitalist discourse, and one way in which Acosta incorporated Chicano ideology in *The Autobiography* is through his rejection of the traditional upward mobility narrative. Even though Oscar does achieve class ascension, leaving behind an impoverished rural up-bringing through military service and then a law degree, his attainment of a middle-class livelihood cannot counter a lifelong internalization of racism and an awareness of economic injustices. Philip Bracher observes that while Benjamin Franklin models self-betterment in his seminal American autobiography, Oscar is "the antithesis of the American Dream: he is an unreliable, irate wreck of a man with serious alcohol problems and a severe drug addiction, bent not on self-perfection but on self-destruction."[51] Jeanne Thwaites reads the fact that Acosta "does not present himself as the book's hero, but as its villain" as an ironic reinterpretation of the upward mobility form.[52] That Acosta portrays himself as constantly anxious, physically sick, and overwhelmed—as a Legal Aid attorney in *The Autobiography* and then as legal counsel for Chicano activists in *The Revolt*—negates any belief that this class ascension has provided existen-tial or emotional rewards. Similar to Browning, he expresses disillusionment with institutional avenues for social change. His return to the legal profession illustrates his attempts to work with the ideology of civil institutionalization in trying to achieve Chicano movement goals. One major difference (among many) between these novels, however, is that Acosta's texts foreground intra-ethnic class distances, narrating them in psychological terms.

Acosta does not portray cross-class politics as something that is just a mat-ter of deciding and acting; rather, he delves into the psychological underpin-nings of how Oscar is constantly trying to make sense of himself as a professional in relation to a working-class collective. Through formal analysis, we can see these psychic taxes manifest in the way Acosta constructs moments of self-monitoring. At the beginning of *The Autobiography of a Brown Buffalo*, Oscar is serving as a Legal Aid attorney in Oakland in the late 1960s, salaried under Lyndon Johnson's War on Poverty efforts. Oscar expresses how ineffectual he feels in truly helping his clients: "Does anyone seriously believe I can battle Governor Reagan and his Welfare Department even with my fancy $567 red IBM? Do you think our Xerox machine will save Sammy from the draft? Or that our new set of Witkin law books will really help turn the tide in our battle against poverty, powdered milk and overdrawn checks?" (28). His feelings of inadequacy and the amount of clients that come in seeking his help are over-whelming. He describes a phone call on behalf of a client whose car has been repossessed. He is unsuccessful in getting her an extension and expresses what torments him the most:

> But the worst is the horror of the look in her eyes as she sits quietly while I beg for an extension of time. What has caused me numerous sleepless nights, pains in my legs, raw nerves at my neck; what has been the absolute worst of it all is the sleepy yet knowledgeable look she gives to me when I'm on the phone, the way she *notices* my red $567 IBM typewriter on my mahogany desk . . . that I cannot handle. (29)

Oscar physically feels his psychic stress. Obviously, he is unaware of his client's thoughts, but she becomes a mirror that induces "horror" at his reflection. Why does he say "horror" instead of "guilt" here, since his reference to what she notices specifically—his expensive typewriter—indicates that he feels guilt at owning an expensive machine while she is struggling to make ends meet? In *Guilt: The Bite of Conscience*, Herant Katchadourian cites one of the common definitions of guilt, stating that it "results from the violation of a moral code that entails *crossing* a line—a trespass."[53] One way of reading Oscar's guilt is that he both fears and yet lays claim to his trespass, for doing so keeps him accountable to the people he has committed to work for. He feels guilty for crossing over into the middle class as a result of his profession while the majority of Latina/os and Blacks have more in common with his client. These are feelings worsened by the fact that he can do little for them given that their real problems are structural. Further exacerbating his guilt are thoughts that he does not even deserve his position, indicated when he imagines the voice of his psychiatrist, Dr. Serbin, telling him, "'Oh, of course, you can't give them any false hope. After all, you're just a little brown Mexican boy'" (25). Guilt's more public counterpart is shame, an emotion that tends to result from public exposure, and "from failing to measure up to a personal and social standard."[54] We can see then, that when Oscar tells us about his client's "sleepy yet knowledgeable look," he is revealing that the worst of it all has been the way his private guilt has turned into public shame. But of course this frightening public exposure is one of his own projection, which implies a desire to feel accountable to a gaze that will shame him, that will raise the stakes of his class trespass. Once those stakes have been raised, the shame can either be debilitating or be channeled.

Rather than seeking an activist outlet as he does in the sequel, at this point in his story Oscar seeks escape, which he does when the stress gets too much for him and he quits his job and ventures on an alcohol-and-drug-infused cross-country journey of self-exploration. It is a journey that, as Héctor Calderón has observed, is part satire, part road trip narrative, and part Christian confessional all rolled into one.[55]

The road trip in *The Autobiography* reaches a pivotal moment at the end of the novel when Oscar has an epiphany that he can combine his individual desires to be a writer of revolutions and to actually participate in one by going to Los Angeles and joining the Chicano activists. The night before he leaves for L.A. he reads some magazines "to get in shape for [his] new career" (197):

In the January issue of *Look,* there is a story written by a lawyer who worked for Senator Dodd. He stole his personal files and exposed his corruption . . . a spy. An undercover agent for the good guys. The perfect front. Get a straight job. Work for the man as a cover. Hell, they'd never expose me. I am too tricky. I can make any kind of face you ask. After all, I've been a football man, a drunk, a preacher, a mathematician, a musician, a lawyer . . . and a brown buffalo. (197)

Oscar fantasizes about playing the role that Freeman does in Greenlee's novel—an undercover agent who will pretend to be a part of the system in order to subvert it. Both are imaginative reinterpretations of civil institutionalization, of attempting institutional reform through undercover intelligence work.

In actual life, and as depicted in his second memoir, *The Revolt of the Cockroach People*, Oscar (who now goes by the name Brown Buffalo to indicate his newly awakened political consciousness) opts for a more open challenge to the system by serving as legal counsel for Chicano activists. It also shows him, like Freeman, pitted against other people of color who have chosen to work within the system. Michael Hames-García remarks that by including the "many antagonistic Mexican American bailiffs, judges, police officers, and police informants encountered throughout *The Revolt of the Cockroach People* . . . Acosta sought to point out that in the early years of the Chicano movement, crucial questions about identity and the relationship between shared political interests and social location were not being asked."[56] Acosta's novel paints a spectrum of Mexican American professionals whose class positions would make them invested in upholding the social order, challenging "the assumption that solidar-

ity follows automatically from identity."[57] Acosta and Greenlee's novels express
similar denunciations of those in the minority middle class who are willing to
accept individual success over the collective cause, especially those whose work
directly undermined their efforts, since infiltration by undercover police was a
real and realized fear for Chicano and Black activists.

Through these other Mexican American professionals who work to uphold
the status quo, Acosta highlights Brown Buffalo's radical politics as emblematic
of someone who is using his professional status strategically to help the Chicano
militants and who identifies with the working class and with outsiders. James
Smethurst argues that Brown Buffalo's attraction to the *vatos loco* (crazy dudes),
whom he hangs out with and who are part of the Chicano movement, stems
from the fact that other Mexican American figures are connected to "'Anglo'
institutions and ideologies" while the *vatos* are "resolutely Chicano" and "are
in permanent conflict with these institutions, particularly the police and the
various aspects of the legal system."[58]

Furthermore, Stephen Schryer reads Brown Buffalo's union with the *vatos*
as a way he reconciles his class anxieties in gendered terms. Schryer points out
that Oscar's abject descriptions of his female clients on welfare in *The Autobiography* emphasize that their "excess physicality . . . underscores their incapacity for discipline and self-denial" and reveal that he is reproducing the same
stigma against women on welfare evident in public policy discourse.[59] And,
since Oscar uses similar language toward himself to convey that he "has not
been able to discipline his unruly body and behavior,"[60] his need to abject the
welfare mothers reveals that he fears he is too similar to them. His marginalization as a minority antipoverty lawyer and the associations white-collar work
has with feminization further exacerbate Oscar's need to distance himself from
marginalized women. By joining the *vatos* in *The Revolt*, however, Brown Buffalo is able to "return to lawyering, now re-imagined as a virile, militant, distinctively Mexican American activity rather than as a feminine submission to
Anglo social policy."[61] Joining the Chicano militants cannot so easily override
class distances, however, for as Schryer puts it, "The problem he faces is that
none of his efforts can erase that his utility to the movement lies precisely in
the fact that he is different from his clients and can mediate between them
and Anglo-dominated courts."[62] The novels discussed in the previous chapter
launched critiques toward members of the Black bourgeoisie who distanced

themselves from the Black masses. *The Revolt*, in contrast, depicts a Chicano character whose class privileges distance him from fellow Chicanos without him wanting them to.

Even as Brown Buffalo identifies with working-class politics, Acosta depicts how this identification is constantly undermined by how others treat him because of his professional status. Moreover, this identification is undermined by Acosta's own narrative tactics, which create distancing effects to foreground Brown Buffalo's class privileges. The first distancing technique is the use of the third person. *The Revolt* opens with an account of the demonstration that took place in Los Angeles on December 24, 1969, when several hundred Chicanos protested church corruption outside of St. Basil's Roman Catholic Church. Brown Buffalo narrates that the demonstrators gather peacefully but get barred from entering the building. After a police officer posing as an usher tells them there is no room for them, Brown Buffalo and a couple of men find an opening into the basement. At this point the novel shifts between the third and first person: "'Come on,' our lawyer exhorts. I strange fate, am this lawyer" (14). The phrasing expresses a key tension: that Brown Buffalo is *a part of* but also *apart from* the group as a result of his class status. Once they get into the church, violence breaks out. Right before the police come in, Brown Buffalo again refers to himself in the third person, revealing that, "The lawyer stands and watches" (16). It is an interesting moment of self-monitoring with Brown-Buffalo-as-revolutionary narrating that he is watching Brown-Buffalo-the-lawyer watching the group. Removed from the action, Brown-Buffalo-as-lawyer is portrayed as an observer rather than as a participant.

The account continues to highlight the distance between the two "figures" represented in the conflict. Brown Buffalo narrates,

And there is swinging and screaming and shouting and we are into a full-scale riot in the blue vestibule of the richest church in town. *But I am standing stock still.* All around me bodies are falling. . . . Black Eagle has squared off with two ushers. One squirts Mace in his face while the other kicks him in the balls. Down and down he goes, crashing to the velvet floor. *I watch it all serenely* while the choir and congregation entertain. *I wear a suit and tie. No one lays a hand on me. I take out my pipe and wade through the debris.* (16–17, emphasis added)

Not only is he now merely an observer, he also maintains an emotional distance from the conflict. In order to understand the significance of all these distancing tactics, we can contextualize them within the ideals held by one of the Chicano militant groups, the Brown Berets. Historian Ernesto Chávez explains the Brown Beret's three-part motto, which was "to serve, to observe, and to protect":

"To serve" meant giving "vocal as well as physical support to those people and causes which will help the people of the Mexican-American communities," while "to observe" required keeping "a watchful eye on all federal, state, city, and private agencies which deal with the Mexican American, especially law enforcement agencies." As for the words, "to protect" they meant working to "guarantee . . . and secure the rights of the Mexican American by all means necessary."[63]

Brown Buffalo's description of himself during this scene makes him into a betrayer of all these goals. Héctor Calderón reads both novels as satires,[64] and indeed, we can see how Acosta also satirizes the middle-class revolutionary. Brown Buffalo is not serving the interests of the group by being immobile, silent, and detached. And rather than vigilantly observing the law enforcement, he serenely watches the conflict in a caricature of a professional analyst like the psychiatrist Dr. Serbin, who constantly interjects throughout *The Autobiography*.

Moreover, because his "suit and tie" signal professional status, he is treated differently and does not face the same repercussions for trying to protect his fellow Chicana/os. After one of the Chicanas gets accosted by the police, he tries to prevent them from hitting her. He writes, "I move. I grab the arm of one of the cops. He turns to slug me with his baton, but Armas stops him. 'Leave Brown alone! He's their lawyer.'" Sergeant Armas, who is also Mexican American, prevents him from getting injured. In their interaction we have another scenario between an ethnic militant and an ethnic gatekeeper, a parallel to the confrontation played out between Freeman and Dawson at the end of *The Spook Who Sat by the Door*. But here, to the angst of the ethnic militant, the gatekeeper protects *him*, because of their shared professional status. Now Brown Buffalo urgently expresses how important it is for him not to be treated differently: "I run down the steps, toward the street. Cops hold me back. I struggle, I shove, I kick away. For God's sake, I want to be arrested! 'Don't touch the lawyer,' they say to one another" (19).

If in *The Autobiography* Oscar feels guilt for not being able to do enough for his working-class clients as a government functionary, in *The Revolt* he expresses guilt over what he does to them as a lawyer who engages in radical politics but who is not treated the same way because of his professional status. After the arrests following the demonstration, he goes back to his office and calls his journalist friend. He wants to tell him about the events so that he can write about them. The phone call ends with the following exchange:

"And you were one of the leaders?"

"In all modesty, yeah."

. . .

"Are you *serious*? Do you see what you've done?"

"Yeah, sure, I've upped the ante."

"You mean you've dumped it on your buddies," he says softly.

I don't remember hanging up the phone. When my mind finally thaws, I find myself alone in my tiny legal office on the tenth floor, high above the cockroaches on the streets of spit and sin and foul air in downtown LA. (21)

Conveying the class separation between himself and other Chicanos, Brown Buffalo has created distance through the use of the third person and by describing himself as emotionally and physically detached, which is taken to another level here—literally and figuratively—in depicting himself in his high-rise office far above other Chicanos. It is a distance he cannot tolerate. In the aftermath of the church protest, he quits his job as part of the Chicano Legal Defense funded by the Ford Foundation because he starts to get pressured by the board of directors over his involvement in political cases:

So to hell with the plush offices. To hell with the fat checks, the IBMs, the Xerox machines, the filing cabinets, the secretaries and the free telephones.

I quit my job and walk out of the Belmont lugging my files, my posters and my souvenirs to the basement of Father Light's Episcopal Church. I set up shop alongside the Chicano Militants and *La Voz*. (80)

To show solidarity with the Chicana/os, Brown Buffalo leaves the comforts of his job and makes a symbolic statement through his spatial reconfiguration in leaving his high-rise office and joining the Chicana/os in a basement. This is Acosta's depiction of Brown Buffalo's enactment of class suicide, of a renunciation of material comforts and material aspirations in the service of working-class politics. There is an American literary history of authors and characters endorsing downward mobility and exhibiting "virtuous restraint as the basis of right conduct over against a society valuing material advancement," as Lawrence Buell observes in tracing this countercultural impulse of "voluntary simplicity" from Thoreau to Wharton to contemporary self-help books.[65] Acosta's novels fit within this literary history and also expand it to include representations of downward mobility undertaken by an individual who does not come from privilege. Further, any spiritual rewards Brown Buffalo might have gained through his act of material renunciation are negated by his constant guilt. He feels this pressure as he immerses himself in protests, sit-ins, legal trials, and the bombing of a courthouse, "tired of being a legal spokesman, a leader who is always exempt from danger" (82). It is a guilt that reveals how deeply tied he still feels to an ethnic working class. However, he retains an awareness that he has privileges that the majority of them do not. In this sense, he is self-reflective about what ethnic affiliation means across classes, with the novels suggesting that it cannot completely override class distances.

Contributing to the guilt he has as a mediator and the conflicted feelings he has as an artist are the suspicions that he will be profiting from telling the Chicana/os' story. Brown Buffalo describes facing criticism as a writer:

The book offer has made me enemies. That I would think to make money off the struggle for freedom of the Cockroaches has made some people whisper traitor, *vendido, tío taco*, uncle tom and a capitalist pig to boot. . . .

I have explained it a thousand times. I have no desire to make a martyr out of Zanzibar. I know he has been murdered. . . . But now there is no Zanzibar to tell our story, no way for us to use the media to get us back our land. I shouted it to the rooftops: we *need* writers, just like we need lawyers. Why not me? I *want* to write. (230)

"Zanzibar" is Acosta's allusion to Ruben Salazar, the *Los Angeles Times* reporter who was killed during the Chicano Moratorium, and here Acosta moves from the criticism coming from other ethnics to the potential physical cost of trying to be an ethnic writer producing politicized content. Acosta attempts to answer the criticism and brave the repercussions through Brown Buffalo's assertion of the need for writers, but his qualified answer comes through all the self-policing moments, conveying that the need he sees is for writers who will be self-reflexive and critical. Thirty years later, another Mexican American writer, Salvador Plascencia, would echo Acosta's self-critical stance by depicting himself in his novel *The People of Paper* as an author who has received grant fellowships to write about the plight of migrant farmworkers and who profits from the "commodification of sadness," but whose characters have revolted against his authoritarian control over their lives.[66] Rather than romanticize cross-class politics or depict Chicana/os or Mexican Americans as uniformly working class, Acosta and Plascencia mark themselves as middle-class professionals and police their character depictions through guilt, shame, and parody.

Tragically, Acosta did not survive long after the militancy period of the Chicano movement died down. He disappeared in 1974 while in Mexico and was never heard from again. He left behind portraits of Oscar/Brown Buffalo that are revelatory for their insights into a period of intense activism and cultural nationalism. They also reveal the difficulties of being a Mexican American writer and a professional during a time when there were so few published and so few in positions that could help other underrepresented people. Oscar/Brown Buffalo expresses his preference for artistic mediation over social mediation, but Acosta as author saw the need for both.

Ultimately we see that the symbolic and material wages of class are not enough for Brown Buffalo, Browning, and Freeman. Freeman traded in the symbolic wages of his class (his educational cultural capital and his status as a professional) to execute a plan for Black collective liberation. He paid a tax on his upward mobility by living a double life with the ultimate cost of his life. Browning initially seemed ready to commit class suicide but decided to go the route of civil institutionalization.[67] The tax he had to pay was figuring out how to implement his ideological beliefs in his institutional life. Finally, Oscar/Brown Buffalo tried the route of civil institutionalization but still had a contentious relationship with the legal system and even participated in the bombing of the courthouse at the end of *The Revolt*. His tax is revealed through his class guilt and the conflicted feelings he has about being an artist and mediator.

These are significant historically situated stories of men testing out distinct paths to enact social change that attempt to imagine ways of not being tempted by and beholden to material rewards. And because they reflect the racial, class, and gender politics of their time, they do not question the androcentric revolutionary leadership position that they explore.[68] Their gender portrayals reinforce how the revolutionary novel tends to be a masculine genre while the degree of male mobility—Freeman's travels across continents and Browning and Brown Buffalo's travels across the country and the ability they all have to move between occupations—is also characteristic of nonmarriage-plot upward mobility narratives that tend to center on male protagonists because flexibility of movement historically has not been as available to women. Taking into account how gender largely shapes opportunities or restricts them does not discount the novels' engagement with social issues. The way in which they depict the challenges of working within and around institutions still makes them important texts that shed light on their historical moment, when activists took different political approaches but radicals and moderates alike were surveilled, jailed, or assassinated.

Black Power and Chicano movement ideology informed civil institutionalization in various spheres, and the question of how to work within institutions, whether governmental, business, or academic, to carry out the redistributive aims of these movements is still relevant. Discussing how in the wake of these movements the affirmation of minority difference became an effective management strategy, Roderick A. Ferguson cautions us from thinking that the "entrance of minority subjects and knowledges into spheres of representation and valorization signaled a new Eden for minority culture and identity. Indeed, that entrance was part of a larger effort by modes of power to keep minoritized grievances from compromising the itineraries of state, capital, and the academy."[69] Ferguson traces how the "institutionalization of difference" legitimized minority difference but also made institutions like the academy the ones offering that recognition, which has enabled the quest for recognition, as opposed to redistribution, appear as a political end in itself.[70] He also wants us to remember how "radical movements promoted the inseparability of the two" in calling for both recognition and redistribution.[71]

The novels discussed in this chapter are products of that dual aim, in that they all feature protagonists opposed to characters who have settled for recognition. These are characters highly aware that economic inequalities intersect with social inequalities. They focus their attention on addressing an immediate need to get more people of color in spheres of power—to redistribute empowering knowledge and resources in Freeman's case; transform institutions of knowledge in Browning's case; and make the judicial system more representative and just, in Brown Buffalo's case. The scenarios that they reference—underrepresentation, widespread poverty along racial lines, police violence toward Blacks and Latina/os, and prejudicial treatment against these groups in the judicial system, are still, even after half a century after these movements, pressing issues. They remind us that a politics of recognition is not enough to counter these effects. In order to secure collective gains, they foreground what one must individually give up.

# CHAPTER 3

# CULTURAL BETRAYAL

"Jesus, when did you become so bourgeois, huh?"

*My Family / Mi Familia*

## THE FORMATION AND MAINTENANCE OF IDENTITY GROUPS

According to social scientists Michael L. Schwalbe and Douglas Mason-Schrock, in order to form and maintain group identities, groups must *define* themselves, *code* particular behaviors and traits to differentiate themselves from other social groups, and *affirm* certain group attributes. In addition, they must enact identity work that *polices* the boundaries of their shared culture.[1] As a way to construct collective identities in opposition to white supremacy, Black and Chicano cultural nationalism inspired the production of art and literature affirming historically denigrated markers of difference such as race, the working class, vernaculars, and folk cultures to form empowered subjectivities rejecting marginality, subordination, and assimilation. In the previous chapter, I discussed how Oscar Zeta Acosta explored identities in tension and what it meant to be both middle class and Chicano during the Chicano movement. Reinforcing Chicano as a working-class identity while revealing cracks in that construction, Acosta expressed guilt and shame and employed parody whenever his character likeness found himself to be, or was interpreted as, more privileged than the collective. As a result, he emerged as a character-narrator who exhibited the range of narrative tactics that go into reinforcing group solidarity. In this chapter, I explore how Chicana/o cultural production has, like Acosta's novels, coded, affirmed, and policed the boundaries of Chicana/o group identity when it comes to class.

Acosta had the challenge of not having an available Mexican American literary tradition from which to draw since the publication of Mexican American literature took off only in the Chicano and post-Chicano movement years. These were the years during which the Mexican American middle class grew—but, at the same time, Chicano ideology contributed to a sense that upward mobility meant cultural betrayal. While scholarship has examined class variation in the post-1960s African American population and intra-group policing rhetoric, this has been sparsely analyzed in Chicana/o studies.[2] Tracing the way in which upward mobility has been correlated with cultural betrayal in Chicana/o cultural production, I demonstrate how this association informs Chicana/o texts even after the Chicano movement.

Two texts produced in the 1990s, Gregory Nava's film *My Family / Mi Familia* (1995) and Helena María Viramontes's novel *Under the Feet of Jesus* (1995), reveal how Chicana/o class representational politics were reaffirmed during a transitionary time—in the aftermath of the Chicano movement but before the mainstream circulation of middle-class Mexican American identity, which will be a subject of the next chapter. While *My Family* explicitly engages in policing mechanisms that shed light on representational practices in Chicana/o cultural production at large, *Under the Feet of Jesus* abides by the conventions of Chicana/o class politics but encodes a desire for upward mobility and depicts it obliquely. This analysis reveals more sharply how Chicana/o texts acknowledged and responded to the reality of economic heterogeneity—and the threat of ideological divisions—within its ethnic imaginary.

## *MY FAMILY'S* INSIDERS AND OUTSIDERS

In the Chicano film *My Family/Mi Familia*, one scene features two of the Sánchez siblings, Toni (Constance Marie) and Jimmy (Jimmy Smits), bickering over Jimmy's refusal to marry a woman he has never met.[3] Toni has just tried to persuade Jimmy to marry Isabel, an undocumented woman from El Salvador who is working in the United States as a nanny, so that she can avoid deportation back to her home country. But Jimmy remains unconvinced and refuses his sister's request: "Go through the motions? You're talking about marriage, *carnala*. That's marriage. That's out!" he roars, prompting Toni to levy what she assumes would be an appropriate insult when she snaps, "Jesus, when did you become so bourgeois, huh?" Implying that Jimmy's stance is antithetical to working-class immigrant politics, Toni's remark loses its ideological bite when Jimmy misunderstands the epithet and answers back, "Hey, fuck you, and don't ever call me 'bushwhacked' again, *cabrona*, whatever the fuck that means." To understand the logic of Toni's accusation, we first must understand that Toni equates "being bourgeois" with betraying working-class politicized solidarity. Such an accusation seems nonsensical: Jimmy has just been released from prison and is unemployed, hardly the profile of someone who is bourgeois. But Toni's insult correlates Jimmy's actions with an ideological position that pits him against his family's working-class roots and suggests he has a lack of empathy for other working-class people.

Jimmy's response—"don't ever call me 'bushwhacked' again, *cabrona*, whatever the fuck that means"—offers not an outright disavowal of bourgeois affiliation but an expression of nonrecognition. He does not recognize the term *bourgeois*, although he understands its use as an invective.[4] He therefore deflects Toni's attempt to question his class commitments with a declarative statement that she cannot call him "bushwhacked." In one sense, *bushwhacked* means "ambushed," so he unknowingly refutes the fact that Toni has just ambushed him with her surprise demand. In another aspect, *bushwhacked* references the verb meaning to live in or travel through wild or uncultivated areas, so his assertion that he *is not* bushwhacked ironically signifies that he *is* bourgeois, given the association of the bourgeoisie with a lifestyle of comfort and cultivation. Yet the fact that he does not understand the word *bourgeois* (or, for that matter, *bushwhacked*) affirms his nonbourgeois status, and Jimmy's alignment with the working class only strengthens once he marries Isabel. Thus an anxiety about class betrayal as cultural betrayal plays out in *My Family* through a comic exchange of accusation and nonrecognition, two discursive strategies that appear often in premillennial Chicana/o texts.

In considering the function of those who stand in for cultural disavowal in Chicana/o texts, it is useful to return to the sociological interpretations of group formation. Ethnic solidarity, which allows individuals to claim an affirmative identity, can also be the basis by which ethnic groups catalyze collective action to protect their social, political, and economic interests. The policing that Schwalbe and Mason-Schrock identify as part of the process of group formation can occur through rhetoric and images designating distinctions between insiders and outsiders. The other form of gatekeeping can therefore apply to the negative charges attached not only to outsiders who threaten the economic and social well-being of those within the ethnic group but also to those inside the community who deviate from its norms. The inside/outside distinction is not a binary but can occur along a spectrum, with measures taken to distinguish the more "authentic" from the more "assimilated." Policing can therefore take the form of a "collective sense of distrust among the more ethnically identified toward the assimilated coethnics who are derided for having 'sold out' to the white mainstream."[5] Ethnic groups may even have particular figures who symbolize ultimate cultural and group betrayal, such as "Uncle Tom" for African Americans or Malinche and "Tio Taco" for Mexicans and Mexican Americans. In contemporary discourse, the censuring label "sellout" evokes the process of cultural betrayal: an individual sells or exchanges his or her communal identity or the community itself for membership in the dominant group. Such individuals might get material earnings from the sale or symbolic ones in the form of dominant group membership or recognition. Aware of the delimiting but also necessary function of such labels, legal scholar Randall Kennedy argues that "sellout rhetoric and its concomitant attitudes, gestures, and strategies can prompt excessive self-censorship, truncate needed debate, and nurture demagoguery. But ostracism, or at least the potential for ostracism, is also part of the unavoidable cost of collective action and group maintenance."[6] Kennedy thus acknowledges that "sellout" and its accompanying discourses, while serving as a means of evasion and silencing, are also useful in the project of creating a shared identity, maintaining group solidarity, and securing and protecting socioeconomic benefits for the group.

*My Family* offers an example of how cultural betrayal becomes associated with middle-class status within a family that is symbolic of the Chicana/o community and, in the process, demarcates the behaviors of those within and outside the family through the use of the four figural types found in ethnic upward mobility narratives. Toni's gatekeeping and opprobrium of Jimmy contains an accusation of selling out. In the portrayal of another brother, Memo

(Enrique Castillo), the film depicts an actual betrayal of culture. Memo, short for Guillermo, is the youngest of the Sánchez children in *My Family*. After he becomes a successful attorney, his family learns that he has adopted the name Bill and intends to marry a white woman, implying that he has completely assimilated.[7] Since Memo has always been, according to the film's narrator, the family's "pride and joy," his assimilation becomes an issue only when he denies his cultural and class origins. When Memo brings his fiancée and her family home to meet his own in East Los Angeles, he downplays his family's immigrant history in order to prove to his Bel Air in-laws that he is not so different. When his father proudly begins recounting his story of crossing the border, Memo interjects and reassures his guests, "Actually, I've never been to Mexico. I've always lived here in Los Angeles, like yourselves." The choice to identify as more American than Mexican is explicit, and Memo's actions earn a rebuke when the scene is interrupted by Jimmy's young son, who jumps onto the coffee table completely naked except for an indigenous headdress and insults Memo and his guests by calling them "pinche gabachos!" (damn white people). Humorously acting out a scene of colonial resistance, the boy exposes the tacit boundaries between those who uphold their familial affiliation (all sitting on one side of the room) and Memo, who is embarrassed by them. Through Toni and Jimmy's tense conversation about Jimmy's supposed bourgeois conversion and the representation of Memo's actual one, *My Family* represents the standards by which Chicana/o familial-communal bonds can be measured, including political actions to prove one's working-class sympathies and pride in Mexican cultural origins.

With Francis Ford Coppola as one of its executive producers, and developed through New Line Cinema, *My Family* was no indie film like Nava's 1983 *El Norte*, which had brought him critical acclaim and an Academy Award nomination for best original screenplay. Chicano in theme but made for wide distribution, *My Family* does, as a result, compromise in topics and tone, which Richard T. Rodríguez describes as the result of "Nava's Faustian pact with Hollywood."[8] Critiquing the film's muted treatment of institutional violence and its depiction of patriarchal family values, Rodriguez reads these aspects as the means by which the film caters to a mainstream American audience. Film scholar Rosa Linda Fregoso, meanwhile, highlights the film's patriarchal family values as part of the film's Chicano nationalist imagery.[9] We can consider the film's depiction of class politics as another way in which it juggles a mainstream palatable message with a Chicana/o sensibility. The film does, for example, present an immigrant success story: starting from poor rural backgrounds in Mexico, the immigrant parents come to own their own home in East Los Angeles and raise kids who have helped the family integrate into the U.S. economic and social order. Among the remaining five children, two work in law or legal aid and two work in a family restaurant owned by one of the sisters. Of the two brothers who exhibited potentially anti-establishment behavior, one gets shot by the LAPD and the other goes to prison and, when freed, is reformed.[10] And even though it is clear that Toni disagrees with immigration policy, she still works within the legal system by encouraging her brother to marry Isabel so the latter can get citizenship through marriage. The film diffuses any overt oppositional elements. It does so even while conveying a message about the necessity of reinforcing familial-community bonds around working-class affiliation, a strategy that underwrote Chicano movement oppositional politics.

The film shows a commitment to Chicano working-class politics and polices this commitment via its representation of the second generation. Memo is clearly the status seeker in the film. *My Family* is reflective of 1990s multiculturalism, which saw mainstream celebrations of ethnic difference, and as such, it correlates status seeking with assimilation, depicting a son's purposeful suppression of his family's immigrant status. In Chapter 1, I explained that the status seeker is marked by the group's history of racialization and subordinate status. The status seeker's quest, therefore, is not just higher or elite status; it is informed by a desire to *not* have a denigrated, pathologized, and criminalized status. As critical as depictions of status seekers often are, they are representing proven paths of social incorporation and financial solvency. Individuals historically have benefited from signaling higher status through lighter skin; positional goods; professional degrees; institutional affiliations; Anglicizing their names; and distancing themselves from the poor, racialized, and immigrant. Status seekers reveal the conditions by which society bestows recognition or enables inclusion and how cultural producers have represented individual and communal strategies for social incorporation that accept prevailing value systems. However, *My Family* also offers siblings standing in for alternatives to status seeking.

As an activist, Toni is a mediator who uses her knowledge of the legal system to help the undocumented. Paco (Edward James Olmos) is the artist in the family, writing down and recounting all of these events. He opens the film in a voiceover and provides commentary throughout the film. It is through his perspective that we learn that Memo went from being the family's "pride and joy" to the family's disappointment. The film is set in the present with flashbacks, and there is no sense that in his middle age he is conflicted about wanting to be a writer, since one scene opens with Paco at his typewriter and his voiceover addresses criticism that we can infer he has received: "So what's wrong with wanting to be a writer? You got a problem with that?" But he also reveals that his father was right in voicing concerns about pursuing writing as a livelihood, and the next scene shows him working as a waiter in his sister's restaurant. The artist-versus-status-seeker relationship that was played out as a generational conflict in *Brown Girl, Brownstones* and *Linden Hills* is enacted in this film as sibling difference, which indicates that the film envisions the second generation as more susceptible to the ideologies of American individualism and materialism and offers alternatives via Toni, Jimmy, and Paco.

Since the film follows its family members into maturity and across generations, it can dramatize the complex interaction between identity, status, and politics. By contrast, many well-known Chicana/o literary texts do not offer explicit depictions of upward mobility since they do not venture into adulthood. For example, in *Pocho*, *. . . y no se lo tragó la tierra* / *. . . And The Earth Did Not Devour Him*, *The House on Mango Street*, and *Under the Feet of Jesus*, inclusion in mainstream society and class ascension through education exist only on the horizon and are never part of the actual story plot.[11] The narrative arcs begin with children from working-class families who register a yearning for class mobility and end with young protagonists still aspiring to a different kind of life. The promise of class mobility implicit in these novels nevertheless holds out hope for a possible resolution to some of the conflicts in that the protagonist is usually one who represents an artist figure or a mediator.

These novels end before they answer the question of how to represent their adult protagonists once they have integrated into mainstream society. A notable exception to this pattern is the "proto-Chicano" novel *George Washington Gómez*, written by Américo Paredes in the late 1930s.[12] Nicknamed Guálinto Gómez, the protagonist embarks on a trajectory toward assimilation that reads as a complete betrayal of his community. He does not grow up to be the "leader of his people," in fulfillment of his proclaimed destiny, but instead opts to

work for the U.S. government as a spy stationed along the U.S.-Mexico border. Marking his transformation into an assimilated subject, he discards his
indigenous-sounding nickname, Guálinto, in favor of his Anglophone baptis-
mal name, George, and marries a white woman—gestures similar to those of
Memo-turned-Bill in *My Family*. Just as Memo's family sees him as a sellout,
at the end of the novel Guálinto is ridiculed by former friends who are disappointed by his new identity. After George rejects his friends' pleas to help
them elect Mexicans to office because he has no time to "dabble in politics,"
his childhood friend Elodia calls him "Vendido sanavabiche" (son of a bitch
sellout) (294). Pre- and post-Chicano movement texts have often followed these
paths. While novels about working-class childhoods often sidestep the question of what happens in adulthood, texts like *George Washington Gómez* and
*My Family* express concern about the effect that upward mobility has on one's
cultural and familial attachments and explicitly present those adults who attain
middle-class status as traitors to their culture and history. This anxiety about
cultural betrayal can be seen in postmillennial Chicano novels such as Salvador
Plascencia's *The People of Paper* (2005). The Mexican American narrator alludes
to but avoids venturing into detail about what life is like for him as a creative
writer in an MFA program in Syracuse, New York, and instead focuses most of
the narrative attention on a previous generation of farmworkers. The narrator
also both is accused of being a sellout for writing about Mexican immigrants
for personal profit and accuses his ex-girlfriend of being one because she is in
an interracial relationship.

## CHICANA/O CLASS POLITICS

There are interrelated reasons for the conflation of class ascension with cultural
betrayal. First, middle-classness often connotes whiteness. Second, and elabo-
rating on the points raised at the beginning of this chapter, Chicana/o cultural
producers and intellectuals have strategically identified with the working class
as a basis for ethnic solidarity. And third, Mexican ethnic authenticity is correlated with immigrants and the working class. Clarifying the first reason, historically in the United States, the middle class has been predominantly white
due to physical, systemic, and epistemic factors. Nonwhites have been killed,
assaulted, and jailed; have had land and property confiscated; and have been

denied equal opportunities in education, employment, and housing—all factors affecting a family's ability to attain financial stability and pass on savings to subsequent generations. People with lighter complexions have historically enjoyed class privilege[13] and, for those that can, there has been much incentive to incorporate into whiteness. Therefore, identifying against the hegemony of whiteness and ideas about the middle-class have been effective mobilizing strategies for marginalized populations. As discussed, sellout rhetoric encompasses attempts to police group boundaries that might be breached to the harm of the racialized ethnic group. Américo Paredes dramatizes and historicizes this scenario in *George Washington Gómez*. After the adult George assimilates, he does not *just* leave. Instead, he returns to threaten his community when he starts working against them as a spy on behalf of the repressive state apparatus. His family and former friends, disappointed by his betrayal, turn their backs to him. The novel warns of ethnic subjects who are moving up or moving out— not just that they will identify with whites, but also that they will work with whites to the detriment of the community. Thus, in *George Washington Gómez* white mainstream culture is represented as having the ability to turn people of color into agents working against communities of color.

Second, regarding Mexican Americans specifically, the negative association of middle-classness with whiteness is strengthened by the concerted effort to affirm the brown working class, a stance that comes directly out of the 1960s and 1970s Chicano movement. The celebrated image of the brown working class and the nationalistic rhetoric that invigorated a new wave of Mexican American politics were a reaction to the continued denigration of Mexican Americans. But they were also a response to a sense that the conservative tactics of the preceding generation had failed: that earlier activists, middle-class Mexican Americans working for middle-class interests, had accepted instead of contested the value system of white America.

This earlier wave of activism came out of the political shift that occurred in the 1930s and 1940s, one driven by what historian George J. Sánchez has called the "second generation," the children of immigrants who migrated to the United States during the upheaval of the Mexican Revolution (1910–1920).[14] Sánchez argues that the second generation was the first to turn its attention to U.S.-based politics, in contrast to their forebears, who tended to gaze back toward the homeland. Historian Richard A. Garcia identifies 1930s San Antonio as a paradigmatic site of this shift and of the emergence of a Mexican American middle class within a three-tiered class structure. At the top were *los mexicanos*, elite Mexican nationals who left Mexico as a result of the revolution and who "wanted to continue to see themselves as Mexican citizens in exile and not as Mexicans accommodating to their new environment."[15] At the bottom was the Mexican laboring class, consisting of migrants and agricultural workers struggling to survive. And in between there were the merchants and professionals, who made up a growing Mexican American middle class that was starting to become conscious of itself. As Garcia explains, they embodied a new dual identity, one that could embrace a collectivist consciousness rooted in a Mexican heritage along with an American philosophy of liberalism and pragmatism.

Emerging Mexican American civic organizations reflected and shaped this middle-class ideology. LULAC, the League of United Latin American Citizens, was founded in 1929 in San Antonio to articulate the concerns of Mexican descendants who wanted greater integration in the United States. As Garcia explains, it was the first major organization to act as the "the conscious vehicle of the [Mexican American] middle-class mind."[16] Raising consciousness through education and political activities, LULAC offered a program for acculturation. The eleven-article constitution, for example, spelled out a plan for how Mexican Americans could Americanize (by claiming citizenship, securing equal rights, speaking English) while still maintaining ethnic ties (by showing pride in racial origins, educating other Latin Americans, and fighting racial prejudice). The document also revealed the rhetorical strategies used to distinguish the Mexican American middle class from Mexican nationals and the laboring class. By privileging the labels "Latin Americans" and "Americans of Latin American descent," LULAC members disassociated themselves from the pejorative connotations of *Mexican*—pejorative because of the ways in which lower-class Mexicans affected the perception of all Mexicans. A non-Mexican American observer who attended LULAC meetings and is cited in Garcia's book notes three reasons why LULAC saw lower-class Mexicans as a threat to their gains and well-being: "first, they took jobs away from the middle class; second, they also lowered the standard of living; and third, they created racial prejudice by not knowing American customs or American laws."[17] This statement captures how the group accepted the value system of a white America that also saw Mexican laborers as lesser. The distancing through naming was a tactic used to differentiate those in the middle class from those perceived as threats to their enfranchisement.[18]

As has been well documented, the trajectory of Mexican American activism took a new turn in the 1960s with the Chicano movement. Historian Rodolfo Acuña recounts how the civil rights movement broke with the kind of institutional politics pursued by the middle-class leaders of LULAC and the GI Forum (the latter consisting of veterans):

The rise of identity politics challenged their leadership and the acceptance of assimilation as a goal. . . . [T]he civil rights, antinuclear and anti-Vietnam movements, along with community action programs, legitimated a spirit of confrontation, creating a new awareness among Chicanos that resulted in a demand for self-determination by los de abajo (the underdogs) and youth.[19]

In contrast to LULAC, Chicanos in the 1960s and 1970s took direct political action through protests, boycotts, and legal efforts to fight for fair wages, equal rights, and much-needed social programs. Yet, despite distinct politics, they were addressing the same problem as their predecessors—what Marcial González has described as the proletarianization and racialization of Mexican Americans that occurred after the U.S.-Mexican war of 1848.[20] Both generations, the founding LULAC generation and the Chicano movement activists, were responding to the perception and treatment of Mexican Americans as a proletarianized racial group, though they took opposing approaches, with the former fighting against this image and the latter embracing it as the visualization of the most disadvantaged. During the Chicano movement, identification across class lines with working-class politics emerged as a strategy for collective advancement. Making a call for such cross-class identification, Rosaura Sánchez wrote in 1977, "It is imperative . . . that those few Chicano women attaining professional status or higher education recognize the low economic status of the majority of Chicano women and identify with their struggle rather than with middle class feminist aspirations, for most of us Chicano women have strong working class roots."[21]

Since promoting working-class politics and empowerment through visibility was a dominant concern in the Chicano movement's fight for justice, there arose along with direct action a visual social platform designed to heighten awareness of communal ties and create a shared mythos as a basis for solidarity.[22] Taking their cue from Mexican cultural nationalism, Chicana/os drew on a cache of politicized symbols, including those evoking the Mexican indigenous past and the Mexican Revolution, and disseminated them in posters, murals, chapbooks, and poems. One of the most potent symbols was that of the Chicano family, akin to the Mexican family but serving as a bulwark against Anglo-Americanization. Since part of the Chicano social vision entailed a rejection of American individualism in favor of collectivism, the family, with its biblical counterpart the Holy Family, was a powerful unifying symbol. As Rosa Linda Fregoso points out, the depictions of the Chicano family found in Chicano-movement works, and even in contemporary films such as *My Family*, "defined [family] in terms of heterosexual marriage, nuclear bloodlines, and gender hierarchies."[23] The result has been an obscuring of difference in order to uphold the traditional patriarchal and heteronormative family. Conceptualizing the Chicano community as a family has also masked class difference, denying a more complex social stratification among Chicana/os. As stated in the previous chapter, José Limón has argued that the erasure of the middle class in Chicana/o texts is a result of a "broader Western intellectual legacy of maligning the middle class," sentiments that informed cultural studies and, by extension, Chicana/o studies.[24]

Finally, though Chicana/os can be economically middle class, many of them still identify with either their working-class roots or the immigrant community, or both. The rise of a Mexican American middle class was closely associated with the economic expansion following World War II and legislation passed in the mid- to late twentieth century. Postwar economic conditions increased the number of jobs available, while the 1944 GI Bill, followed by civil rights legislation in the 1960s, made it possible for more Mexican Americans to gain access to college degrees, middle-class jobs, and home ownership. The 1986 Immigration Reform and Control Act granted millions legal status, and with greater geographical mobility, many Mexican Americans settled in new immigrant destinations, pursuing opportunities in previously untapped labor markets. However, the dearth of scholarship and representations of the Mexican American middle class does not reflect the social mobility that has occurred over time. Many Mexican Americans who entered the middle class through the university system did so during and after the Chicano movement, which helped institutionalize Chicana/o cultural production and scholarship based on working-class identity. It is in this historical context that middle-class membership came to signal cultural disconnection at best, as when the middle-class protagonist of Luis Valdez's play *I Don't Have to Show You No Stinking Badges* (1986) admits to being an "Ivy League snob," and betrayal at worst.[25] Viewing the middle class as reactionary or apolitical can be strategic, along the lines of Rosaura Sánchez's call to identify politically with the working class. But identifying with and representing the Mexican American working class might also stem from the fact that it is more closely associated with marked characteristics of ethnicity, markers that get reinforced by recent immigrants. Sociologist Tomás Jiménez's theory of "ethnic replenishment" explains that the ongoing reconstitution of the working class through continuous immigration helps replenish the cultural practices and symbols that have come to characterize the Mexican American population.[26] Replenishment accounts for why Mexican Americans, even those several generations removed from immigrant status, may, in their cultural practices (food, music, and clothing) and also in their discursive representations, reaffirm portrayals of a homogeneous folk or working-class Mexican community. With middle-class identity likened to assimilation to whiteness, a negation of working-class sympathies, and a disavowal of collective cultural practices, accepting and depicting middle-class Chicana/o identity becomes a fraught endeavor. This raises the question of what Chicana/o identity means in an era when more Mexican Americans are able to join professional ranks than ever before, but when data also show that Mexican Americans on average have lower income levels than whites, Blacks, and Asian Americans, as poverty endures even into the fourth generation.[27] In the next section, I detail how novelist Helena María Viramontes addresses this double bind—reflecting desires for and the possibility of class mobility while also raising awareness of working-class struggles—through a narrative that explicitly depicts the latter while allegorizing the former.

## METAPHORS OF MOBILITY IN
### *UNDER THE FEET OF JESUS*

Set in the Central Valley during the 1970s, *Under the Feet of Jesus* follows a family of Mexican American migrant workers. Suggesting the start of a metaphorical journey, the first sentence sets up the novel as a question about what the destination will entail. "Had they been heading for the barn all along?" wonders thirteen-year-old Estrella (3). It turns out that they do stop near the barn and set up camp. The barn will, by the end of the novel, become the marker of Estrella's internal growth, and, as I will show, the site through which the novel culminates its encoding of class mobility and communal identification.

The plot revolves around the actions of four central characters: Estrella; her mother, Petra; her stepfather, Perfecto; and her friend and romantic interest, Alejo. Over the course of the novel, Estrella and Alejo develop a friendship and talk about life in and beyond fieldwork, Petra realizes she is pregnant, and the elderly Perfecto considers leaving the family and returning to Mexico before he dies. The turning point in the novel comes when Alejo is sprayed from overhead with pesticides from a plane that has arrived ahead of schedule. Petra tries to care for him, but he still falls gravely ill. Estrella promises to help Perfecto tear down the barn in exchange for taking Alejo to the clinic. At the clinic, the nurse in attendance takes their only money while doing nothing more than recording Alejo's vitals and telling them to bring him to the closest hospital. Frustrated that the nurse did so little and did not even consider allowing Perfecto to do repair work instead of taking their money, and anxious that they have no money for gas to even get to the hospital, Estrella grabs Perfecto's crowbar from the car and demands their money back. After frightening the nurse and securing their funds, Estrella and her family are able to get Alejo to the hospital. Afterward, a newly empowered Estrella climbs to the roof of the barn, where, there with the stars over her head and her heart beating with courage, the final scene implies she has developed a new elevated consciousness as well as a new sense of self.

Before the novel catalyzes Estrella into action, it emphasizes the stasis the characters experience as racialized laborers. The narrative draws out the various bodily, environmental, and institutional factors that ensure that their mobility is one of subsistence and survival rather than one that is upward: because of clotted veins, painful boils, tired feet, stalled cars, searing heat, and low pay, and as a result of teachers with lowered expectations, agents patrolling the border, and employers concerned more with the output of their workers than the conditions they endure, the characters in *Under the Feet of Jesus* experience constant curtailed mobility.

In its depiction of a migrant family experiencing class stasis, the novel extends motifs and imagery developed in another Chicano novel, Tomás Rivera's

*. . . y no se lo tragó la tierra / . . . And the Earth Did Not Devour Him.*[28] Eschew-
ing linear plot development, Rivera's *. . . And the Earth Did Not Devour Him*
enacts the motif of waiting through its vignette form and in its portrayal of
a late-1940s–1950s migrant farmworking community in a state of delayed action. Adults pray and wait for God to end their suffering (108–9), children wait
for Christmas in hopes they will receive presents for the first time (134), a boy
waits in vain for a racist barber to cut his hair (103), agricultural laborers wait
for the person promised to teach them job skills (107), and families wait for the
portraits they commissioned unknowingly from a con artist (138). Through the
vignette "Los niños no se aguantaron / The Children Couldn't Wait," the novel
shows catastrophically what happens when some stop waiting: in this story, a
child is accidentally shot when he disobeys his employer's orders not to take
a water break. The vignette "Cuando lleguemos / When We Arrive," delivers
the most lengthy depiction of waiting and also provides access to the hopes the
migrant workers are holding onto in the process of marking time. After a truck
transporting a group of workers breaks down in the middle of the night, the
workers find that they will have to wait there until dawn. The entire vignette
is then filled with their thoughts as they decide what they will do once they
arrive at their respective destinations, which range from a desire to lay down
after standing for the whole ride, to working in hopes of buying a car, to leaving for another city where the work might be less exploitive. Ramón Saldívar
notes that the mood of the story "is like the tense of the verb [lleguemos] in
Spanish, a conditional one: the completion of the action has been deferred."[29]
The recurring sentiment is that of anticipation, of a hope based on the promise
that once they arrive, things will be better and they will have options. It is one
strain of thought from an unnamed individual that interrupts and expresses a
different viewpoint:

When we arrive, when we arrive, the real truth is that I'm tired of arriving. Arriving
and leaving, it's the same thing because we no sooner arrive and . . . the real truth of
the matter . . . I'm tired of arriving. I really should say when we don't arrive because
that's the real truth. We never arrive. (145)

"Arriving" acts as a metaphor for class mobility. The speaker is double-voiced,
speaking at once literally (about the truck arriving wherever it is headed) and
metaphorically (about the attainment of a better socioeconomic status). The

refrain "when we arrive" is thus cast as futile illusion, as the voice here expresses that arriving is temporary, a marker of a destination that will soon become another departure when the labor to be done is completed. It is a disillusionment echoed in *The House on Mango Street*: that novel begins with references to Esperanza's family's constant movement from one run-down dwelling to another, never arriving at the idealized home that Esperanza hopes they will eventually reach.[30]

Raymund A. Paredes has read the expression of disillusionment in Mexican American literature as part of the tradition's critique of the American Dream and materialism. He argues that writers such as Cristina Mena, Josephina Niggli, and Mario Suárez dealt with these issues through characters who rejected assimilation, while others like José Antonio Villarreal showed "that money, even in relatively small amounts, is all the more ruinous in the hands of those unaccustomed to it."[31] Paredes links several concepts: the American Dream, assimilation, and materialism; his interpretation conveys that believing in the American Dream means assimilating into a value system of materialism. Reading Mexican American literature as Paredes does in this article reinforces class-mobility-as-assimilation-as-cultural-betrayal as moving away from one's Mexican roots. However, as John Alba Cutler has argued, the "idea of assimilation as boundary-crossing, [as] a choice to divest oneself of ethnicity in exchange for full participation in mainstream American life, is persuasive in US culture and looms over Chicano/a literature," which does not accurately reflect how assimilation is a dynamic process, with individuals assimilating aspects of the host culture and the host culture assimilating aspects from immigrants.[32] Chicano texts are themselves products of assimilation, produced out of bicultural experiences. Moreover, rather than refuting the American dream, they are offering bicultural reinterpretations of it. Cutler prompts us to recognize how often assimilationist discourse gets juxtaposed to ideals of authenticity, and here we see that . . . *y no se lo tragó la tierra / . . . And the Earth Did Not Devour Him* and *Under the Feet of Jesus* do not romanticize poverty, equating it to a more authentic version of culture. Instead, the novels register an intense desire to get out of poverty, endorsing class mobility in collectivist, not individualist, terms.

Scholars have marked the thematic and imagistic similarities between Viramontes's and Rivera's novels, both centered as they are on migrant communities with child protagonists.[33] Scott A. Beck and Dolores E. Rangel, for example, read Viramontes's novel as a feminist re-visioning of Rivera's, focusing on the differences between the existential crises the protagonists in each novel experience. They interpret Estrella as a much more proactive character, one who "is not as blindly hopeful when she experiences her existential crisis and passage into adulthood. Unlike Rivera's protagonist, she remains angry and prompted to action by the injustice of it all."[34] Offering another point of comparison, I propose that Viramontes's text extends Rivera's treatment of metaphors conveying the lack of and necessity of increased mobility, in particular through its figural rendering of blockages, falls, and ascension.

Viramontes metaphorizes class mobility by giving image to the objective and subjective aspects of social class as they bear weight on her characters. Explaining how metaphors operate, cognitive linguist George Lakoff and philosopher Mark Johnson argue that metaphors have the capacity to structure our actions and thoughts, arising out of experience and also influencing how we interpret.[35] In other words, the way in which we describe an object or activity reflects and shapes the way in which we perceive it. Following their argument, we can see that the language surrounding class indicates that it is viewed as part of a process, not static. To metaphorize class mobility means to work within our understanding of class as a journey within a hierarchical system—one can move up or down according to an increase or decrease in resources. In Viramontes's novel, class mobility and immobility are metaphorized through imagistic references that are actually more evocative of transverse mobility, namely that of cars and roads, a way in which the novel can relate an amorphous concept like class through a relationship with tactile and perceivable objects in motion.

While Viramontes would not centralize traffic metaphors until her next novel, *Their Dogs Came with Them* (2007), with a plot structure that mirrors a freeway, they are present in her first novel, even as it is set in rural San Joaquin Valley rather than in urban Los Angeles. Deborah Clarke, analyzing the role of the car in the lives of the characters, remarks, "What's striking about this family group is their rootlessness; they are never referred to by family name and never—except for the elderly Perfecto—identify any place as home. Given how often their place of residence changes, it becomes clear that the car is the only constant. Although they rarely literally live in the car, it constitutes the only home they keep coming back to."[36] In viewing the car as their "only constant" Clarke does not take into account that the family was carless before they met Perfecto Flores. She reads the car as a home and marker of identity for the family, illustrating what she calls "automotive citizenship." While I agree that the car plays an important role in the lives of this family of migrant workers, I do not read the cache of metaphors related to the car as indications that Viramontes is constructing a new sense of citizenship, detached from Mexican or U.S. identity, but rather find that she employs them to depict class mobility as a process influenced by race and gender. As a single Mexican mother, Petra is more impoverished and less mobile, for instance, before she marries the handyman, Perfecto Flores.

The novel presents images of cars, traffic, and roads that are employed to convey the difficulty of movement without resources. Started in medias res, the novel includes flashbacks that describe life before Petra met and united with Perfecto. Abandoned by Estrella's father and left in poverty, in one scene Petra walks with her children along the highway in search of a place to stop and get groceries, and we get insight into her thoughts about the difficulties of traveling without a car:

Petra knew the capricious black lines on a map did little to reveal the hump and tear of the stitched pavement which ascended to the morning sun and through the trees and no trees, and became a swollen main street and then a loose road once again outside the hamlets that appeared as splat dots on paper. (103)

Here Petra reflects on the differences between actual roads and those depicted on a map, seeing the lines as belying the physical reality of traveling without resources and on foot. The scenario of her family walking in the searing heat with little water and looking for an opportunity to cross the freeway in order to get to the gas station on the other side also suggests a parallel to border-crossing immigrants, alluding to the toil of travel and the risks involved in trying to get to a place with resources. At one point Estrella's brother, Arnulfo, asks "Should we wait?" and as he says this he is "looking down the slithery road" and thinks to himself "It looked as flat as a crushed, dried snake" (104). Arnulfo's fear is that they could all end up like a crushed snake he has a memory of and echoes Petra's distrust of their journey. While the highway is felt tactically (it is hot, rough terrain), it is also experienced psychically, as the road becomes a way to access the thoughts of characters who are not thinking consciously of their social and class statuses but who have distresses that reveal the difficulty of a journey that is difficult precisely because of where they are in a hierarchical social and class system.

The association of roads with danger is employed in another scene to get at the same ends—the psychic distresses related to a lack of resources, albeit obliquely, as this scene takes place before the family undergoes their experience along the highway and is a foreshadow of what's to come. Set during the time when they are still living in an apartment and seemingly stable, Petra sees the "freeway interchange right above their apartment [that] looped like knots of asphalt and cement" and thinks of it as a "car wreck waiting to happen" (16). Meanwhile her husband is getting ready to leave, and when he does, he wrecks their marriage and leaves her and the children to fend for themselves, forcing them to start moving again in search of food and shelter. Petra's fears of a car crash were actually displaced fears of her own impending lack of safety and stability.

Once Petra and her children are forced to leave the apartment and start moving from place to place, they experience periods of extreme hardship and relief. It is a dynamic that is replayed throughout the novel as images of constriction and respite get figured through transportation passageways like roads, and inner-body transportation systems like veins. In the passage mentioned earlier, Petra describes how the capricious black lines on the map became "a swollen main street and then a loose road" (103). Like this image of the road with backed-up and then relaxed traffic, so too are Petra's veins described as "vines choking the movement of her legs" (61), which see some relief with her intake of garlic. Perfecto also dreams of his veins containing blockages, with "his veins like irrigation canals clogged with dying insects" (100), which is a feeling that gets dispelled when he awakes. Through these references, the novel depicts a sense of mobility that is full of fits and starts (like Perfecto's old Chevy that periodically stalls and even gets stuck in the mud in one scene) while also drawing heightened attention to the conduits of mobility that go unnoticed unless you actually experience constricting forces.

Alejo plays a pivotal part in the narrative in that he provides the catalyst by which Estrella moves forward at the end of the novel and he also introduces and enacts a series of key metaphors. He is the character with faith in what we traditionally think of as upward mobility, believing, as Paula Moya has pointed out, in the American Dream and independent entrepreneurship.[37] And though the novel is moving away from this kind of self-made-man glorification by not focusing the narrative on him solely, it does value him as a character, causing narrative tension when he falls ill due to the pesticides. One of Alejo's major contributions to the narrative is his role in encouraging Estrella to think about social mobility in the first place, here alluded to through a reference to cars and gasoline:

If we don't have oil, we don't have gasoline.

Good. We'd stay put then.

Stuck, more like it. Stuck.

Aren't we now? (86)

At this point in the narrative, Estrella expresses pessimism about their situation, accepting stasis as part of their condition because she is being realistic in thinking about how little they have and how dependent they are on even their current position for food and shelter. In their budding romance, she even tries to forget the perpetual cyclical nature of her family's movement "trying not to think of Exits and Entrances, of Stop signs and Yields" (89). Here, through the use of traffic metaphors, the narrative repeats Rivera's portrayal of, as Ramón Saldívar has put it, the "economic life of the migrant farmworker bound to the seemingly endless cycle of arrival and departure."[38]

Even though Alejo has been the optimistic one, working in hopes of making enough money to attend school and study geology, his plans for mobility are countered by the reality that his working environment treats his body as disposable. When he gets sprayed with pesticides he envisions an extreme stasis, and the novel overlays Alejo's metaphorical association with gasoline with one of tar pits:

He thought first of his feet sinking, sinking to his knee joints, swallowing his waist and torso, the pressure of tar squeezing his chest and crushing his ribs. Engulfing his skin up to his chin, his mouth, his nose, bubbled air. Black bubbles erasing him. Finally the eyes. Blankness. Thousands of bones, the bleached white marrow of bones. Splintered bone pieced together by wire to make a whole, surfaced bone. No fingerprint or history, bone. No lava stone. No story of family, bone. (78)

Being stuck takes on a different meaning here as Alejo's memory of the tar pits becomes a way for him to think about the burning pain he is feeling because of the chemicals. The fragmented sentences in this description also convey stilted articulation, as would come if one were really prevented from moving and were being engulfed. In addition to the slow death the passage also expresses a fear of not leaving a memory: "No fingerprint or history" and of being completely erased. In likening social and physical death with a sinking into the tar pits, with a slow movement into the ground, Viramontes creates an image of mobility that is, like the traffic metaphors, employed to depict the cyclical nature of subsistence migrant work as one of stasis.

By describing engulfing stasis as occurring after being exploited for one's work without regard to one's personhood and likening it to a deprivation of a personal agency and imprint, Viramontes creates a link between class immobility and recorded history. She carries this narrative thread out in another scene in which personal documents serve as indications of Petra's family's past and its potential trajectory. In the novel, documents are very carefully guarded, as Petra puts all her family's papers literally under the feet of the Jesus statue she owns. The documents comprise birth certificates, baptism certificates, a social security card, an "Identification card—NOT A LICENSE" (166), a first communion certificate, an award certificate given to Estrella for an essay, and Petra's marriage certificate. The narrative states that "Petra folded the creases of the documents with the same care she folded a Phillips 66 map" (167). For migrant workers, a roadmap would be as necessary as the vehicle for transportation that would get them from one campsite to the next. The documents underneath the statue are like a roadmap. They reveal where the family has been and where they could potentially go; as long as they have proof of birth in the United States (and stated on the birth certificates themselves) they can enter school, secure employment, perform jury duty, enter the military, and own property. The documents thus serve as another way in which social and class mobility are referenced (and also valued if not possible) in the novel.

We get insight into Petra's yearning for class mobility when she and her family are at a gas station where they have stopped to get groceries. This is before they have met Perfecto, so they have been traveling on foot. At the gas station she spots a man filling up his car:

Petra crossed her arms and looked at the Bermuda's plump seats. The white plush carpeting was so white, it was obvious no one ate in the car. She envied the car, then envied the landlord of the car who could travel from one splat dot to another. She thought him a man who knew his neighbors well, who returned to the same bed, who could tell where the schools and where the stores were, and where the Nescafe coffee jars in the stores were located, and payday always came at the end of the week. (105)

To own a car that nice means, to Petra, being able to own one's own home, being able to separate the acts of driving from the acts of eating and sleeping. To be able to drive a car like that means having the luxury of staying in one place long enough to become familiar with one's surroundings, enabled by the regularity of a weekly paycheck. While Petra desires a car and the life it symbolizes, what she is really seeking is upward mobility. By including all these images of mobility, fraught, feared, and longed for, the narrative registers its characters' desire for social stability.

These metaphors of mobility—cars, roads, and gasoline—also figure in the most pivotal scene in the novel, helping to describe the impetus that Estrella needs to demonstrate agency. After the nurse—who stands in for a white gatekeeper of resources—has checked the gravely ill Alejo and has taken their remaining nine dollars as her fee without offering him any treatment or accepting Perfecto's offer to do repairs as payment, Estrella mulls over her options: "She tried to make her mind work, tried to imagine them back on the road with an empty gas tank and wallet and Alejo too sick to talk" (147). The turning point comes when she remembers her conversation with Alejo about tar pits and thinks of the "Energy money, the fossilized bones of energy matter. How bones made oil and oil made gasoline. The oil was made from their bones, and it was their bones that kept the nurse's car from not halting on some highway" (148). Here she starts realizing, as Moya argues, that the labor her family and others like theirs exert are what enable the mobility of others, allegorized as their bones creating the oil for gasoline, but also more immediately by the produce they pick and which others consume.[39] Estrella realizes that she, her family, and Alejo deserve to be mobile themselves, and with this knowledge she takes a crowbar and demands their money back, smashing the objects on the nurse's desk in the process and expressing a newly empowered identity.

Along with encoding a desire for class ascension through metaphors, the novel illustrates how Estrella undergoes developments that could enable her to attain upward mobility in the future, arising out of an awareness of a collective struggle. First is the development of literacy. In demonstrating how Estrella comes to learn how to read texts and the world around her and how she comes to understand that words have material effects and gain meaning through and in relation to others, Moya argues that the novel depicts an "expanded notion of literacy," one that is "embodied, intersubjective, and egalitarian."[40] Building on Moya's analysis, Jeehyun Lim reads Estrella's literacy as intersubjective and focuses on the role that bilingualism plays in Estrella's development, since it is the Spanish-speaking Pefecto who teaches her that words can be instrumental.[41] Lydia Cooper, meanwhile, sees Estrella as an "artist-creator [who] seizes the symbols in the world around her and inscribes them with meaning, learning in the process to inscribe herself."[42] Cooper highlights the aesthetic capability of Estrella's literacy, which can equip her to fashion a more empowered identity. And as a character with an artistic sensibility, Estrella aligns with the artist type often present in upward mobility narratives, the one who orients the narrative's ethical perspective. Her literacy is artistic and transforming because it is embodied, intersubjective, egalitarian, and bilingual—qualities that expand the way she sees herself and the way things could be done. She thus models how literacy can be empowering as well as ethical. While access to institutionalized education can facilitate upward mobility in the traditional sense, in the novel we get a representation of how a literacy gained through social knowledge (knowledge of one's location in a system of hierarchies and of how others are classed, racialized, and gendered) can enable one to develop and maintain an ethical sensibility even if one does become more empowered.

Crucially, even after Estrella has asserted herself and taken another step in her journey toward becoming more self-empowered, she still places value in the collective. After they leave the nurse's trailer, Alejo tells Estrella that he is not worth the act of violence she just committed. Estrella responds, "What a thing to say," and then thinks of bell peppers, a thought she sees as "odd" (152) but is actually very fitting with her developing consciousness. She

remembered how the brilliant red and green and yellow bell peppers were stacked like layers of granite stone into small and solid pyramids. The colors became something so completely breathtaking that one had to stop and ask why, why would anyone want to create an incandescent mosaic out of something as nondescript as bell peppers? Estrella wanted to tell the mother, to say, Mama take a look at that, but a woman walked in the store and toppled the peak by removing the top single red one, shiny as new love, and it was as easy to dismantle all that work as it was to kick a can on the road. (153)

Estrella is awed by the organization of seemingly "nondescript" bell peppers, an organization that is as solid as stone and as beautiful as a mosaic. The collective ensemble transforms the peppers into something grandiose, yet Estrella's recollection is careful to note the individual elements that go into its makeup. The use of conjunctions in place of commas to separate each of the descriptive markers in "red and green and yellow" helps emphasize the differences between the peppers and also their unity. She also remembers that when one was lifted off the top, the entire collection got dismantled; this is the image that comes to mind when she thinks about Alejo's claim that he does not matter enough for Estrella to demand justice on his behalf. Her unarticulated thoughts are telling her that each individual does matter, and when individuals organize, they can create something stronger and more beautiful. Yet the image reminds her that there is the risk that the shiny red pepper at the top, or an individual, could be plucked away, could leave or could be tempted to leave perhaps, and of the necessity of being conscious of the collective. In reading this scene, Moya argues that "Alejo's lack of understanding and his condemnation of Estrella's actions make evident the individual nature of Estrella's socially constituted knowledge."[43] Now that Estrella is beginning to see the world in a new way, her challenge will be trying to get others to see the world and themselves differently as well. And at this point, recalling the bell peppers becomes a way for Estrella to think about collective organizing and specifically about the importance of recognizing individuality along with the needs and strength of the collective.

Through Estrella's budding awareness of racialized class groups, the novel endorses mediating on behalf of others. Although most of the novel is set apart from urban spaces and non-Spanish speakers, when the family must interact with the nurse, we see the role that Estrella assumes as the one who has been educated in the United States and as the one who strongly advocated to bring Alejo to the clinic in the first place. There is the language barrier that she must cross, but also, as Lim explains, "the barter system of her family and the money economy of which the nurse is a part."[44] As a representation of an ethnic intermediary, Estrella acts as a "cultural broker." Extending sociologist Jennifer Lee's work on cultural brokers, Jody Agius Vallejo found through her studies on Mexican Americans that "all the 1.5 and second generation who grow up poor, and some of the second generation who grow up middle class, provide some type of social support to their families, primarily when they act as 'cultural brokers' between their families and the English-speaking public."[45] Like these socially mobile Mexican Americans who are in positions from which they can help their families, Estrella attempts to broker her family's interaction with the nurse, but she realizes that even speaking the same language as the nurse does not mitigate the wide chasm between their priorities (Estrella's to save Alejo's life and the nurse's to pick up her kids from baseball practice). Estrella consequently learns that in dire circumstances there are other ways of being heard, and that mediation does not always mean diffusing conflict: instigating it could achieve more effective results.

In this self-assertive act, Estrella begins to become conscious of a new sense of self, one that embodies knowledge of how things have been done but also acts with knowledge of how things could be done. Right after she has recouped the money from the nurse, she "felt like two Estrellas. One was a silent phantom who obediently marked a circle with a stick around the bungalow as the mother had requested, while the other held the crowbar and the money" (150). The narrative implies that Estrella does not suddenly become a new person, nor does she leave her past self behind, but she embodies both Estrellas: the daughter who passively obeyed, was superstitious and guarded what her family had, and the other Estrella that is instead forceful and is now equipped with the resources for mobility. Embodying both implies that her journey will continue to be a negotiation between traditional ways of doing things and learning new ways of acting in the world.

While Estrella does not achieve upward mobility (in the traditional sense) within the text, she has at this point started to develop the tools (literacy, class consciousness, a sense of agency, a collective identity) to potentially better her circumstances and fight for those who could use her help. Had the novel continued it would not be a stretch to imagine that Estrella had gone on to college and/or become a farm worker activist, like Ernesto Galarza. Without explicitly saying so, the novel does want to establish that Estrella is changed, and she now has abilities that will give her greater mobility in the future, as illustrated in the final scene of the novel when she ascends to the top of the barn.

Estrella's ascension at the end of the novel is made all the more acute by the images of stagnation and also falling that have occurred throughout the narrative. Her mother and Perfecto are both stuck in their lives of subsistence, with no way out. Even though Petra desires a stability enabled by upward mobility, she has no way to attain it. The much older Perfecto, meanwhile, has given up and wants to make his way back to Mexico to get ready to die. And while Alejo has been the one to express a desire to attain the American dream through hard work and entrepreneurship, his vision is individualist in scope, and is not the one that the novel endorses.

This is evident in how his physical immobility leads to Estrella's development of agency. He serves as a narrative sacrifice, in the sense that as a character, he is sacrificed in the service of both the development of the plot and the transformation of consciousness of the protagonist. As part of his role, Alejo experiences several falls throughout the novel. Just as "arriving" is a metaphor for attaining increased socioeconomic resources, "falling" is a metaphor for losing the ability to attain them. Alejo falls out of the peach tree when he sees Estrella swimming in the river (40), he almost falls when the pesticides spray down on him and he thinks of sinking into the tar pits (78), and he even dreams about falling, a dream he recounts to Estrella (117). Meanwhile, two piscadores are said to have fainted as a result of the heat (83). All these scenes help convey that the world of the migrant workers is precarious, that their lives are unstable, and their health is at risk due to their working conditions. Even though as an independent male Alejo would have had more opportunities than Estrella to improve his life, he becomes the character who bears the brunt of their fragile economic state in order to enact movement from a character who might otherwise accept stasis as a permanent condition. Juxtaposed to Alejo and these scenes of falling is Estrella on top of the barn at the end of the novel, the edifice that has both frightened her and evoked her curiosity.

The barn has been read as a symbol of decay[46] and a symbol of language,[47] but we could also read the barn as a symbol of both the elevated consciousness that Estrella develops during the course of the novel, and also the potential for upward mobility that is made possible as a result of that consciousness. The first time we read a description of the barn, Estrella and her siblings are said to be in awe of it. It was "a cathedral of a building," and while her siblings take in its size, "Only Estrella studied the door with its flaked white paint" (10). From the very beginning Estrella had wondered how to enter it, a realm imposing in its stature and guarded by a door marked by its whiteness, like

the power behind many U.S. institutions. In an interview, Viramontes illu-
minated the inspiration behind her portrayal of the barn as a forbidden space:

I was reading Erlinda Gonzales-Berry's *Las Paletitas de Guayaba* and she was writing
about how these young girls were not allowed to go into a barn. Well, that immediately raised my attention because every time something is prohibited because of gender, you know, primarily *mujeres*, I begin to think why, why is that? I always think the
opposition is because there is something that they don't want us to know or something
they want to keep away from us. That's how I started *Under the Feet of Jesus*, with the
question of a young girl not being able to go into a barn and the desire of her wanting
to go in. . . . When I'm so incredibly angry at how people have been treated, the racism and sexism, it becomes almost a surreal thing.[48]

Citing gender and racism as ways in which girls like Estrella have been barred
social inclusion, Viramontes portrays a scene in which Estrella not only enters a
forbidden space but also climbs to the top. Before Estrella enters the barn, she
puts on her "work trousers" (170), indicating that there will be labor involved.

The labor involved in ascending onto the barn's rooftop is a labor of identity as well, as this scene allegorizes the struggle of overcoming class and social barriers. Once in the middle of the barn, Estrella rests her lantern on the
ground and lets it flicker on low. As she endeavors to climb the chain that has
been hung from the middle of the ceiling, she can see the light below and only
darkness above. Leaving behind the familiar and climbing to the unknown,
Estrella climbs up the chain bearing her own weight while also dealing with the
"taste of soil rolled in her mouth, and a speck water[ing] her eye" (173). For a
migrant laborer, the soil would have particular resonance for Estrella, as it has
for Chicana/o cultural producers who employ the land as a powerful symbol of
pride, unity, and origins for Chicana/o identity. The novel certainly participates
in this tradition of strongly linking land and identity, but it does not glorify land
imagery. Rather it portrays the physical toll on the laborers who must tend to
it, who are by their lack of options forced into a life of subsistence. Along these
lines, the soil is not an unobtrusive smudge on Estrella's cheek nor a deliberate
mark; it is a "taste rolled in her mouth" that makes her climb all the more ardu-
ous yet also heightens another of her senses. Likewise, other aspects of Estrella's
upbringing, such as patriarchy and religious faith, are like the soil in that they
are part of the foundation upon which her identity is formed and are sparking

within her a heightened awareness of how they are involved in perpetuating social inequalities. And even as she is striving for something different, the narrative suggests she will still face elements from her past circumstances since those are still the conditions in which she and her family live.

Her task is not even complete when she finishes climbing, for she still faces a barrier and has to work to counter its resistance. She reaches the loft but finds the trapdoor that would take her onto the roof shut tight. Struggling to open it, "She pressed her back like a shovel against the door and pushed up once again. Again and again until whatever resistance there was gave way to her back" (174–75). This image of her back revisits a trope from women of color feminism, articulated in the anthology coedited by Cherríe Moraga and Gloria Anzaldúa, *This Bridge Called My Back*. In the preface, Moraga employs the metaphor of the back to exemplify her "theory in the flesh."[49] Moraga posits the body as registering the material effects of lived experience, serving as a means toward self and social knowledge and as a bridge between women of color. In Viramontes's novel, this metaphor shifts in image. Estrella's back as a shovel connects her with the project of women of color feminism and acts as a symbol of resistance emerging out of the laborious process of self-realization rooted in her background as an agricultural laborer.

The labor of her back also enables her to work toward a kind of payment. Estrella makes it onto the roof where she is "stunned by the diamonds" (175), feeling enriched by the new perspective she has attained. But her earnings— the "diamonds," also register her symbolic wages, distinct from the symbolic wages of class, which subjects could try to access through status symbols like actual diamonds. Estrella's wages instead are composed of the symbolic value that working-class and oppositional characters have in reinforcing collectivity in Chicana/o cultural production. At this point, Estrella is upwardly mobile but also ethnically identified. The wages, therefore, operate as a narrative payoff as well—how the novel reconciles individual identity with group affiliation.

The events in the novel got her to the position from which she could envision climbing, and this last scene has shown her again that she has the courage as well as the mental and physical capabilities to overcome obstacles. Now at the top, "she felt gravity pulling her but she did not lose her footing" (175). Having come this far, "No longer did she feel her blouse damp with sweat. No longer did she stumble blindly. She had to trust the soles of her feet, her hands, the shovel of her back, and the pounding bells of her heart"(175). In sum, this entire description of her ascension has included references to physical and mental labor, land and upward movement, and in this negotiation between striving for ascension while maintaining a relationship to and gathering strength from one's origins, we see the indirect communication of values that undergird a collectivist upward mobility.

Furthermore, the barn scene evokes religious symbolism and reconfigures religious iconography to culminate the relationships of identification that have occurred in the novel. The last line of the novel leaves us with the image of Estrella standing on the roof with beating heart: "Like the chiming bells of the great cathedrals, she believed her heart powerful enough to summon home all those who strayed" (176). In showing how Petra's faith in Catholicism has not been enough to change her family's circumstances and even having her Jesus statue fall to the floor and break, the novel has by the end depicted religious ideology as insufficient to address their needs. Héctor Calderón's summation of the break with religious faith that occurs in . . . *y no se lo tragó la tierra / And The Earth Did Not Devour Him* applies to Viramontes's novel as well, as the novel depicts a protagonist "no longer totally immersed in a natural world of spiritual forces or ruled over by myth, religion, and abstract notions of fortune."[50] This break is symbolized by Estrella's stance at the end of the novel, not under the feet of Jesus but on top of her own cathedral. Whether Estrella is read as a Christ or Virgin of Guadalupe figure, the narrative draws on the familiarity of Catholic iconography to represent Estrella and her new pragmatic and collective consciousness as an alternative to religious faith, a way in which the traditional is reconciled with new political imperatives. If Petra's way, which is resigned to a patriarchal family structure and subsistence living and affirmed by her faith in religion, represents a traditional way of doing things, Estrella and her youth represent an alternative model.

Consider how Estrella stands in for an ethnic mediator who is also mobile, and who also stands in for how ethnic texts mediate relationships between readers and issues pertaining to ethnic communities. Her function as a hybrid symbol, as an amalgamation of the traditional Catholic with a feminist consciousness, is illustrative of the kind of work Chicana authors and artists have undertaken to resist and reinterpret iconography upholding oppressive patriarchal structures (the family and the church) while reinventing them to promote feminist values.[51] These symbolic forms have enabled Chicanas to forge empowering iconography while drawing from ethnic culture and reinforcing its saliency. Estrella's symbolic function as part of a call to identify is signaled by the way in which she is said to believe "her heart powerful enough to summon home all those who strayed" (176).

That Estrella is calling out to those who have "strayed" suggests that the novel is trying to reaffirm a sense of shared values among even those who would have trouble identifying with the exigencies and collective politics depicted in the novel. In an interview, Viramontes alluded to this possibility in explaining the type of audience she envisions in writing her work:

The type of audience I want is comprised of readers like my daughter and son who did not grow up in the protest movement or in the civil rights movement and who think of all this stuff as very alien to them. Who, when we go back home, or even when we lived in Southern California and went back to East L.A., it was still very different for them because they are upper middle-class Chicanos. So different from the way Eloy [her husband] and I grew up. There is no way to artificially raise them the way we grew up. It would become self-denial.[52]

Viramontes expresses a desire to reach out to those who are distanced by time, geography, and class from the realities that sparked the civil rights movement, and yet who have the potential to become more aware of the social inequalities that led to the development, in the novel and in actual life, of ways of resisting and ameliorating those inequalities. While Rosaura Sánchez reminds us that a novel "like all texts—is not analyzable in terms of the author's intentions, but as a product of those social and cultural practices and ideological discourses which interact to determine the experiences of the individual who actually writes the work,"[53] the practices and ideological discourses that are embedded in Viramontes's works are tied to the fractured nature of collective identity, to the fact that not all the members of an ethnic group share the same experiences or have similar ideological outlooks. Reading this novel as an allegory of upward mobility helps us understand the role novels like it can play in speaking to those who are marginalized and also to those who disidentify with the plight of the racialized poor and working class. By eliciting an empathetic connection to Estrella and the other characters, the novel has put out a call that is similar to other Chicana/o novels, which ask for a response in the form of identification with working-class politics.

As we have seen, in reinforcing an identification with working-class politics, Chicana/o texts have tended not to depict class mobility or have portrayed Mexican Americans in the middle class as cultural betrayers. But Viramontes's novel gestures toward an alternative to individualist middle-class incorporation, which was symbolized by Memo in *My Family*. Héctor Calderón has stated that "within the present historical conjuncture Chicano narrative is the product of recent literate elites who are reworking artistic forms to reconcile Native American, mestizo, Spanish, Mexican, and Chicano realities with present social contradictions."[54] Viramontes's novel speaks to class contradictions in ethnic cultural production broadly, as upward mobility is both desired and regarded warily; it might enable access to resources, but it might also decrease working-class affiliations. *Under the Feet of Jesus* offers a way in which to reconcile these contradictions, offering an allegory of ethnic-affiliated upward mobility that models a process of attaining a consciousness that demands access to resources as well as values a collective identity. The novel does not romanticize the working poor, showing how a mobility of subsistence exerts dire effects on the characters. It also does not valorize leaving the working poor to pursue independent goals. But it does show how education and independence can be instrumental for self- and communal empowerment.

The novel leaves open a question, however: What would Estrella's story be in adulthood? Part of the tax Viramontes pays in order to depict class conflicts with an optimistic ending is leaving Estrella in childhood. To leave her there avoids the possibility that Estrella would physically have to leave her community, which would open up complications that the novel would not be able to resolve as easily. As we move further into the twenty-first century, we see the emergence of more Mexican American protagonists who reflect the economic heterogeneity of the Latina/o population, including protagonists who show what middle-class status looks like in adulthood, or who have inherited it as children. Mexican American and African American texts are continuously grappling with the question of what ethnic identity means in light of intra-group class stratification and in the context of attempts to enforce or resist cultural essentialization. In the next chapter, I examine texts explicitly addressing these issues to discuss how they try to reconcile ethnic identity with middle-class status for a mass market.

# CHAPTER 4

# STATUS PANIC

> Prestige involves at least two persons: one to claim it and another to
> honor the claim. . . . In the status system of a society these claims are
> organized as rules and expectations which regulate who successfully
> claims prestige, from whom, in what ways, and on what basis. The
> level of self-esteem enjoyed by given individuals is more or less set by
> this status system. . . . [T]he enjoyment of prestige is often disturbed
> and uneasy, that the bases of prestige, the expressions of prestige claims,
> and the ways these claims are honored, are now subject to great strain,
> a strain which often puts men and women in a virtual status panic.
>
> C. Wright Mills, *White Collar*[1]

> I think I kinda compromised myself a little bit in some of the material
> coming up because you gotta get in. I don't think I was as hard edge
> in the beginning as I kinda like to be now. You know I've been in
> meetings with Warner Brothers where I wasn't particularly happy with
> what I was hearing. And the Chicano would say you know fuck this.
> Fuck you guys, I'm leaving. But when you leave you're out. So I'd
> make myself stay. And probably a lot of people would say that's selling
> out. But it isn't selling out. It's the way the business is set up.
>
> George Lopez, *Brown Is the New Green*[2]

## ETHNIC STATUS PANIC FOR A MASS MARKET

In a 1988 *Los Angeles Times* essay, Richard Rodriguez shares a conversation he
has with a Princeton undergraduate who proposes, "What's missing from the
Chicano novel . . . what we really need . . . is a novel about a Mexican kid who

grows up in the suburbs; who hangs out at the mall."[3] Rodriguez sympathizes and tells us that he has been looking for such a novel for most of his life. The rest of the essay is a compilation of stories from actual "Mexican American lives that might inhabit an imaginary novel," derived from interviews Rodriguez had with middle-class Mexican Americans in Los Angeles, including a financial analyst, a film maker, a community-foundation president, a couple of lawyers, and an academic, among others, who discuss their ethnic background in relation to their current class status. Rodriguez frames his foray into these stories by citing the argument that the "cliché never changes: We don't speak English. We drop out of high school. We live on some wrong side of town. We work as maids or gardeners." To contest these stereotypes, Rodriguez takes an approach different from that of Chicana/o cultural producers, who have humanized, or valorized, the working class to counteract flattening and negative representations. Counter to the "perception of Mexicans as poor," Rodriguez instead wants to make it known that there is a Mexican American middle class. He is not alone in wanting to document economic heterogeneity. A 1997 policy report would later provide evidence of an "Emerging Latino Middle Class," describing it as "one of the major, if largely ignored, components of Southern California's middle class."[4] And in addition to informing Rodriguez's own first memoir, *Hunger of Memory* (1982), the desire to represent middle-class Mexican Americans drove the production of the ABC sitcom *George Lopez* (2002–2007) as well as the publication of Michele Serros's young adult novel, *Honey Blonde Chica* (2006).

Aimed at a broad audience, these texts do certain kinds of work in articulating shifts in ethnic and class formations. For one, they put the identity and aesthetic label *Chicano* under pressure when it comes to accommodating varied class experiences by foregrounding the fact that Mexican Americans and Chicana/os are not monolithic in life or in representational tactics. As I discussed in the previous chapter, the link between upward mobility and cultural betrayal in Chicana/o cultural production often led to the evasion or critical depiction of the Mexican American middle class. Rodriguez's memoir, Lopez's sitcom, and Serros's novel respond to this history in how they articulate a minority identity in relation to majority culture affiliations. Just as these texts work to dispel the idea that Mexican ethnicity means "poor," they labor against the idea that the "mainstream" or "middle class" means "white." The outcome is not just more color added to mainstream depictions of middle-class life, for along with their portrayal of Mexican Americans, these texts centralize ethnic and class conflicts, and in the case of Lopez and Serros, they do so in genres in which one would not necessarily expect to find them.

Moreover, they illuminate that a characteristic in these mainstream depictions of ethnic upward mobility is a version of what sociologist C. Wright Mills in 1951 termed "status panic."[5] Though written more than half a century ago and concerned mainly with a white middle class, Mills's observations in *White Collar: The American Middle Classes* remain a relevant description of the fluidity and crisis of status recognition. For one, Mills identified the twentieth century as largely shaped by capitalist-driven changes in the occupational structure of society. Seeing the "old middle class" of the nineteenth century as one composed of independent farmers and small businessmen, Mills argued that the "new middle class" emerged as a result of the increasing "centralization of property," which transformed the nation from one of "small capitalists into a nation of hired employees."[6] Within organizational business industry came constantly shifting hierarchies, in which the basis for status became increasingly unstable. Mills elaborates on how white-collar workers' claims to prestige depended on the status of their workplace, title, and dress, and most important, on recognition by others. In this chapter, I examine what the articulation of status panic in Rodriguez's, Lopez's, and Serros's texts indicates about the status of mainstream ethnic representations. I argue that they depict status panic and also express it, revealing how they negotiate acceptance by a potentially hostile readership and viewership.

Even though there is a longer history of mainstream depictions of a Black middle class,[7] the dramatizations of status panic in the ABC sitcom *black-ish*, which first aired in the 2014–2015 season, demonstrate how it too is grappling with the fact that such depictions are still going against the grain of dominant perceptions about race, ethnicity, and class. At the end of this chapter, I discuss how *black-ish* juggles being both atypical and representative of Black families and the strategies it takes to enact and reconcile status panic. Rather than seeing depictions of status panic as just pertaining to an individual character's anxieties about misrecognition, I read these affective moments as reflective of the texts' endeavors as a whole in responding to pressures of exclusion and assessment. For these reasons, I see these depictions as emerging in response to anxieties about people of color in historically exclusionary spheres such as workplaces or network television, the effects of and backlash toward affirmative action, and the use of authenticity discourse in reinforcing and policing ethnic identity. The figural types enable cultural producers to depict these tensions, along with scenarios that attempt to reconcile them, sometimes in the cultural text itself, or for a readership and audience.

## *HUNGER OF MEMORY*'S INSISTENT NEGATIONS

At the beginning of his literary career, Richard Rodriguez capitalized on his middle-class experiences with the six autobiographical essays that make up *Hunger of Memory: The Education of Richard Rodriguez*. Written from the standpoint of an assimilated "middle-class American man" (1), *Hunger of Memory* was the first of a trilogy chronicling Rodriguez's life, each from a different angle. According to the author, *Hunger of Memory* focuses on class; *Days of Obligation: An Argument with My Mexican Father* tackles ethnicity; and his third volume, *Brown: The Last Discovery of America*, wrestles with race.[8] It soon becomes clear, however, that these three social categories cannot be so easily unbraided, since each text shows how all three categories are intertwined in the author's understanding of self and society.

*Hunger of Memory* has received much popular and critical attention, largely due to its controversial claims about minority identities. In this account of his early life, Rodriguez recalls his educational journey as a dark-skinned child of Mexican immigrant parents who is schooled into an American public identity. Rodriguez's guilt and nostalgia form a complex web once he realizes that he knowingly embraced the very means by which he became estranged from his parents' language and customs. He states that as a child, "I was reminded by Spanish of my separateness from *los otros, los gringos* in power" (14). He discusses how his family's conscious decision to make the children learn English dramatically altered the dynamics of familial intimacy: "We remained a loving family, but one greatly changed. No longer so close; no longer bound tight by the pleasing and troubling knowledge of our public separateness" (22). The benefits of assimilation and the separation it entails become central themes for Rodriguez. He continues in subsequent chapters to narrate his process of upward mobility and educational achievement, showing that he is constantly threatened with the stigma of separation that is often imposed upon minority identities. At stake for Rodriguez are the dominant assumptions about minorities, and particularly minority students. In "Profession," in which he explains his opposition to affirmative action, he declares that he was unfairly labeled a minority student by the university system, the very system that had assured him nonminority status through the educational process. Having taken pains to develop his public voice in school and professionally, Rodriguez wonders why some people still want to categorize him as disadvantaged. Ultimately, he argues that just because he is a racial minority that does not mean he is a cultural minority.

Rodriguez's sociocultural interpretations, employed to validate his journey away from cultural minority status, and his denunciations of minority programs such as bilingual education and affirmative action were roundly criticized by various Chicana/o intellectuals. They did not object to Rodriguez's claim to be middle class; rather, they took issue with his conservative politics and his seeming complicity with the structures of dominance that continued to marginalize Mexicans and Mexican Americans. Referring to the negative terms in which Rodriguez frames his language and cultural origins, Tomás Rivera described *Hunger of Memory* as the product of a "colonized mind."[9] Similarly, Norma Alarcón assessed Rodriguez as a "shepherd playing the aristocrat."[10] Paula Moya argued that Rodriguez's false belief in the concept of a universal human and his acceptance of the "bourgeois heterosexual Euro-American male subject as the standard of universal humanity" prompted him to conclude, mistakenly, that he had to disavow his racial identity in order to achieve universality.[11] The particularity of Rodriguez's experience, or rather his propensity for taking his own experience as proof of a larger social argument, inclined Ramón Saldívar to argue that there is no dialectic between Rodriguez's individual identity and a collective ethnic identity, given that Rodriguez only interprets cultural political events through his personal experience, not the other way around.[12]

While Rodriguez's later works would be received more favorably, the early relationship between Richard Rodriguez and Chicana/o intellectuals was discursively contentious.[13] At the time he wrote *Hunger of Memory*, Rodriguez did not acknowledge that even middle-class Mexican Americans could still be racialized, gendered, and classed in a way that was out of their control. Moreover, the civil rights movement made it possible for ethnic minorities to claim affirmative identities; they did not have to relinquish their ethnic identity in order to get ahead, and so the fact that Rodriguez did so anyway made his position as a Latino spokesperson all the more contested. While we can read

Rodriguez's disavowal of ethnic identity as an interpretive error,[14] in examining the strategies he employs to narrate his middle-class status, especially how he distances himself from Chicana/os and the poor, we can also understand how his interpretations are driven by a deep vulnerability as well as by anxieties over marginalized collective identities.

Rodriguez rejects the minority label *Chicano*, thereby framing his middle-classness as his primary identity and signaling his membership in and loyalty to a majority culture. In *Hunger of Memory*, he chastises Chicanos for looking to the past rather than facing the reality of the present. In the book's prologue, he communicates his distaste for what he later accuses Chicanos of enacting: a romanticization of the past that he calls the "middle-class pastoral," in which middle-class Chicanos deny their "difference from the lower class [and] attempt cheap imitations of lower-class life." Like the poet who ventriloquizes through the voice of a shepherd to sing the praises of an idealized country landscape, Rodriguez argues that Chicanos seem to be saying, "But I still *am* a shepherd" (5). At another point, Rodriguez describes the uncomfortable nearness of some fellow Chicano university students wearing serapes in a "clownish display" (171). In *Days of Obligation*, he again characterizes Chicanos as Mexican Americans with a penchant for dressing up in order to self-identify:

Mexican Americans of the generation of the sixties had no myth of themselves as Americans. So that when Mexican Americans won national notoriety, we could only refer the public gaze to the past. We are people of the land, we told ourselves. Middle-class college students took to wearing farmer-in-the-dell overalls and they took, as well, a rural slang to name themselves: Chicanos.[15]

Notably, his critique of Chicanos is based solely on examples of visual display. He avoids any mention of Chicano literary, artistic, or political action and reduces Chicano identity to mere spectacle. He casts them all as a self-indulgent group reveling in romantic fallacy and denying their difference from those truly disadvantaged. What Rodriguez recognizes, and what is useful, is his observation that, contrary to appearances, there were participants in the Chicano movement who were middle class (or on their way via college degrees). However, Rodriguez fails to acknowledge that not all Chicanos who went to college were or would become middle class; even more crucially, he ignores the fact that many did not identify culturally as middle class, since that could entail identifying with an antagonistic mainstream culture. Consequently, by generalizing Chicano expression with so much disdain, he might have also reinforced a commitment from Chicanos to *not* be like Richard Rodriguez—that is, to not be elitist or disconnected, serving as a cautionary tale for those wanting to strengthen working-class political affiliations.

The seeming separateness of Chicana/o identity threatens the mainstream inclusion for which Rodriguez admits striving. He uses Chicanos in his project of asserting his integration into majority culture by countering their visual display with his own literary display. In *Hunger*, his literary references flaunt his mastery of the English language and its literature, including nods to Shakespeare, the Renaissance, the Romantics, and the Victorians. He fights the implicit accusation that he has sold out by claiming that he is the one who is true to his culture—that is, the culture into which he has been educated—and that middle-class Chicanos are operating under false pretenses by trying to deny their middle-class cultural capital. Thus he ironizes the script of cultural authenticity. Whereas Chicanos asserted authenticity through poverty, and by speaking from the position of an oppressed people, Rodriguez bases his claim to authenticity on his ability to write erudite essays about what it means to be poor and look indigenous rather than having to culturally identify with either. In other words, he admits that he muses about those who live on the margins of society rather than pretending to know or be one of them. The only time *los pobres*, as he refers to the oppressed poor, make an appearance in *Hunger of Memory* is when he works with a group of construction workers hired from Mexico. Rodriguez then constructs the Mexican poor as illiterate and silent in order to reinforce his own literacy and public voice.[16]

Rodriguez is adamant that he is not poor, not a Chicano, and not a minority.[17] Still, underlying Rodriguez's rhetorical moves and the impulse to distance himself from Chicanos and the poor is a fierce anxiety about being perceived as an "other" himself. His writing exhibits poignantly what Mills described as "status panic." Rodriguez asks his readers to recognize him as a writer worthy of prestige, one who can attest to the cumulative effects of his education. Yet the threat of overdetermination hangs over his head—the fear of being seen as just another Mexican, as just another ethnic writer, or as accruing undeserved rewards because of affirmative action. These fears come to a head when he narrates his experiences on the academic job market. After a white colleague confronts

Rodriguez over the many offers he received, he tells us, "I felt disgust. The job offers I was receiving were indeed unjustified. . . . All I was saying amounted to a frantic self-defense. It was a lie. I tried to find an end to my sentence; my voice faltered to a stop" (184). While Rodriguez ended up leaving the academy, his response turned out to be a literary one. *Hunger of Memory* served as a contextualization of his status panic, revealing a fear of being misrecognized and mislabeled. If the majority of Mexicans are thought to be illiterate laborers, then his intellectual production speaks to a vastly different experience. And if one of the pervasive assumptions about Mexican Americans is that they are all immigrants or are a threat to white American culture, then Rodriguez is an adamant example to the contrary. Consequently, he fashions the middle-class Mexican American experience as in danger of being misunderstood. At the crux of this strategic representation is a need for validation, as if his writing were a response to the question, How do you represent the assimilated Mexican American if there is no context for his kind of experience in the American literary imagination?[18] In the end, Rodriguez seeks status within the mainstream and renders acculturation as a process accompanied by deep pain. He reverberates awareness about what status seeking is costing him, and yet he justifies that cost as one that must inevitably be paid in order to have a public voice and an accepted status in American letters. He accepts the tax in order to accrue the symbolic wages of esteemed instead of denigrated status. A conflicted artist as well as a status seeker, his embodiment of both is the source of tension at the heart of *Hunger of Memory*.

Richard Rodriguez searched for ways to narrate the experiences of education and upward mobility for Mexican Americans at a time when such writings seemed anomalous in relation to Chicana/o texts. His vocal claims of being assimilated and middle class and his disdain for Chicano identity, and the resulting reception of his politics and identity claims, have, however, served to reinforce the association of upward mobility with cultural disavowal. His writings and the discourse around them also shed light on the assumed parameters of Chicana/o identity. Attempting to define these parameters, for instance, Henry Staten has referenced Rodriguez's story to reflect on Chicano identity, suggesting that there are degrees of ethnic identification:

Rodriguez is wrong to think that someone who grows up in a migrant worker family or a working-class barrio family and then goes to college has no grounds for identification with the culture of origin. . . . While pointing toward the plight of the most oppressed ethclass, Chicano or Chicana is primarily available as a self-description to those who have begun to emerge from the condition or who are capable of articulating the potentially Chicano-Chicana community for itself; this stage is not where one stops being a Chicano or Chicana but in some sense where one starts. Yet I believe that at some point the identification ceases to be valid, that one cannot stretch the threads of affiliation indefinitely thin. One can be a Chicano who goes to Harvard, but can one be a Chicano whose parents went to Harvard?[19]

Staten's implicit answer is that at a certain point on the upward path, Chicano identity becomes incongruent with one's social position. Research by Susan Keefe and Amado Padilla conducted around the time of Rodriguez's early writings did find that education and socioeconomic mobility tend to correlate with a lessening of cultural awareness, which they define as knowledge about cultural history, language use, and identification with group labels such as "Mexican American" and "Chicano."[20] Their research also reveals that even when one controls for generation, factors such as gender, neighborhood, and to a certain extent religion help predict cultural affinity, with women, those who live in ethnic neighborhoods, and Catholics having higher levels of cultural awareness. Notably, these studies were done in an era when there were no representations of a Mexican American middle class, except for the ones usually associated with cultural betrayal. Cultural production in the 2000s not only reflects how the Mexican American middle class has relationships with both the mainstream and ethnic communities but may also be shaping beliefs that this is possible.

The representation of Mexican American identity has become more capacious, with the increase in the Latina/o population and the changing face of media having ushered us into a new discursive stage. Cultural critic Herman Gray has argued that the waning dominance of the big three television networks in the 1980s due to competition from cable, video games, and videocassettes led networks to develop a strategy of "narrowcasting," which led to more shows targeting specific demographics.[21] While the 1990s saw the rise of shows featuring all-Black casts, in the 2000s Latina/os started gaining more traction in the realm of television. No doubt this shift was enabled by 2000 census data, which revealed the vast numbers of Latina/os in the United States, leading media outlets to take the representation of this population more seriously. As a result, we have seen the rise of successful Mexican Americans like the comic

George Lopez, who inherited the ideology of the Chicano movement, who identifies as Chicano, and whose cultural production reveals a negotiation between Chicano identity and mainstream conventions.

## GEORGE LOPEZ'S MAKING OF A MIDDLE-CLASS HERO

George Lopez's television hit, *George Lopez*, aired for six seasons on ABC from 2002 to 2007, bolstering Lopez's career as a mainstream comic by giving the viewing public a show about a middle-class Latino family. When the actress Constance Marie found out she had landed the role of George's wife, Angie Lopez, she reportedly exclaimed, "Finally—we're Latinos on TV, but we're not in the barrio! And we're successful!"[22] Indeed, the show was unique in setting Latino culture in the suburbs and dealing with the growth and development of a Mexican American father, a Cuban American mother, and their two assimilated children.[23]

On the show, George plays a manager in a Los Angeles airplane parts factory whose personal growth is constantly challenged and then signified by his ability to reconcile his current middle-class status with his working-class upbringing. George is respected by his employees and is integral to the running of the factory, but the show does not paint his ascent to the middle class as conflict free. Abandoned by his father and raised by his acerbic blue-collar mother, Benny, George struggles to maintain his success as a father in a loving family and as an admired factory manager. To dramatize how far George has come from his unhappy working-class childhood, the show employs flashbacks or has characters recall memories of a young George suffering from neglect and low self-esteem. By the end of such episodes, George comes to terms with these memories and grows as a person, one means by which the show, following the sitcom tradition, creates a correlation between working-class life and dysfunction and posits middle-class status as enabling self-realization. In addition to how he handles personal issues, his character is also showcased by how he engages with the ethical battles that arise from his intermediary position at work. In "Profiles in Courage," George is asked by the Powers brothers—the factory owners—to demote an Arab worker because they believe that his ethnicity might cost them government contracts in the post-9/11 era.[24] Episodes like this one foreground George's middle status: he is the middle-class Chicano who is neither an owner of the factory nor one of its workers and who is, in turn, uniquely positioned to either uphold or ignore workers' rights. The show strives to paint George's virtues as stemming in large part from his commitment to negotiate with those he works for on behalf of those who work under him.

The show's entire narrative arc follows the advantages and crises George experiences as an intermediary figure who has to arbitrate conflicts at the factory. As the series begins, he has just been promoted to his position as manager of Powers Bros. Aviation after sixteen years on the assembly line. The central question in the first episode is whether he will remain loyal to his fellow workers or change now that he is part of management. This question arises again in the series finale, when the factory has been bought out by a Mexican corporation headed by a businessman played by Chicano actor Edward James Olmos.[25] Olmos's character plans to shut down the factory but offers George a six-figure salary at a job in Phoenix. In these opening and closing episodes that bookend the series, George is offered privileges that allow him advantages over others, but they also offer him the chance to prove that despite moving up, he has not sold out. In both cases he demonstrates his support for his fellow workers. At the end, he manages to keep the factory open and running.

The question of selling out is also explored in the episode "Token of Un-appreciation."[26] In this episode, the Powers brothers ask George to go back on the assembly line when they are behind in production. Not only does he feel unappreciated and disrespected by his employers, he fears that his value as a manager will not appreciate (in the economic sense) if he can be demoted at whim. The conflict intensifies when George is offered a job at Aerocorp, a competing company that wants to hire a Latino to improve its chances of receiving government contracts. Tempted by the promotion, George never-theless declares that he does not want to be a token Latino. We can compare George's portrayal to Richard Rodriguez's to get a fuller understanding of how ethnic status panic differs from the kind of generalized status panic discussed by Mills in his account of the white-collar worker. Like Rodriguez, who won-ders why people still see him as a minority, George protests how others see him. An upset George finally confesses to his bosses how frustrated he is: "I spent fifteen years trying to get off the line and in a blink of an eye you send me back down. You know how that makes me feel?" (Figure 1). George's pro-test echoes Richard Rodriguez's insistence in *Hunger of Memory* that he be

FIGURE 1. George confronts the Powers brothers. Source: "Token of Unappreciation," *George Lopez*, aired October 9, 2002.

recognized for his merits: the note of status panic is clear and reverberating. Both men express anxieties about being disrespected and unappreciated, and both cite their mobility stories as justification. Both are responding to class-inflected stereotypes that correlate Mexicans to manual laborers and subordinate status—in other words, not white collar.

Furthermore, their protests are directed toward various depicted and implied gatekeepers of approval, ones who offer distinct kinds of status recognition. Remember that throughout the show, George faces the question of whether he will "sell out" as part of management, and acts in ways that reassure the other characters—and potentially viewers—that he is still concerned about the status of the workers. In *Hunger of Memory*, Rodriguez describes a moment that taps into similar anxieties about ethnic loyalty and authenticity. While he is finishing his dissertation and teaching at Berkeley, some Latina/o students come to his office and ask if he will teach a "minority literature" course at a community center. He tells them he does not believe that there is such a thing as minority literature and gives reasons why, but then feels anxious at their dismissal of him: "I saw one of my listeners yawn. Another sort of smiled. My voice climbed to hold their attention. I wanted approval; I was afraid of their scorn. But scorn came inevitably. . . . After that I was regarded as comic. I became a 'coconut'—someone brown on the outside, white on the inside."[27] Another aspect to their panic, then, is the questioning of their status by assessors of ethnic authenticity and loyalty.

A third aspect to ethnic status panic, portrayed on *George Lopez*, is concern about the status of the group as a whole. Despite the scorn he receives, Rodriguez does not affiliate with the racial protest movements. George, however, is represented as concerned with how he is perceived by those without power and how they are treated.[28] While his status panic is motivated by evidence that his employers view his position in the factory hierarchy as flexible, he is also worried about the status of the workers. We can see, for example, that after George confronts his bosses the question remains: How can George assert his individual value while remaining loyal to his community? Community in this sense is his community of workers, many of whom are racial minorities. Moreover, how can George assert his individual worth when his community may need him on the shop floor, or on the production line?

The affirmative action ploy is introduced as one possible option. The show's take on affirmative action can be summed up as follows: affirmative action is a way to advance professionally through institutional practices rather than through one's own merit. George insists that this would compromise him ethically, and indeed the show presents a rather cynical portrait of affirmative action by not bringing up its progressive political possibilities. Instead of acknowledging that the Aerocorp job could enable George to hire other racial minorities or change the working environment, the show limits the advantages of the new position to a bigger salary, an on-site gym, and contained acts of playful subversion. In order to be a middle-class hero with working-class consciousness, George has to find an alternative solution. Instead of leaving his community for a better position, he airs his grievances to his bosses and asks them to join him and the workers on the assembly line in an act of solidarity. The answer the show offers is that in times of hierarchical crisis, nonhierarchical production can defuse individual and collective ire. This is the same strategy that enables George to keep the factory open when it is threatened with closure. In the final episode, George puts his new job offer on the line and joins the workers in a protest, forcing Olmos's character to reconsider shutting down the factory. These episodes, beginning and ending the series, endorse the politicized potential of the intermediary position, specifically of class mediation. The push of his moral attributes as a sitcom character come into stark relief when compared to a character Lopez plays in the film *Bread and Roses*. In this film, Lopez plays an exploitive office building manager named Perez who bullies the janitorial staff into working overtime, threatens them against joining a union, and coerces a female janitor into sleeping with him in exchange for hiring her undocumented sister.[29] While looking to a sitcom for messages about a politicized Chicano identity might seem fatuous, by ignoring the messages in commercial media we would be falling into the trap that David Román has noticed in Chicana/o and Latina/o studies, whereby scholars engage in a "romance with the indigenous," meaning that they prefer alternative, grassroots, and community-based performances and art because these are seen as more authentic and real and are "presumed to have remained uncontaminated by commercialism, commodity culture, or mainstream tastes."[30] If we take seriously the premise that *George Lopez* is a politically charged cultural production, we can see its contributions in expanding the representational realm of Latina/os and how it is trying to counter dominant portrayals of the middle class as apolitical. We can also see the compromises it makes to get those messages across.

For example, even as the show represents the politics of collectivity, it mocks Chicano cultural performances. In one episode in particular, the show distances itself from and parodies Chicano community theater. "Meet the Cuban Parents" revolves around the Christmas visit of George's Cuban in-laws.[31] It depicts the friction between George and his father-in law, Vic (Emiliano Díez), who he feels has always looked down on him for not being a professional, wealthy, or Cuban. Through the conflict between George and Vic, the show represents Latinos as coming from various national and class backgrounds, acknowledging that these distinctions can be sources of tension. During this particular visit, George's frustration begins when Vic hands him a wad of bills so that he can take his daughter "out on a nice date." George's exasperation increases when Vic mocks the size of George's Christmas tree and then buys George's son, Max, the bike that George and Angie had intended to get him for their Christmas present. George's anger finally spirals into an all-out Christmas showdown when he uses his salary bonus to buy the family a new Christmas tree and a cascade of presents, and then unveils a backyard full of Christmas decorations and artificial snow. Rather than granting George the satisfaction of having provided the family with the best seasonal display, Vic criticizes him for buying a "department store" Christmas, adding that while he can show the kids Cuban traditions, it is up to George to make sure that they know Mexican Christmas traditions. This leaves George in a tough spot, since his mother has never taught him any specific Mexican Christmas traditions. So when his secretary suggests he take his family to a community play, he eagerly agrees after reading the flyer aloud, which states, "The César Chávez Teatro de la Communidad in association with Tenochtitlan Productions Presents: 'A Chicano Christmas Carol, starring Moctezuma Cuauhtémoc.'" George grins and adds, "Nothing is more Mexican than this!"

The play turns out to be a parodic rewriting of *A Christmas Carol* with stereotypical barrio figures. Instead of Ebenezer Scrooge and his clerk Bob Cratchit, they see a drug lord and one of his dealers, and in place of Tiny Tim there is Timoteo, who gets shot in the first act. Once home, Angie expresses her relief that they left after the "pitbull mauling" as the rest of the family grumbles about the horrors of the play. In her brief spell as a writer for the show, Michele Serros penned this episode, continuing a running theme in her work—a critique of what she portrays as Chicano clichés. It is reflected in George's discomfort with what is essentialized as stereotypically Chicano: a hyperbolic representation of poverty, violence, and fatalism. This is not the image of Chicano or Mexican culture he is seeking. Rather, he wants a Christmas that is not determined by the demands of ethnic authenticity, one that is not Cuban or Mexican, but is just a family Christmas. Here the show avoids a deeper engagement in ethnic identity by simply resorting to the ambiguous notion of a holiday stripped of culture. Constrained by the conventions of the sitcom format, the show frequently slips into such sappy narrative closure, unable to address adequately the complexities of class and ethnic affiliation, which in this episode are displaced in favor of emphasis on the nuclear middle-class family.[32]

This flattening of Chicana/o cultural production into mere spectacle echoes Rodriguez's appraisal of Chicanos as enacting a "clownish display" and suggests that in this sitcom as well, reducing the ideological project of Chicana/o cultural production into theatrics (literally) and distancing oneself from it becomes a means of establishing majority-culture affiliation and mainstream palatability. In that fall 2002 season, two other shows aired starring Latino males, and both were on FOX: *Luis*, featuring Luís Guzmán, and *The Ortegas*, featuring Cheech Marín. Lopez's show was the only one that made it past that first season, and sociologist John Markert suggests that this was due to Lopez's show being more subtle in its representation of ethnic differences while the other two were more blatantly stereotypical.[33] In his content analysis, Markert found that jokes against whites were rare and much more prevalent were inter-ethnic jokes, occasioned by pointing out differences between George as a Mexican and his wife and father-in-law as Cubans. In the Christmas episode, the jokes between George and Vic could be considered both inter- and intra-ethnic barbs, since they point out differences between and within Latino groups, while the jokes launched at Chicano popular culture exemplify intra-ethnic jokes made at the expense of the history of Chicana/o politics and art.

Serros, who wrote this episode, served as a cast writer for *George Lopez* for one season and has explained that her limited time on the show was due to behind-the-scenes power dynamics. Her experiences serve as a reminder that even a Latino-themed sitcom featuring a Mexican American star, and including a Mexican American writer like Serros on its staff, would still be subject to the pressures of conforming to a white middle-class viewership. In a column for *Fox News Latino*, Serros hints at why she left the job: "Just as the second season was picked up, I did a Chappelle and quit the show abruptly. In my case, it was due to medical reasons; the environment and the process of comedy writing for a major network were literally making me sick."[34] By referencing the sudden departure of the *Chappelle's Show* host and star, Serros alludes to the power dynamics between racialized performers and white audiences. Chappelle reportedly quit his show because he was no longer sure that white viewers were laughing with him instead of at him as he interrogated racial stereotypes in his comedy sketches.[35] Serros describes how uncomfortable it made her to watch Lopez have to negotiate the portrayal of ethnic identity with writers and producers:

I often felt badly as I witnessed him, the star of his own show, relegated to nearly begging for permission for any and all scraps Chicano. One time he was firmly reminded, in almost a condescending manner, that he was not to use Spanish slang. "Now George, we talked about this. There will be no Spanish." The exchange seemed like a flashback to a 1970s classroom in Texas.[36]

The production of *George Lopez* exemplifies how ethnic sitcoms are constrained not just by genre conventions but also by the management of ethnic differences by white financiers, writers, and directors. According to Lopez in his autobiography, he also felt pressured to conform to expectations of what a Latino home should look like and recounts the words of a network executive who urged him to make the set appear more ethnic:

"George, there's nothing in the kitchen that tells anybody that a Mexican family lives there." They wanted to put in a tortilla maker. I don't even know what that is. My grandmother was my tortilla maker. So I told them, "What about the Mexicans in the kitchen?"[37]

Amid furnishings that look like they could appear on any family sitcom, ethnic markers like a tortilla maker along with a few Latina/o art pieces on the wall could have been attempts to make the home look ethnic but still familiar enough for a mainstream viewership. Yet Lopez's attempts to make the subjects on the show more vocally ethnic was met with resistance. The portrayal of a middle-class Latina/o family on network television was, as Serros and Lopez reveal, one largely out of their control.

More blatantly conforming to mainstream ideology is the fact that the representation of the admirable middle-class character is forged in contrast to the portrayals of the working-class characters. The show structures power hierarchies through humor as well as economic positions. George is the middle-class hero, a champion of the workers, but he is able to keep his position because of the workers. Humor on the show is often at the expense of George's working-class employees, who function as his comic foils, playing into a long history of negative representations of the poor and working class. Among the factory workers are his mother, whom he frequently ridicules for her bad parenting and loose morals; his best friend Ernie, a dim-witted sidekick; and, at the beginning of the series, his secretary, Marisol, a comic rendition of a chola. The fact that George is always able to tell the better joke and have the last laugh reinforces the idea that he is more qualified than they are. George's status on the show is consistent with Erica Scharrer's research, which finds that working-class fathers are often made out to be buffoons while middle- and upper-class fathers like Cliff Huxtable appear wise and authoritative.[38] George appears somewhere in the middle: capable of making mistakes, a failing often attributed to his single-parent upbringing, yet smarter and more of a leader than his working-class employees. By situating George as a middle-class hero bolstered by working-class supporting characters, the show reinforces a hegemonic valuing of the middle class.

It conveys this message while simultaneously countering dominant portrayals of the middle class that reinforce white families as representative of society at large. In watching *George Lopez*, viewers are presented with a family whose members come in different skin shades, as in many Latino families. George is visibly the darkest one in the family and, notably, was bigger in size at the beginning of the series than when it ended. The combination of his color and size was something Lopez understood could prevent his acceptance in the entertainment world. In the documentary *Brown Is the New Green: George Lopez and the American Dream*, he shares how he tried to mitigate people's perceptions of his appearance: "Well the fact that I was big and brown and . . . a little overweight, a lot bigger than I am now, is I had to smile a lot because when I didn't smile it'd look really intimidating."[39] Responding to fears of racial difference, Lopez had to make George a nonthreatening presence on television. And in order to diversify sitcom families racially, his show apparently had to appear nonthreatening to the hierarchy of class. The show was ultimately canceled in 2007, with ABC arguing it would be financially costly to renew it for a sixth season. Lopez saw the cancellation as further evidence of ABC's mistreatment of the show, with the network moving its time slot four times over five years and putting it against the ratings powerhouse *American Idol*.[40]

Both George Lopez's show and Richard Rodriguez's memoir depict and enact status panic in showing that their merit and acceptability by a mainstream audience are not something they can take for granted. Just as characters seeking status register socioeconomic conditions, so does ethnic cultural production seeking mainstream status. In appealing to broader audiences, Richard Rodriguez's memoir and George Lopez's sitcom distance themselves from and mock Chicano culture, and assure audiences that they do not condone affirmative action. They reduce a social protest movement to theatrics, and pose individual merit at odds with a policy that opens up opportunities for historically excluded groups. In appealing to mainstream palatability, the two cultural producers also open themselves up to accusations of selling out, and Lopez's character counters this reading by continuously showing George as tied to the working class. Offered several opportunities to move up at the expense of his racialized working-class community, George stays and works on its behalf. In effect, he is a middle-class character with a working-class consciousness, a televised possibility played out in the realm of the ideal, vastly different from the middle-class man depicted in Richard Rodriguez's memoir. Of course, the sitcom genre demands resolution of conflicts and integration back into the community, while the memoir allows for melancholy, ambiguity, and estrangement. Ultimately, the reach of these cultural producers signals greater acceptance for their representations, but the strategies they employ in speaking to the mainstream and to the history of ethnic politics discloses the conditions upon which that acceptance rests. Their status panic registers an anxiety about the instability and newness of the class and social status they are representing and also indexes the status of middle-class Mexican Americans in the contemporary American cultural imagination. In the next section, I examine how Michele Serros, a "Generation X Latina," also depicts status panic in a narrative featuring an untraditional Chicana protagonist.[41]

## *HONEY BLONDE CHICA* PUTS THE *GO* IN GOMEZ

Despite her brief stint as a television writer on *George Lopez*, Michele Serros is most known for her literary production. Her works include a collection of poetry, *Chicana Falsa: And Other Stories of Death, Identity, and Oxnard*, and a novel, *How to Be a Chicana Role Model.*[42] *Chicana Falsa* includes the poem "La Letty," in which Letty calls the speaker a "Chicana Falsa" for speaking "sloppy Spanish" and being a "Homogenized Hispanic." Serros's poem added an alternative voice to Chicana literature by interrogating the politics of authenticity in its questioning of the dominant notions of what it means to be a "true" Chicana. Having pried open for herself the door into oppositional representation and critique within the Chicana literary community, Serros continued to write against the grain by producing fiction for the commercial teen market and by focusing on characters that bear little likeness to the traditional child protagonists found in the works of earlier generations, such as *Barrio Boy*, *Pocho*, or *The House on Mango Street.*[43] Her novel *Honey Blonde Chica* depicts the teen angst of Evie Gomez, an upper-middle-class Mexican American living in Southern California.[44]

Evie's story is not an immigrant narrative or an assimilation tale. She is a fourth-generation Mexican American: her father owns several bakeries, her stay-at-home mom spends her time shopping, and her older sister attends Stanford. When asked by National Public Radio's Debbie Elliot whether the choice to represent Mexican Americans in this way was a conscious decision on her part, Serros answered,

I grew up reading a lot of young adult novels and being an author, and going into middle schools and high schools I was seeing a lot of the same books that I read and they follow a similar theme, and that's a theme I call the "Three Bs." It was always about barrios, borders, or bodegas and I wanted to present a different kind of life. A life we don't always see in the mainstream media.[45]

Here Serros disassociates her work from what she sees as the prevalent themes in Latina/o literature, which include working-class sites like barrios and bodegas and the immigrant experience of crossing the border. Like the works of Richard Rodriguez and George Lopez, Serros's novel represents the heterogeneity of the Mexican American population and the practices and identity conflicts that come with upward mobility.

The novel's reconciliation of status panic is tied to Evie's personal growth and acquisition of maturity, which in turn is tied to her acceptance of the value of labor. According to the novel's narrator, "the Gomezes were a very focused, ambitious family. They accentuated the *Go* in Gomez, all of them, that is except for Evie, who felt more of a personal connection to the lagging z as in Gomezzzzzz" (4). With Evie's family already well off, the novel stresses the necessity of maintaining aspirational values. While the rest of her family adheres to a strong work ethic, Evie at the beginning of the novel prefers to spend her time with her friends the "flojos," flip-flop-wearing surfers who "shared one thing in common, and that one thing was the absolute, all-consuming unending desire to . . . do absolutely nothing" (7). Exhibiting traits similar to the young, fashionable characters found in teen fiction like the popular *Gossip Girl* series, Evie and her friends engage in a culture of parties, promiscuity, underage drinking, and brand-name consumption. Amy Pattee has argued that the "raison d'etre of the *Gossip Girl* characters involves consumption and display," and for the most part, Serros's novel appeals to readers of this type of commodity-loaded genre.[46]

However, even if Evie starts off as just another loafer among the rich and idle of her set, she undergoes a transformation by the end of the novel. After the valuable lessons she learns about friendship and individuality (this is a teen novel, after all), the last pages describe her finally getting up early enough to make the 6:30 a.m. surfing run with her friends and using her designer surfboard for the first time. With her friends cheering her on as she paddles through the ocean, she prides herself on at last "putting the 'Go' in Gomez! . . . She was carrying on the family name!" (298). These closing lines summarize the novel's denunciation of her previous indolent lifestyle by telling us that "Evie Gomez suddenly felt alive, focused, and had only one thing on her mind and that was the absolute, all-consuming, unending desire to leave the lagging, lazy z of her last name behind her . . . for good" (298). Whereas Evie had defined herself in terms of her uselessness and nonproductivity as a member of the flojos, she now identifies with her family's values of personal responsibility and active self-assertion. Since this morality tale begins and ends with references to how Evie resists and then exemplifies the "Go in Gomez," her identity transformation reveals the novel's investment in her as a reformed character who moves from the leisure-class habits of immobility and waste toward a bourgeois ethic of personal drive and perseverance.

"Putting the Go in Gomez" then arises as the novel's ethos and a motto of Mexican American class mobility. The novel questions the stereotypes that affix laziness to working-class Mexicans; rather, it associates laziness with socio-eonomic privilege (those who have resources and leisure time can be lazy) and links a strong work ethic to Mexican ethnicity—to those with names like Gomez. The novel also focuses on a character who needs to internalize the values that make middle-class maintenance possible. In effect, what Evie has to learn is to counteract complacency, exemplified by the "lazy z," which, as part of her name, can never be totally left behind. Thus, even though the novel devotes narrative space to Evie's other identity conflicts—the question of which hair color best represents her true self is a running leitmotif—the weightier conflict is the one that goes unsaid if we read Evie as the child of a new class of Mexican Americans that is anxious about preserving its newly attained middle- and upper-class status.

This depiction of Evie's status insecurity aligns with Barbara Ehrenreich's theorization of the middle class. Ehrenreich has argued that the U.S. "professional middle class" is characterized by a "fear of falling."[47] Ehrenreich bases her definition on the group's professionalism: since this group cannot pass down professionalism like property, each subsequent generation shares in the fear of returning to the working class. While Evie does not explicitly express this fear, and in fact there is no mention of her ever having experienced a nonmiddle-class existence, her striving to live up to her family's values of hard work and achievement points to the anxiety that middle-class parents might pass on to *their* children. No wonder, then, that at the beginning of the novel the flojos are cheekily but also pointedly described as being part of "Generation YBother?" (7). The message seems to be that instilling and adopting a hard work ethic is a source of generational conflict and a cultural challenge.

The novel also shows how for racialized minorities, the fear of falling is compounded by status panic; in fact, the two go hand in hand, but the latter includes an anxiousness that one's status will not be recognized correctly. In *Honey Blonde Chica* this is linked to the struggle between the "haves and the have más" (24), signaling where the real conflict lies in the novel. It is not in Evie's relationship to the working class. The only working-class character in this novel is the family's housekeeper, who is rather seamlessly incorporated into the family's home life. Instead, the novel's conflict centers on Evie's relationship with upper-class characters who are not Mexican Americans or white Americans but girls from Mexico City who attend her boarding school. This clique of girls, even more affluent than Evie, displays an extravagance and elitism so extreme that Evie's leisurely loafing seems like a minor indulgence. They even call into question Evie's class membership by deriding her father for "selling doughnuts." The novel accesses all the stereotypes about rich, catty, mean girls via this group of progeny of the Mexican elite.

The status panic that Evie experiences is due to the taunting and dismissal by her wealthy Mexican classmates, and through the inclusion of these characters the novel itself expresses an anxiety that Evie might be dismissed by the reader if there were no characters who allowed her to appear in a sympathetic light. After all, Evie is characteristically lazy, has a maid to pick up after her, and frets over frivolous crises about her hair color. But by including the characters from Mexico, the novel appears to anticipate and forestall a critical dismissal of Evie's character: she interacts with characters whose greater wealth and privilege make them even less appealing. In other words, the novel evades critique of its Mexican American character by displacing any negative connotations of wealth onto the Mexicans. In the end, this articulation through national difference is used to present Evie as a marketable and viable literary character. It also foregrounds a transnational economy in which class structures from the United

States and Mexico intersect and provoke crises of status and inclusion. While such concerns are evident in Serros's previous works in relation to her status as a Chicana-in-question with "sloppy Spanish," here they broaden to include a critique of transnational hierarchical social structures, with the upper classes dysfunctional on both sides of the border. The novel also points to how the conditional nature of ethnic inclusion is a transnational dynamic, with native-born populations, recent immigrants, and wealthy transnational subjects all expanding and helping police the boundaries of ethnicity.

Most Chicana/o cultural production is examined through an oppositional frame of analysis, but analyzing untraditional and commercial protagonists such as those created by Serros and Lopez involves considering the compromises cultural producers make in order to appeal to a mainstream audience. Ralph Rodriguez has noted that Chicana/o studies have tended to focus on locating "resistance" within texts and calls for a consideration of other formal and thematic elements, ones that might be missed if the focus is on the familiar.[48] Attuning to these other elements enables us to see how depicting Evie and George as status seekers and George as a mediator allow the novel and sitcom to illustrate power dynamics and ethical issues while depicting characters who, like most people, do not entirely contest the structures that they depend on for their livelihood and well-being. I am not claiming that these texts are beyond oppositional politics; rather, I am, like Raphael Dalleo and Elena Machado Sáez, arguing that we have to take into account artists and characters that reveal "the market's centrality in the creation, dissemination, and reception of virtually all contemporary cultural texts."[49]

Are these characters then not actually Chicana/o? We can recall Richard Rodriguez's conversation with the student who wanted a "Chicano novel" about a "Mexican kid who grows up in the suburbs." Since "Chicano" is often used interchangeably with "Mexican American," he might not have been referencing the politicized history behind Chicano representations in saying "Chicano novel" instead of "Mexican American novel." But the history of Chicana/o cultural production and scholarship asserts that there is a difference. And since Serros is so adamant about distancing herself from Chicano conventions, it would not be a stretch to see her as exemplary of a post-Chicano aesthetic. Doing so would reinforce her generational distance from earlier Chicano writers. We could also include George Lopez in this camp, since his ventures in television and film also move away from traditional Chicano representations. In his next foray into television sitcoms, he moved up in class even more by playing a wealthy entrepreneur on the quickly canceled show *Saint George* (FX, 2014). But affixing "post" to these cultural producers might occlude the fact that like Chicano texts, they are highlighting power disparities, delivering ethical critiques, and exploring issues of identity in a society stratified by race and class. So it is a "post" that is very much in dialogue with Chicana/o politics and aesthetics. Viewing them solely as "Latino" texts would also elide the history of Chicana/o class politics that shapes their narrative choices. Texts like theirs could be seen as an end, or as a beginning: an end to traditional Chicana/o representations, or an expansion of them into new territory to reflect contemporary social and market dynamics—what Dalleo and Machado Sáez call "post-sixties" Latinidad. A valid critique is that these ethical engagements are muted, and ultimately, because they cater to a mass audience, they uphold American mainstream values. As Rafael Pérez-Torres remarks, "Chicana culture is often most valued when it manifests the quality of most resistance." He cautions, "one cannot presume, however, that the entire history of Chicanas has been one of opposition and resistance. This presumption simply re-creates the subject-position of the Chicana as a perpetual saintly-victim, long-suffering but ultimately short on agency."[50] While Mexican American cultural production has traditionally exhibited an anxiety about representing upward mobility, these works foreground intra-ethnic class tensions to portray heterogeneous Mexican American identities who represent a spectrum of political engagements. Not accepting upward mobility as cultural betrayal, as an attempt to keep up with the Joneses, these texts prompt us to consider class and ethnic formations in the United States through the Rodriguezes, the Lopezes, and the Gomezes.

## *BLACK-ISH* RE-CODES RACE

Like the previously discussed texts, *black-ish*, the ABC sitcom that premiered during the 2014–2015 season, also asks us to consider class and ethnic formations, through the Johnsons, a family challenging assumptions about experiences and expressions of Blackness. The Emmy-award-winning show features Andre "Dre" Johnson (Anthony Anderson), an advertising executive, and his

wife, Rainbow "Bow" Johnson (Tracee Ellis Ross), an anesthesiologist, along
with their four kids and Dre's parents. Set in an upper-middle-class Los Angeles
suburb, the show explores what race means when individuals can be generationally removed from class and civil rights struggles. Observing that his kids often
reveal a lack of knowledge about Black history and culture, Dre worries that
his family is losing authenticity because they are well-to-do, and that they are
not fully Black anymore, but only "black-ish." When it first aired, the show's
title was criticized for being explicitly about race.[51] In response, showrunner
Kenya Barris has explained the title as an inclusive "dynamic adjective."[52] Note
how the show presents itself as a working definition, a qualification to the term
*Black*, every time it airs its title after an opening sequence:

'**black** • *ish*

/*blak* • *ish*/, [adj]

Along with the terms *post-Black* and *post-soul*, *black-ish* can be understood as
part of an ongoing attempt to provide a lexicon for identifying cultural production self-consciously departing from the essentializing discourse associated
with the legacy of Black cultural nationalism. Therefore, generational and class
differences within the Black population are dominant features of the "post"
aesthetics and of *black-ish*.

From the beginning of the series, the show has straddled between present-
ing this elite Black family as representative of and as atypical of "what Black is
today."[53] In the opening voiceover to the pilot episode, Dre frames his upward
mobility story in triumphant but measured terms: "I guess for a kid from the
hood, I'm living the American Dream. Only problem is, whatever 'American'
it was who had the 'Dream,' probably wasn't where I'm from."[54] As he picks up
his mail outside of his beautiful home, a tour bus stops in front of the house
to witness, as the tour guide says, "the mythical and majestic Black family out
of their natural habit and yet still thriving" (Figure 2). This comedic sketch
playfully mocks several historic power dynamics in the entertainment industry: the phenomenon of racialized people being exotic to white audiences, the
expectation that a racialized family will be representative of the race ("the . . .
Black family"), and yet an understanding that depictions and experiences like
those of the Johnsons are still few and far between, and the show is staking its
appeal on that atypicality.

THE MYTHICAL AND MAJESTIC BLACK FAMILY
WHITE NEIGHBORHOOD
(CIRCA 2014)

1640

FIGURE 2. The Johnsons viewed from the tour bus. Source: "Pilot," *black-ish*, aired September 24, 2014.

The question of how representative this family is becomes a source of humor throughout the series, and in the first episode, there is a subtle jab at Dre's attempts to see himself as a representative for the race. Like the pilot of *George Lopez*, *black-ish* begins with a promotion, or rather the promise of one. Dre is confident he will be promoted to the position of senior vice president at his advertising firm, which would make him the first African American to hold that position. As he enters the firm, he is greeted by other Blacks, including a security guard, a receptionist, two maintenance men, and what could either be another agent or an intern. His voiceover states that because there are so few of them there, when "one of us made it, it was kinda like we all did." He mentions that if others saw him as the Jackie Robinson of advertising at the firm, "they wouldn't be wrong." Meanwhile, the Jean Knight song "Mr. Big Stuff" can be heard in the background, its opening lyrics as follows:

Mr. Big Stuff

Who do you think you are
Mr. Big Stuff
You're never gonna get my love

Now because you wear all those fancy clothes
And have a big fine car, oh yes you do now[55]

Even as Dre muses that all the Black people at the firm are part of a "family" and sees himself as being a symbol for all of them, the audio undermines the visuals and his fantasy, hinting that he is naïve in thinking that he has the other Black people's "love" just because he is Black.

If this scene builds up and checks Dre's rise as symbolically significant, the next scene reveals the extent to which Dre sees his ascent as more personally advantageous and exhibits the show's exemplary moment of status panic. Dre is a status seeker in the televised tradition of George Jefferson, and throughout the series, many episodes highlight his desires to achieve and signal elevated status, particularly through titles and conspicuous consumption.[56] He declares that at his firm, a distinction exists between lower and upper management, as a clip shows the two groups seated across from each other at a conference table. Predominantly comprising people of color, lower management snacks on Cheetos and grape soda while the all-white upper management enjoys a medieval feast. Dre's motives for ascending, he makes clear, are to be able to partake in the feast too. What a letdown for Dre when his promotion turns out to be for senior vice president, but for the "Urban Division." This new division has been formed to secure an account with the L.A. tourism board, but Dre understands how *urban* can be used as a racialized code word (for example, ABC suggested "Urban Family" as a title for the series),[57] hence his troubled look and status panic when he reacts to his boss's announcement of his promotion and thinks to himself, "Wait. Did they just put me in charge of Black stuff?" In this chapter, I have been tracing how mass market representations of a nonwhite middle class articulate status panic: affective moments that stand in for how the text as a whole is straining to communicate the challenges of disrupting assumptions about race, ethnicity, and class. This episode dramatizes how racial identity operates as currency for Dre (and is analogous to cultural creatives who produce content that is racially themed) but also marks the tax on that deployed currency if Dre's ascent will be circumscribed by assumptions about race and class.

The texts discussed in this chapter demonstrate how status panic can be induced by institutional gatekeepers, but they also show status panic occurring as a result of how one is perceived by the ethnic group. Dre embodies and reacts to this type of gatekeeping; his expressions of lament are played up for comedic effect every time his family seemingly departs from what is considered authentically Black. In the pilot, Dre's exasperation is evident when his son wants to go by "Andy" instead of Andre or Dre, opts for field hockey instead of basketball, and wants to convert to Judaism in order to have a Bar Mitzvah. The last prompts Dre to don traditional African dress and to make his son wear some too, as part of "operation keepin' it real," in which he attempts to convince his son to have an "African rites of passage ceremony" for his birthday instead. We can link this scene with the moments in *Hunger of Memory* and *George Lopez* whereby cultural nationalism gets framed as theatrical; here *black-ish* parodies Black cultural nationalism's endeavors to affirm and root Black identity in African origins. If in *George Lopez* George's status panic gets relieved when he confronts his employers and when he proves himself to be a capable mediator, in *black-ish*, Dre takes the strategy of re-coding the terms that induce status panic. Since he cannot convince his son to reproduce his version of Black identity, he compromises by offering his son a culturally hybrid birthday party: a "Bro Mitzvah." Following the logic of the show, the party will be "black-ish." Further, Dre asserts that his take on "urban" for the marketing campaign will be to translate it as "hip, cool, and colorful just like my family." Dre—and the show—may not be able to do away with standards of assessment informed by race and class, but it will offer an expanded vocabulary and accompanying dramatizations to shake up the cultural imaginary.

The thematic significance of status panic gets reinforced in another episode from season one, "The Gift of Hunger," but through Bow.[58] Here, Bow's relationship to whites gets paralleled to Dre's attempts to prove status, even though they are often juxtaposed as having distinct views on race. Her views about race are not as fixed as Dre's are, a difference attributed to her mixed-race background and bohemian upbringing. However, this episode reveals that despite her self-perceptions, she still cares about the perceptions of others, especially when it comes to class. The episode also explores how ethnicity is most recognizable as working-class culture. Its premise stems from another example of Dre's frustration at how far removed his family is from his experiences; his kids do not appreciate the steak restaurant he grew up going to on special occasions because their experiences with food and comfort have been so different. To get his kids to understand struggle, he makes them all get jobs. The youngest, a pair of twins, end up begging for food from the neighbors, prompting Bow's own status panic when the neighbors start thinking the family is experiencing financial difficulties and offer them charity. Troubled by the "pity casserole" they have just received from the neighbors, she rebukes Dre, "I have worked too hard, and I went to school for too long and I took way too much affirmative action money . . . the point is I will not let my image be destroyed." As Dre attempts to teach the kids the value of hard work, a subplot focuses on Bow's attempts to demonstrate her wealth around the neighborhood in fine dresses, jewelry, and a sports car. The Johnsons want their kids to appreciate working-class hardships, but they do not want to be read as working class. In this situation comedy, Bow's antics are played for laughs, but she is depicting a situation that many professionals of color find themselves in, as their status is called into question because of dominant perceptions of race.

Even as *black-ish* depicts class and cultural heterogeneity disrupting assumptions that there is a singular Black community, the show has developed to engage with issues affecting the group as a whole. In particular, the show's take on police violence has altered course since the first season. In that season the show's message about racial profiling seemed to convey that racism was a thing of the past. On the episode about Martin Luther King Jr. Day,[59] a holiday the family celebrates with its annual ski trip, Dre tries to convince Andre Jr. that racism still exists after he finds that his son does not know about the March on Washington or the Montgomery Bus Boycott. The episode, however, makes it seem as if racism just exists in Dre's head, after repeated attempts to point out signs of racism turn out to be absurd, including a friendly interaction with a police officer who has stopped them on the road not because he has racially profiled them as Dre gloatingly thinks and points out to his son, but because of an expired registration.[60]

Fifteen years prior, another Black upward mobility sitcom, *The Fresh Prince of Bel-Air*, devoted an entire episode to racial profiling. The popular NBC series (1990–1996) featured Will Smith's character (also called Will Smith), a working-class youth from West Philadelphia, and his acculturation into his wealthy Bel-Air uncle's family. The show made clear that the family learned from Will as well, and often highlighted the contrast between Will and his cousin Carlton in terms of their life experiences. On "Mistaken Identity," the two are on their way to Palm Springs when they are pulled over, arrested, and jailed for being suspected of stealing the Mercedes they are driving, a car lent to them by Carlton's father's legal partner.[61] The show plays up Carlton's naïveté in not realizing the gravity of the situation, and ends with him sorely wanting to be assured that the "system works" and that they were not pulled over because of race. Carlton's father, a lawyer who in the course of the series becomes a judge, gives him no such assurance. If *The Fresh Prince* communicated that class does not insulate one from racism, in its first season *black-ish* conveyed that it does. During *black-ish*'s first season, the Black Lives Matter movement was increasing in visibility throughout the country, making the series' take on police treatment of Blacks strikingly out of synch with the sociopolitical climate. As an example of how racial profiling can occur despite one's class, Chris Rock was taking selfies every time he was pulled over by the police and posting them on social media.[62] Creator Kenya Barris reportedly had pitched the idea of doing an episode based on Henry Louis Gates's 2009 arrest, which occurred when police were called because he was perceived to be a burglar even though he was trying to get into his own home, but ABC did not want Barris to do any jokes about the police.[63]

Season two's "Hope"[64] seemed like a do-over for the show and one that was widely praised on social media[65] for tackling systemic anti-Black violence and by critics for "its embrace of the Norman Lear tradition of political theater."[66] As a critic for the *New York Times* stated, "'Hope' managed to work in a stunning amount of American racial history (and current events) into a single episode without coming off like a sitcom Wikipedia page."[67] Barris, who has talked about his own experiences with police violence, wrote this episode.[68] It still portrayed the family as insulated from police violence; the younger generations have learned about the many cases of unarmed Black people being killed by police via the news or, as Andre Jr. has, from Ta-Nehisi Coates's *Between the World and Me*. The episode is set entirely in the family's living room as they watch news coverage of the potential indictment of an officer who repeatedly tasered an unarmed Black man. The stationary element of the episode underscores the question of how the family might move forward: How does this family make sense of the systemic violence? And what will they do about it? In response to the first question, the show depicts how much experiential and ideological variance can exist within a family. For example, Bow is certain that that the judicial system will side with the victim and wants to shield the youngest kids from these stories in order to maintain their innocence, while Dre and his parents vehemently disagree. The decision falls in favor of the police officer, at which point an incredulous Bow does not know how to make sense of it. Zoey, the teenaged daughter, echoes her reaction. She has come across as apathetic, but reveals she does care but does not know what to do about it. To the extent that the show can offer a resolution to an ongoing problem, it resolves the paralysis the family feels when Bow suggests that the entire family join the protests that are occurring. The show depicts individual moments of status panic, but these are tied to perceptions and treatment of the group as a whole.

One of the striking aspects to *black-ish* is that in offering its take on race and class, it references so much Black history and culture. It can add the qualifier "ish" because representations of "Black" are so widespread and mainstream; as Barris explains, Dre also sees American culture becoming "black-ish."[69] Any episode might contain references to well known Black icons (such as Malcom X, Martin Luther King, Oprah), Black musical genres (for example, jazz, soul, R&B, hip hop) and musical stars (Marvin Gaye, Michael Jackson, Beyoncé, Drake), Black writers (James Baldwin, Toni Morrison), Black TV (*Good Times*, *The Cosby Show*) and films (such as by Spike Lee, Lee Daniels), and Black cultural practices (for example, "the nod" and going to the barbershop). As a result of the way in which so much of Black cultural production is part of popular culture, the show can reference and riff on it as part of its comedic appeal, even if its audience is "three-quarters nonblack."[70] The high visibility of Black cultural production facilitates the deployment of parody and satire in representational endeavors to disengage race from class. In the next chapter, I examine texts that like *black-ish* use satire and parody to counter class-inflected perceptions of "Black," while depicting how much individuals and industries are invested in reinforcing race as class.

# CHAPTER 5

# RACIAL INVESTMENTS

> The anomaly of my social position often appealed strongly to my
> sense of humor. . . . Many a night when I returned to my room after
> an enjoyable evening, I laughed heartily over what struck me as the
> capital joke I was playing.
>
> James Weldon Johnson, *The Autobiography of an Ex-Colored Man*[1]

## SATIRIZING RACE AS CLASS

In November 2005, *The Onion* published a piece from the point of view of
a cutting-edge trendsetter who bemoans the fact that others keep failing to
see how "ironic and hilarious" his fashion sense is.[2] The first in his neighborhood to wear iron-on T-shirts in the 1980s and electroclash paraphernalia in
the 1990s, the white narrator is practically giddy over his ability to don hip
wear and abandon it once everyone else catches on. So proud of his tongue-
in-cheekiness, he decides at twenty-five to make the ultimate nonconformist fashion act by wearing a suit. He tells us, "A lesser man might have just
snagged a cheap suit at Goodwill, but I went all out, choosing a conservative,
gray three-button suit and having it fitted by the best tailor in town. I even had
my hair cut in a short, non-descript style parted to the side. I mean, who the
hell does that? I looked like a fucking senator!" Fully accessorized and ready to
make his fashion mark, he hits his usual city spots only to be met with stares
and resistance. Irked at not getting the laughs he deserves, that others are not
getting the joke because they think that he is dressing like this *for real*, the
narrator decides to perfect his look until it is as "hilarious as it could possibly
be," since looking like every other trendsetter would be selling out. He there-

fore buys a briefcase, fills it with actual legal briefs, moves out of his loft and into an Upper East Side co-op, joins a corporate law firm, becomes a partner with a corner office, and as his ultimate act, marries a girl from Connecticut and has two "ironic" children.

Deriving its humor from the extremity of the act and the fact that this scenario happens all the time—that people convince themselves that they are not selling out—the comedic factor is also bolstered by the fact that no one else understands his parody. In many respects, *The Onion* article's concern with an ironic approach to asserting principled beliefs through a classed performance parallels the actions of the main character in *Erasure*—Percival Everett's satiric novel about authorial identity and artistic production.[3] Like the suit-wearing hipster, *Erasure*'s upper-middle-class protagonist, Thelonious "Monk" Ellison, decides to assert his nonconformity by parodying the very thing that he most contests. In his case, it is the pressure on Black writers to produce sensationalized stories about the ghetto and Black poverty. Due to industry preferences, Monk cannot get published: his novels, which include obscure rewritings of Greek tragedies and poststructuralist reveries, supposedly lack African American authenticity. Out of frustration and protest, Monk produces a parody of Wright's *Native Son*, which he titles *My Pafology* and later renames *Fuck*, a fictitious memoir featuring a wayward urban youth with "fo' baby mamas" and a propensity for crime and violence. Yet the parodic novel is quickly picked up by a publisher, becomes a commercial and critical success, gets a movie deal, and wins a national book award. Clearly, no one is getting the joke here either.

In both narratives, the joke relies on an understanding of social assumptions about race and class. Moreover, both the fashionista and Monk profit from their ironic performances, succeeding materially if not artistically. They demonstrate that the conflation of race and class, in which whiteness is associated with wealth and Blackness with poverty, is so strong a frame of reference that their protagonists fail to disrupt it with their individual acts. This chapter focuses on two texts, *Erasure* and Lynn Nottage's play *Fabulation, or the Re-Education of Undine*,[4] that use satire and the figural types to depict Black characters trying to oppose classed connotations of race, yet in the process play out the deep investments that individuals and industries have in Black pathology narratives.

*Erasure* and *Fabulation* share similarities with the narratives analyzed in Chapter 4, which staged status panic to highlight fears that one's racialized otherness will still be called into question during social, economic, or artistic appraisal. Like *George Lopez, Honey Blonde Chica*, and *black-ish, Erasure* and *Fabulation* are invested in calling for wider representational schemas when it comes to race and class, and employ humor to do so. But *black-ish, Erasure*, and *Fabulation* differ from the Mexican American middle-class narratives I discussed earlier. Black cultural production has a longer institutional history, and images about and by Black people have circulated more widely. As a result, the use of irony, parody, and satire in these works to reference intragroup cultural tropes is more explicit, responding as they are to the high visibility of certain kinds of Black representations.

The multiplicity of texts in the post-civil-rights period that choose irony over sincerity in their portrayal of Black subjects illustrates the results of what Herman Gray calls the era of "hyperblackness," in which the increase of Black representations in the media has shifted concerns from Black invisibility to contestations over what is now visible.[5] Contemporary cultural producers who challenge dominant perceptions of Blackness have been categorized under various labels, including terms such as *post-Black* or *post-soul*.[6] Bertram D. Ashe observes that these labels apply to Black artists born after the civil rights movement who incorporate mixed-cultural influences in their art and who "trouble" Blackness to "hold it up for examination in ways that depart significantly from previous—and necessary—preoccupations with struggling for political freedom, or with an attempt to establish and sustain a coherent black identity."[7] Part of troubling Blackness has entailed emphasizing heterogeneity within the Black population, and Everett's novel asserts that these correlate to diverse thematic and aesthetic concerns as well. *Erasure* highlights how representations of class and race are glossed over and regulated by commercial expectations when Blackness is coded as underprivileged and art about Black identity is expected to be a documentation of urban life.

Everett's novel joins other novels such as Paul Beatty's *White Boy Shuffle* and Colson Whitehead's *Sag Harbor* in thematizing how until the turn of the century middle-class Black existence seemed anomalous in the U.S. cultural imaginary. When Paul Beatty's protagonist leaves suburban Santa Monica and attempts to integrate into a working-class neighborhood, he finds that his middle-class experiences are at odds with those of his new neighbors: "in a world where body and spoken language were currency, I was broke as hell. Corporeally mute, I couldn't saunter or bojangle my limbs with rubber nonchalance. I stiffly parade-marched around town with an embalmed soul, a rheumatic heart, and Frankenstein's automonomic nervous system."[8] His social life is at a standstill until he finds a way to get over the awkwardness he feels at not having the symbolic wages of ethnicity earned through intragroup markers like language and behavior, while Colson Whitehead's protagonist in *Sag Harbor* declares that he and his friends are living contradictions because they are "black boys with beach houses."[9] Assessing the perceived incongruity of the terms *Black* and *middle class*, Vershawn Ashanti Young argues that

Desegregation may have eliminated separate but equal laws, but it has not eradicated the fantasy wherein race marks class. Thus many contemporary middle-class African Americans experience a psychological dilemma: their class status is linked to a white racial identity, and their racial identity is linked to a lower-class status.[10]

In refuting the racialized class fantasy, Everett's, Whitehead's, and Beatty's novels make a case for the multidimensionality of Black identity, which include markers of class mobility. These texts contest sociological and literary antecedents such as E. Franklin Frazier's *Black Bourgeoisie*, Dorothy West's *The Living Is Easy*, and Gloria Naylor's *Linden Hills*, which decry the Black bourgeoisie for emulating whites and individualist values at the expense of a collective Black identity and Black social progress.[11] They also suggest that racial identity does not necessarily trump class identity, even as it may inform it. *Erasure* presses this issue by exemplifying the experiential and commercial value placed on Black poverty and dramatizing the effects of profiting from the entwinement.

## *ERASURE*'S CAPITAL JOKE

In contrast to traditional African American passing narratives, Monk does not pass in order to leave his race; rather, he passes in order to "return" to his race under a racialized class fantasy. In order to sell his fake memoir, Monk passes in the spirit of what Gayle Wald has called "post-civil rights passing narratives." In these types of narratives, "identity is *assumed* to be performative rather than natural," and these performances occur in an era when race matters but with a difference in a post-civil-rights era.[12] Now that legal segregation is no longer an impetus for passing, the novel showcases the pressures to pass in terms of class. At the beginning of the novel, Monk shares that he is just not Black enough:

Some people in the society in which I live, described as being black, tell me I am not *black* enough. Some people whom the society calls white tell me the same thing. I have heard this mainly about my novels, from editors who have rejected me and reviewers whom I have apparently confused and, on a couple of occasions, on a basketball court when upon missing a shot I muttered *Egads*.(2)

Monk is not recognized as Black, so he writes in order to expand the signification of Blackness even as he points out the restrictions of racial categorization. The novel is aware that passing is not so much about moving from a real self to a fake self as it is a means to an end: passing can be "the point of entry into a discussion of race as performative reiteration."[13] For Monk, passing is not about leaving Blackness to enter whiteness, but about how returning to Blackness as it is conceptualized in the media entails a disavowal of middle-class experiences.

Monk's literary and behavioral passing does not happen willingly nor suddenly; rather, it is a gradual process that lays bare his ambivalence about the commercialization of racial performance. While initially he does not want to perform the identity of Stagg R. Leigh,[14] the author of his fake memoir, *My Pafology*, he begins to do so when the profits to be garnered from the performance outweigh the cost to his artistic integrity. He at first declares that he is "not going to put on an act" (156) for the editor at Random House and speaks as himself. But after she still believes him to be Stagg, he later agrees to a meeting with a movie producer. He muses beforehand, "I would have to wear the mask of the person I was expected to be. I had already talked on the phone with my editor as the infamous Stagg Leigh and now I would meet with Wiley Morgenstein, I could do it. The game was becoming fun. And it was nice to get a check" (213). And yet, while Monk at times takes pleasure in the joke he is playing, he vacillates between enjoyment and despair, at moments wanting to cry (246) and nearing delirium when he hears that his fake novel has been shortlisted for a national award (259). Evidence that he has embraced the role of Stagg in full attire comes when he is asked to appear on the Kenya Dunston show. He leaves his hotel room in "black shoes, black trousers, black turtle-neck sweater, black blazer, black beard, black fedora" (245). The narration tells us, "Stagg Leigh is black from toe to top of head, from shoulder to shoulder, from now until the ends of time. He bops down the carpeted hallway to the elevator, down again, farther down, down" (245). Evoking Ralph Ellison's narrator in *Invisible Man* playing Rinehart, Monk's sartorial change here marks his dramatic behavioral and literary passing as Stagg Leigh. This description, indicating both revelry and the beginnings of a psychic crisis, also gestures to the dissolution of Monk's identity and artistic integrity. It turns out that passing is not something Monk can control. Since passing narratives characteristically represent "the psychological strains of passing" to capture how characters become increasingly more stressed as a result of juggling dueling identities, Monk appears as a parody of a passing protagonist.[15]

This exploration of Blackness occurs against a background narrative about Monk's familial problems, which besides fleshing out his character also provides a rationale for why he allows himself later to sell out and profit from the novel he writes but loathes. During a trip to his hometown of Washington, DC, to deliver an ironic Barthian reading of Barthes's own *S/Z* at a literary conference, Monk is forced to recognize the disintegration of his family and starts shouldering the burden of taking care of its remaining members. His father committed suicide seven years earlier, and only when Monk goes through his papers does he discover his father's long-kept secret—a passionate love affair that resulted in a half-white daughter. Deciding what to do with this knowledge is compounded by the worry over how to care for his mother and their longtime housekeeper now that his mother's Alzheimer's has worsened. In addition, his sister who was a doctor at a women's clinic has just been shot and killed by an anti-abortionist. At the same time, his brother, Bill, has revealed he is gay to his wife and children and is in the midst of a divorce, which leaves Monk the only sibling alive and without a litigation battle to take care of his mother's needs and address his father's past. The melodramatic nature of his familial story makes the fact that he cannot get a novel published even more ironic, since his own life is ripe with novelistic elements. However, Everett does not develop these sensational plot lines. We never know what happens to his half-sister after their meeting, or find out the back story of who killed his sister, or why his brother decided to come out when he did. Indeed, it appears Everett is more interested in highlighting readerly expectation for the sensational than actually fleshing out the characters and plots within *Erasure*.

Since the familial issues arise as the novel unfolds, making money is not Monk's main concern at the beginning of the novel. *Erasure* instead begins with Monk's interest in documenting and affirming his experiences. At the beginning of the novel, Monk announces that he is speaking from the pages of his journal. He begins his self-description while divulging his artistic and literary tastes:

I have dark brown skin, curly hair, a broad nose, some of my ancestors were slaves and I have been detained by pasty white policemen in New Hampshire, Arizona and Georgia and so the society to which I live tells me that I am black; that is my race. Though I am fairly athletic, I am no good at basketball. I listen to Mahler, Aretha Franklin, Charlie Parker and Ry Cooder on vinyl records and compact discs. I graduated summa cum laude from Harvard, hating every minute of it. I am good at math. I cannot dance. I did not grow up in any inner city or rural south. . . . My grandfather was a doctor. My father was a doctor. My brother and sister were doctors. (1)

Behind this list of physical, experiential, and artistic attributes is an implied template of Blackness that Monk has disavowed as applicable to his identity. While he acknowledges the phenotypical and historical reasons why society designates him as Black, he does not relate to the supposed tastes, talents, and class background wrapped up in the idea of Black identity. He challenges how athleticism and geographical origins are used as popular stereotypes of Blackness and positions himself in opposition to these characteristics while preferring some forms of Black music and artistry (Aretha Franklin as the "Queen of Soul" and Charlie "Bird" Parker as a symbol of jazz), which suggests his strategy is one of selective identification. Everett's naming of his protagonist Thelonious "Monk" Ellison, and his character's embrace of a Black musical tradition signify a desire to remain rooted in Black artistic history, while at the same time pushing for a broader scope of Blackness affirmed within the literary world. The fact that Monk writes in the first person signals that he is invested in his experiential authority because he wants his experiences acknowledged and validated.

Monk seems to want it both ways; he is a conflicted artist who wants to affirm middle-class Black identity by contesting the way race gets intertwined with class, yet at the same time chafes against being categorized as a Black writer. Walking through a bookstore, Monk rants over the categorization of literature according to race:

I went to Literature and did not see me. I went to contemporary Fiction and did not find me, but when I fell back a couple of steps I found a section called African American Studies and there, arranged alphabetically and neatly, read *undisturbed*, were four of my books including my *Persians* of which the only thing ostensibly African American was my jacket photograph. (28)

As a writer who does not explicitly write about "Black themes" but who nonetheless is shelved in the Black section, Monk is cast into dusty oblivion, limiting his authorial reach and exposure. The novel's critique is not only that writers get classified as "Black writers" but that Black writing means writing about particular experiences, which has implications for how the mainstream then perceives Black culture. In his denunciation of such racial categorization, Monk's aesthetic politics read as individualist in scope. He is, after all, most concerned with how this marginalization limits his royalties and authorial recognition. He does not worry about how other Black people are treated, only how they are perceived due to the kinds of representations that are popularized and rewarded, and therefore his racial politics are problematically limited to self-interest. Indeed, Monk confesses that he does not think about race, and feels guilty for not thinking about it, but he knows that there are "people who will shoot me or hang me or cheat me and try to stop me because they do believe in race, because of my brown skin, curly hair, wide nose and slave ancestors. But that's just the way it is" (2). What Monk's comment does not take into account is that racism is structural, and not just inflicted through personal prejudice. He manages to simultaneously cast off any interest in race while at the same time assuming the stance of a potential victim of racism, a maneuver that shows how he makes a distinction between race and racialization. Monk acknowledges that one can understand race as a social construction, but one cannot control the extent to which others will act on their racist beliefs, for race has material and social effects. Ramón Saldívar argues that in critiquing race but in keeping it as a term *sous rature*, Everett joins other "post-race" writers in moving away from traditional modes of representing race while acknowledging that the effects of race are still realities with which to contend.[16] However much one may want to be "beyond race," Monk's description reiterates that one can still be racialized.

Dramatizing how middle-class Black identity seems anomalous in the cultural market, *Erasure* not only shows how certain facets of Black identity trump others, it also lays bare how certain genres may dominate other genres. *Erasure*, framed as the recording of Monk's most intimate thoughts, contains a pastiche of narratives: the story of Monk Ellison passing as Stagg R. Leigh; the picaresque novella of *My Pafology* itself; an entire academic essay on Barthes' *S/Z*; and ideas for stories, short sketches, and brief humorous dialogues between famous cultural producers such as Wilde, Joyce, Wittgenstein, Derrida, Pollock, and Moore, among other asides. Often these literary tangents appear as non sequiturs and contrast sharply with the biting racial satire of *My Pafology*. These experiments in form and style consequently offer a critique broadly directed at racial typing and specifically at the publishing world that Monk argues maintains a sense of what real African American writing is and invalidates everything else. It is, as Brian Yost comments, a critique against "the commercial exploitation of the vernacular form, not vernacular and oral tradition itself."[17] The novel therefore provides a literary example of John K. Young's argument in *Black Writers, White Publishers*, in which he contends that "the basic dynamic through which most twentieth-century African American literature has been produced derives from an expectation that the individual text will represent the black experience (necessarily understood as exotic) for the white, and therefore implicitly universal, audience."[18] If to conform to the expectations of Black literature means writing in the style of social realism, *Erasure* issues a challenge by experimenting with a variety of genres.

In the novel, the profitability of social realism and the exoticization of Black experience as urban poverty and pathology is symbolically concretized in the novel *We's Lives in da Ghetto* by fictional author Juanita Mae Jenkins. After receiving his seventeenth rejection letter for his latest novel, Monk finds out that *We's Lives in Da Ghetto* has just been optioned into a movie for $3 million. At one point he reads from the first page of Jenkins's novel, noting its conspicuous phonetic renderings of Ebonics:

My fahvre be gone since time I's borned and it be just me an' my momma an' my baby brover Juneboy. In da mornin' Juneboy never do brush his teefus, so I gots to remind him. Because dat, Momma says I be the 'sponsible one and tell me tat I gots to holds things togever while she be at work clean dem white people's house. (28–29)

Remarking that he felt like throwing up upon hearing about the movie deal, Monks analogizes that it is the same as "strolling through an antique mall, feeling good, liking the sunny day and then turning the corner to find a display of watermelon-eating, banjo playing darkie carvings and a pyramid of Mammy cookie jars" (29). The description acknowledges the appeal of commodified nostalgia, in the comfort of a past that can be trafficked and even bought, yet pivots on the reality that one cannot control what will get commodified if one person's treasure is another person's terror. The past that infringes on the present is equated with novels like *We's Lives in the Ghetto* as a past form that is still haunting the present.

The type of literature that Monk finds so terrifying has been referred to under many names, including "urban literature," "street literature," and "Black Experience novels." These novels, known for their gritty and raw portrayals of the ghetto, have also been categorized as "ghetto realism," a tradition pioneered by writers like Iceberg Slim and Donald Goines in the late 1960s and 1970s. Eddie Stone quotes Greg Goode, who penned an early analysis of ghetto realism, in his biography of Goines, summing up how the dominant theme of Goines's work revolved around the ways that

the ghetto life of the underprivileged black produces a frustrating, dangerous double-bind effect. One has only two choices, neither wholly desirable. One may settle for membership in the ghetto's depressed, poverty-stricken silent majority, or opt for dangerous ghetto stardom.[19]

Everett essentially enacts ghetto realism as hyperbolically as possible in the creation of *My Pafology*. In *My Pafology*, the young narrator's poverty and lack of self-worth lead him into a desperate attempt at "ghetto stardom" through rape, robbery, and murder. The main character is seventeen-year-old Van Go Jenkins, and the novella begins with him having just awakened from a dream in which he repeatedly stabs his mother for calling him "human slough" (65). After waking, Van Go decides to visit one of his four children, Rexall, the one with "Down Sinder" (66), though his main interest is in luring Rexall's mother away from school so that he can rape her. Lest the reader think Van Go stops there, he also gets a job working as an errand boy for the Daltons, a wealthy Black family with a daughter whom Van Go also rapes. The last section then devolves into complete spectacle when Van Go receives a phone call asking him to appear on a talk show; it turns out to be a ruse to get him on set so he can be confronted for his lack of child support. There he is almost apprehended by cops coming to arrest him for raping the Dalton daughter. However, he manages to escape and steal a gun, which he uses to kill a wino who keeps claiming to be his father and also a Korean storeowner. For his last feat, he holds several people hostage in a post office before he is caught by the police. A TV reporter captures him on film as he declares the last lines of the novella: "Hey, Baby Girl. Look at me. I on TV" (131). Ghetto stardom indeed.

The creation of *My Pafology* is rendered in conflicted terms, despite the fact that it is supposed to be a parody. Notwithstanding all of Monk's meditative protest against his unjust treatment by the literary world, his very act of contestation is portrayed as something that he did not do willingly. The literary cold shoulder that he continues to receive, coupled with a culminating incredulousness that the most popular Black writer of the moment is Juanita Mae Jenkins, induces Monk into a state of writer's paroxysms that end in the production of the very thing he despises:

I sat and stared at Juanita Mae Jenkins' face on *Time* magazine. The pain started in my feet and coursed through my legs, up my spine and into my brain and I remembered passages of *Native Son* and *The Color Purple* and *Amos and Andy* and my hands began to shake, the world opening around me, tree roots trembling on the ground outside, people in the street shouting *dint, ax, fo, screet* and *fahvre*! And I was screaming inside, complaining that I didn't sound like that, that my mother didn't sound like that, that my brother didn't sound like that and I imagined myself sitting on a park bench counting the knives in my switchblade collection and a man came up to me and he asked me what I was doing and my mouth opened and I couldn't help what came out, "Why fo you be axin?" (61–62)

The psychology of this passage is striking in its depiction of a muted yearning for protest manifesting as an uncontrollable iteration of a fictional persona, foreshadowing the rest of the novel. Immediately after, Monk begins work on *My Pafology* under his assumed pen name, Stagg R. Leigh. The passage impresses the idea that Monk's actions are forced since he just "couldn't help what came out" and what comes out is an outburst in novel form, one that apparently he cannot rewrite or edit and does not need to since he mimicked the conventions so perfectly on the first try.

Monk hates his novel and is ashamed to be associated with it, though his creation of it is supposed to be parodic. That his subversive act is then expressed as something that is not voluntary is notable considering that after the antagonism he has expressed toward this type of writing, he is not self-satisfied enough to reveal to the world that something he wrote as a parody was in fact taken as truth. Danielle Fuentes Morgan argues that Monk does not intentionally write *My Pafology* as satire and only calls it that retroactively. Seeing Monk as part of an educated elite who actually believes Black stereotypes and who writes the novella as "cathartic invective, possessed by hideous, stereotypical blackness and nothing more," Morgan claims that Monk has to distance himself by calling it satire in order to "absolve himself from wrongdoing for his addition to the canon of black belittling literary exercises."[20] Morgan maintains that Monk's satire thus fails because he did not code it as a satire. The novella is hardly absent satirical cues, however; Monk makes them clear through the references to the archetypical trickster character Stagger Lee and to the Daltons in *My Pafology*, recalling Richard Wright's *Native Son*. I want to suggest instead that Monk's self-distancing from his novella disrupts readerly expectation for signs of resistance in texts. In calling his work a satire, Monk is expressing a protest against power relationships—one of the most distinguishable characteristics of African American literature. Yet by portraying Monk as someone who did not plan to write a protest novel, *Erasure* ironically stages a protest against the expectation that its protagonist will be a recognizable resistant figure.

Valerie Smith discusses the assumptions that African American literature depicts struggle and resistance in her introduction to Andrea Lee's novella *Sarah Phillips*, whose eponymous protagonist grows up in a suburban Black middle-class community.[21] Smith notes that Phillips "cannot be admired either for showing bravery in the face of adversity or for seeking deep truths in the rural South or in the African diaspora," which Smith says has elicited disapproval from readers because they "expected the text to center on a character engaged in a project of political or personal resistance." Like Lee's novella, Everett's novel may strike readers as being politically apathetic. However, just as protagonists can pass from one identity to another, texts may also pass from one mode to another. In this case the novel passes as apathetic, but if we consider the history of Black literary production, it embodies social protest in a very different form. While his is not a sincere proletariat novel or an example of social realism, Everett's novel thematizes the frustrations of aesthetic creation when social protest is narrowly conceived, and how contesting formal requirements can be a method of social protest in itself. My intention is not to recoup Monk for a tradition of resistance; rather, I want to highlight how there is a contestation against power dynamics, but it is delivered through the figure of a conflicted artist who chafes against the tradition of standing in for and representing for the collective, even as he draws from that tradition's collective signifiers and decides to profit from it.

One way in which the novel incites dialogue between power and aesthetics is through the inclusion of *My Pafology* in *Erasure* as a novel-within-a-novel. Monk regurgitates *My Pafology* but Everett embeds it, creating a tension between the inner and outer frame. While formal experimentation is occurring on two levels—by the writer within the novel and the author outside of it, the latter is figured as the one with ostensibly more control. However, both authors cannot actually guarantee how their playful experiments will be received. Within the novel, the only person who is in on the joke that *My Pafology* is facetious is Monk's literary agent. As Monk learns once the novel is published, every other reader of *My Pafology*, white or Black, reads it as a real memoir. The parody may not even be clear to readers of *Erasure*. Critic Michael Knight has written about how he gave *Erasure* to one of his Black students to read but that his student "thought the parody was great. Not a great parody, [but] a great book tucked inside a pretty good book."[22] Or if the novella is understood to be a parody, some readers may prefer it to the rest of the novel. Gillian Johns was struck, for example, by how her students in a course on Black literary humor found the parody "the best (or most pleasurable) aspect of *Erasure*."[23] As to why the novel may elicit these kinds of responses despite its lodged critique, Margaret Russett observes that "While presented as Monk's invention, Van Go ultimately occupies the same fictional space as his fictional creator. And for all its parodic intention, *My Pafology* is for many readers the most compelling section of *Erasure*—fast, mean, and very funny."[24] Clearly, the inner story is quite powerful in relation to its outer frame. *Erasure* has tried to contain and even undermine *My Pafology* and yet may have only elevated it. The reception of *My Pafology* to readers within and outside the novel speaks to the appeal of familiarity in spite of the experimentation that attempts to subvert it and how genres may dominate other genres.

The reason why *My Pafology*'s parodic nature may be unclear to some readers is due to the fact that novels and films like it actually exist and are acclaimed
for their naturalistic depictions of social inequality. Artists must deal with the
question of how to represent social difference but not sensationalize it. There
is also so much pressure and incentive to capitalize on familiar types, as Imani
Perry explains:

There is a good deal of money made, and individual economic opportunity garnered,
through the widespread consumption of the performance of race roles. The thug, the
mammy, the gardener, the tragic mulatto, the Suzie Wong, the nanny, the angel,
the noble savage, the angry Black—these are repeatedly bought and sold. Although
these generate revenue, they also operate to implicitly thwart the recognition of people
who don't occupy such roles. Moreover, the consumer package of the role or performance becomes overdetermined and collapses within it cultural attributes that become
further devalued by virtue of their association with stereotype.[25]

*Erasure* protests against the profitability of race roles that lead to a reinforcement
of stereotypes that have a negative effect on both art and people. When the
wider audience comes to take these representations as more true than others,
the cycle of production and reward continues, and leads to the suppression
of other forms of representation and the devaluing of certain identities. Even
someone like Monk cannot escape the pressures and monetary incentives to
write according to racial scripts.

There is interpretive confusion because the route Monk takes to express
his protest against literary reduction and racial categorization is an indirect
one. Rather than directly confront his frustrations with the publishing world,
his antagonism is channeled into layers of concealment. *Erasure* contains a
tripartite counterattack, pronged as it is through elements of satire (*Erasure*
the novel), parody (*My Pafology*), and irony (acts of misreading). All require
a double audience—one that gets the subtexts and one that does not. Monk's
mistake is that he assumes that the audience that will read his novel will be in
the camp that gets the double meaning. The real irony is that the ones who
end up exalting the novel are not ignorant racists but liberal whites and Blacks
who praise it for its rawness and realness.[26] The novel dramatizes deep naïveté,
demonstrating that the joke might end up being on the joker due to the fact
that playing with stereotypes has uncontrollable effects. Glenda Carpio calls

playing with stereotypes a "volatile artistic gambit" because they can take on lives of their own and carry "the possibility of confirming popular, if tacitly held, racist beliefs."[27] *Erasure*'s dilemma hits home the point that when there is capital, economic *and* cultural, at stake in joke telling, it is impossible to know one's exact gains or losses.

Linda Hutcheon has written about this problem in *Irony's Edge* and ultimately declares irony to be "risky business" because of its "transideological" nature and the fact that people belong to varied "discursive communities."[28] Comprehension, Hutcheon further argues, is dependent on one's membership in the discursive community equipped to decipher the ironic work's hidden meaning. *Erasure* exemplifies this phenomenon, since it ultimately suggests that one cannot depend on irony to get one's point across. Yet I would argue that rather than dismissing irony as a viable weapon against stereotypes, *Erasure* points out how much capital is invested in preserving them.

For example, even when Monk meets with the movie producer, Wiley Morgenstein, to discuss a movie deal of *My Pafology*, and acts in such a way as to neither reject nor confirm any assumption about himself through his speech and dress, he is nevertheless read according to the connotations of stereotypical Blackness. Dressed in khakis and striped shirt with a button-down collar, he sits down to lunch and orders a Gibson, after which

Morgenstein offered a puzzled look to his young friend. "You know, you're not at all like I pictured you."

"No? How did you picture me?

"I don't know, tougher or something. You know, more street. More . . ."

"Black?"

"Yeah, that's it. I'm glad you said it. I've seen the people you write about, the real people, the earthy, gutsy people. They can't teach you to write about that in no college." (217)

Then, when Morgenstein asks Stagg why he did jail time, Monk's strategy is to answer through hearsay: "They say I killed a man with the leather awl of a Swiss army knife," which relieves Morgenstein: "Here I was about to think you weren't the real thing" (218). The reader is cued into the absolute absurdity of Monk's half-hearted play-acting by his choice of weaponry; the leather awl of a Swiss army knife hardly has ghetto credibility. Yet this description speaks to how little effort Monk has to put into his performance. By showing the success of Monk's class passing but the failure of his irony, *Erasure* critiques the fetishization of the Black lower class for profit, which both whites and Blacks buy into. George Lipsitz has written about the "possessive investment in whiteness," explaining how

[B]oth public policy and private prejudice have created a "possessive investment in whiteness" that is responsible for the racialized hierarchies of our society. . . . Whiteness has cash value: it accounts for advantages that come to individuals through profits made from housing secured in discriminatory markets, through the unequal educations allocated to children of different races, through insider networks that channel employment opportunities to the relatives and friends of those who have profited most from present and past racial discrimination, and especially through intergenerational transfers of inherited wealth that pass on the spoils of discrimination.[29]

*Erasure* illustrates that there is a possessive investment in blackness that serves as the corollary to the possessive investment in whiteness. In order for white supremacy to maintain its hold, the most dominant images of the nonwhite have to support the current racial hierarchies. The circulation of images that feature Blacks as impoverished, criminal, pathological, and highly sexualized (and pathologically sexualized, implied by the two titles of the book: *My Pafology/ Fuck*), function in this service.

In highlighting the profitability of this investment, the novel expresses a pessimistic view of Black cultural production. In the introduction to *Black Cultural Traffic*, Kennell Jackson historicizes the increasing reach of Black performers and performances since the 1840s, calling attention to how "black cultural performances and representations of blacks can travel far and wide. [They] have enormous mobility. They can end up in unlikely places, in contradictory alliances, can take on new and unintended forms, and can synthesize radically disparate materials."[30] Even as *Erasure* provides proof of this cultural syncretism in literary terms, Monk represents disillusionment about its reach. Jackson further argues that "[black] cultural traffic involves some system of exchange or commerce. Between black performances and the viewers looking in on those performances, there occurs trade in ideas, styles, impressions, body language, and gestures."[31] *Erasure* cynically depicts this exchange as limited to a commodity transaction that only sells a certain kind of image in which Blackness is a product peddled and bought so long as it lives up to its market value and to its market expectations. It is not just representation but also its mode of delivery that Monk sees as restricted, with satire being one genre that does not get the same kind of traffic as social realism. Darryl Dickson-Carr points out that "literary satire remains relatively marginal, even as its televised brethren (such as *The Daily Show*, *South Park*, *Chappelle's Show*, *The Boondocks*, and *Key & Peele*) have made substantial inroads into the American collective consciousness."[32] *Erasure* illustrates how marginal literary satire is; in order for it to sell for mass production in visual form—as a film—it must pass as social realism.

The scene between Monk and Morgenstein (who himself is reduced to the Jewish stereotype of the greedy media executive) also drives home the point that just mixing linguistic or bodily codes does not work to ensure ironic understanding. What Monk fails to understand is the deep investment that Morgenstein has in the credibility of Stagg. He is, after all, ready to invest millions to turn his book into a film. Therefore, even when he receives information that causes him cognitive dissonance, he takes as assurance anything that will allow him to retain his original ideas about Stagg's authenticity. On one hand, the book can be read as a dramatization of the failure of irony to provoke its intended result. On the other hand, by pitting an ironic act against the commodification of authenticity, the novel shows the disparity of power between an individual act and a system of established conventions. In other words, while the novel does not show how one can execute effective social change, it does play out how ineffective individual efforts can be, especially when changes in social meaning depend on the widening of discursive communities. And this occurs not just through a single book or artwork, but through the collective efforts of cultural producers, media executives, publishers, educators, policy makers, and institutions.

## CAUTIONARY TALES OF CLASS PASSING

As a result of Monk's successful class and genre passing, the novel moves from illusion (Monk's idea that his satire will be understood) to disillusion (Monk's abandonment of any such belief) with the dissolution of Monk's identity. The final scene takes place at the National Book Awards Ceremony, which is the culmination of months of reading and assessment from a committee of which

Monk has also been a part. Even though he detests awards, Monk relates an understanding that these prizes can be gatekeeping institutions: he "complained endlessly about the direction of American letters, [and so] when presented with an opportunity to affect it, how could [he] say no?" (224). However, once it becomes clear that *My Pafology/Fuck* is in the running and the committee members praise it for being "[t]he best novel by an African American in years" and "[a] true, raw, gritty work" (254), Monk realizes the gravity of his error in thinking that he could effect any change through his individual efforts. In the denouement, Monk even starts to doubt himself and the world when it is announced that his novel *My Pafology/Fuck* has just won the National Book Award. "[T]he floor had now turned to sand" (264) is the *Invisible Man* reference and signal description that gives us insight into Monk's state of mind as he makes his way up to the front of the room at the awards ceremony. Then comes Monk's complete absorption into his fictive antithesis, Stagg Leigh (though only temporarily, for the novel is written retrospectively, implying that Monk recovers from his mental lapse):

The faces of my life, of my past, of my world became as real as the unreal Harnet [one of the committee members] and the corporations and their wives and they were all talking to me, saying lines from novels that I loved, but when I tried to repeat them to myself, I faltered, unable to recall them. Then there was a small boy, perhaps me as a boy, and he held up a mirror so that I could see my face and it was the face of Stagg Leigh.

"Now you're free of illusion," Stagg said. "How does it feel to be free of one's il-lusions?" (264)

As Monk loses his illusions he also slips into what Kierkegaard, appropriating and modifying Hegel's phrase, called "infinite absolute negativity," referring to the state at which irony acts as total negation and destruction, and nothing is left stable.[33] Communicating the futility and destructive nature of irony that no longer affirms anything but devolves into perpetual cynicism, Kierkegaard describes it as a form of madness that overtakes the employer of irony.[34] Recall-ing another Ellisonian reference in *Invisible Man* about being free of illusions, Monk also demonstrates that the cost of his own rinehartism—if rinehartism stands for the possibility of forever trading in identities—is the loss of faith in any identity, including his own.

Monk's appearance at the awards ceremony could have been an act of celebratory exposure, with Monk given the opportunity to disabuse the judges and audiences of their own racial preconceptions and deliver an "I got you!" Instead, Monk loses his footing and himself in his disbelief that his irony has been taken as sincerity, and to such an extreme extent. Just like Pierre "Dela" Delacroix in Spike Lee's *Bamboozled*, Monk acts as a sacrificial figure in a cautionary tale.[35] In portraying how a capital joke turns into a *capital* joke, with an emphasis on the profit rather than the punch line, the two works fashion middle-class creative producers who attempt but fail to drive home their challenges to media industries not only because they believed too highly in their individual efforts to make an impact, but also because they lost sight of the fact that race is not just something you can make fun of to dispel. While in *Erasure* the disillusionment Monk experiences leads to the destabilization of his identity, in *Bamboozled* the ensuing fallout from the controversy over *The New Millennium Minstrel Show* results in Dela's death when he is shot by his assistant. These endings leave a conflicted assessment about the effectiveness of humor in dispelling stereotypes. Within the novel and the film, the characters who wield these devices do not fare well. Both Dela and Monk lose control over the reception of their work, and a compromise of art is equated to a compromise of self that eventually results in a loss of self. Yet the texts themselves are satiric, parodic, and ironic works. It is as if, by offering completely pessimistic views of the failures of irony, the works are enacting the worst-case scenario for a cultural producer who is driven by the necessity and lure of profit. Each text then ends with the protagonist punished for selling out, claiming a psyche and a life at the end of the novel and the film, respectively. Rendering class passing with ironic approaches, both texts are able to enact a critique of identity performance while at the same time acknowledging the pressing environmental and social factors that prevent the intelligibility of the irony and therefore of the exigent circumstances that necessitated such behavioral and narrative strategies in the first place. Therefore, they are both sympathetic and antagonistic to characters who pass for what they are not, only withdrawing sympathy once the characters start profiting from the possessive investment in blackness.

Perhaps the figure that is most pressured by the possessive investment in blackness is the rapper. If *Erasure* provides a literary critique of artistic gatekeeping, Donald Glover delivers a musical one. Best known for his acting roles on the NBC sitcom *Community* and the FX drama *Atlanta*, Donald Glover is also a writer, comedian, and rapper and has performed under the name Childish Gambino. He critiques the circumscription of Black identity in several songs on his 2011 album *Camp*. In "Backpackers" the speaker ventriloquizes those who would dismiss him for not fitting the conventions of a rapper: "Nerdy ass black kid, whatever man I'm sick of him. . . . What is this nigga doin—rap is for real blacks." He answers the criticism that he is not "real black" in the song "That Power" by pointing out that any attempts to generalize a racial identity constitute different sides to the same coin of racism: "hated on by both sides / I'm just a kid who blowing up with my father's name / And every black 'you're not black enough' / Is a white 'you're all the same.'" Like Everett's novel, Glover's lyrics take issue with the conflation of race with culture, providing a critique of what legal scholar Richard Ford has termed "difference discourse." Ford assesses such discourse as prescriptive because it "describes social identities such as race as a manifestation of underlying differences—a racial culture—while at the same time generating those very differences."[36] Using different mediums, Everett and Glover respond to the racialization of culture that leads to assumptions about how racial identities should be performed and represented.

Whereas *Erasure* and *Camp* contest the exclusion of Blacks from seemingly white middle-class cultural experiences, the high-grossing film *8 Mile* subverts the racialization of culture to open up white participation in "Black" cultural production.[37] The film, starring and loosely based on the recording artist's real life, features Eminem as an aspiring rapper. Throughout the film, his whiteness and poverty get mocked by a crew of Black rappers. In a pivotal freestyle tournament, however, he upsets the power balance by taunting his main rival for being middle class and Black. When Eminem's character, B-Rabbit, raps to the crowd that his opponent went to private school, that his real name is Clarence, and that his parents have a good marriage, the battle is won. He takes away his rival's symbolic value, which is vested in his street cred. By pitting these two characters against each other, this scene stages and then unsettles how racial identities can carry value in the symbolic and material realm influenced by the connotations of class. Since middle-class status tends to be associated with whiteness and poverty with people of color, B-Rabbit's final rap performance (and Eminem's successful career itself) throws the symbolic value of racialized identities into flux. The battle is one that pits class against race, and the value of white poverty as an authentic rap struggle increases as the Black middle-class rapper's value decreases. In order for Eminem's character to emerge the winner, he needs the predominantly Black audience to shame his opponent, which Harry Elam has pointed out results in a politics with "the black masses [that] is not coalitional but hierarchical and intraracially divisive."[38] The film therefore carves a space for the white underdog dependent on the exposure of the class-passer who has passed for symbolic and monetary value. Even though the film leads toward the triumph of the white protagonist over racialized opponents, the outcome of countless blockbuster films, it also delivers the same cautionary tale that we have seen played out in the texts produced by Black artists whereby the racialized class-passer gets punished for trying to profit from the possessive investment in blackness.

## *FABULATION*'S DISINVESTMENT IN BLACK PATHOLOGY

Lynn Nottage's play *Fabulation, or the Re-Education of Undine* fashions a female class passer in the sense that it centralizes its protagonist's class affectations to highlight her attempts to distance herself from the Black poor. The protagonist, Undine Barnes Calles, is a "smartly-dressed thirty-seven-year-old African American woman" (79) who owns her own successful public relations firm and makes a living, "catering to the vanity and confusion of the African American nouveau riche" (87). Befitting of the description herself, Undine has disavowed her working-class Brooklyn origins by claiming that her family perished in a fire and has discarded her birth name, Sharona Watkins, all on the day she graduated from Dartmouth. Ever since, she has been on a trajectory of status seeking and status-making for those who enlist her services.

Undine readily admits to her self-making but cannot accept she led to her own undoing. The play begins after the suave South American she had married because he gave her "flair and cache" (87) has absconded with her wealth, leaving her at the mercy of creditors who take everything she has. Moreover, the FBI accuses her of identity fraud. The first of a series of run-ins with the law, the encounter with the FBI triggers massive anxiety. It is a condition so chronic for her that she even has a name for the pain in her chest—Edna. The play names and literalizes her status panic through an actual panic attack. In the process of undergoing financial and social descent, Undine vents her status panic and bitterness to a friend, another Black female social climber:

How naïve, foolish of me, to assume that I was worthy of some comfort and good fortune, a better chance. They give you a taste, "How ya like it?" then promptly take it away. "Oh, I'm sorry, we've reached our quota of Negroes in the privileged class, unfortunately we're bumping you down to working class." Working. I'm not even working. I think I'm officially part of the underclass. Penniless. I've returned to my original Negro state. (92–93)

Having worked her whole life to be a counterexample to the way in which race gets conflated with class, wherein Black signifies poverty, Undine here expresses her deepest fears. With her loss of wealth and reputation she feels stripped of agency even in how she gets categorized. Yet, she recategorizes herself a step further downward—from working class to underclass—to emphasize her fall in worst-case-scenario terms that are economic and discursive.

The play then puts Undine through a series of humiliations in which she is made to experience every stereotype associated with the Black underclass. Now poor, she is forced to return home to the Brooklyn housing projects where her family still lives. Her grandmother lives with the family, and everyone thinks she is diabetic, but she has actually been injecting herself with heroin and begs Undine to get her more. Even though her "entire life has been engineered to avoid this very moment" (104), Undine ventures out to a street corner to make the drug purchase and is caught in the act by the police. Sentenced by a judge to six months of drug counseling, Undine has to attend group sessions with addicts. Her real addiction had been to high-fashion magazines, but she participates in the circle and even attracts the attention of Guy, a reformed addict who wants to date her.

Essentially, Undine starts off as one class-inflected stereotype and becomes another, scripted to play, as Aimee Zygmonski puts it, both the "black bourgeois lady and the welfare queen."[39] Examining how in opposition to the "welfare queen" stands the image of the "black lady," Lisa B. Thompson has argued that the Black lady has traditionally stood for middle-class respectability and has had the burden of "concealing sexuality; and foregrounding morality, intelligence, and civility as a way to counter negative stereotypes."[40] The "welfare queen," in contrast, "represents moral aberration and an economic drain," asserts Wahneema Lubiano, who identifies this figure as "the synecdoche, the shortest possible shorthand, for the pathology of poor, urban, black culture."[41] Both types have been used to circumscribe Black women and portray them as dysfunctional. Undine strives to be a Black lady but meets her worst-case scenario when she not only loses her wealth but finds out she is pregnant with her estranged husband's child. The pregnancy forces her to navigate the social services available to poor women—the kind of women from which Undine had tried to distance herself. In contrast to Undine, an alternative route presented in the play is modeled through a childhood friend who has attained professional success but who has not cut ties with her working-class past. Devora is a financial planner with her own brownstone who returns to the projects to visit her sister. Upon seeing her old friend, Devora hands Undine her business card, disclosing she has started a "financial planning program for underprivileged women" like her (119). Undine notes it "gives [her] a slight paper cut, just enough to draw blood" (119). Undine, by this time, is poor, living in the projects, seen as an addict, single, and pregnant, and experiences complete and painful abjection in feeling she has become a stereotype.

As discussed earlier, Percival Everett puts Van Go Jenkins through a similar process of absurdly contrived racialized episodes, except to different ends. Van Go Jenkins is made to conform to stereotypes about Black males in order to critique the media's possessive investment in blackness. Undine is made to experience the stereotypes imposed on Black women to point out how she has actually bought into the possessive investment in blackness in her attempts to distance herself from any associations with the Black poor. Read together, these satiric texts take on the two most pernicious Black stereotypes in the contemporary era, since the "welfare queen and the street criminal are brandished to discredit progressive redistribution, pare back social protections, and justify ever-tougher modes of policing and social control."[42] Racially coded language about criminals and welfare queens influenced the passing of two policies that have had devastating effects on Black communities: the 1994 crime bill, and the 1996 welfare reform act. Published in the early 2000s, Everett and Nottage's texts are intertwined with this sociopolitical vilification of the Black poor. Further, while *Erasure* showcases how racial discourses are profitable, *Fabulation* highlights how these discourses can be divisive. It is only by occupying the positions she had previously feared and rejected that Undine sees that she had accepted a value system in which the Black poor are viewed in negative terms.

She accepts the narrative of Black pathology, on the one hand, and the American cultural narrative of individual self-fashioning, on the other. It is a dual ideological influence encapsulated in the characterization of her "journey that began miraculously at the Walt Whitman projects and led [her] to Edith Wharton's *The Custom of the Country*, an intriguing parvenu discovered in an American Literature course at Dartmouth College" (133). That the housing projects in which she grew up are named after Walt Whitman suggests that she was raised within an ideology of self-declaration and affirmation that is part of American culture. And she could have drawn inspiration from her working-class environment and origins in declaring that affirmative identity. Instead, Undine was inspired by Wharton's novel about a perpetually striving social climber, whose protagonist, Undine Spraggs, serves as the model for her character. Since she found Wharton's protagonist "intriguing," she ended up emulating this striver who, like her, constantly tries to hide a secret from her past that threatens her social standing in the present.

Consequently, Undine must lose everything in order to gain insight that will enable her to be birthed anew—this time not through her own efforts but with acceptance of her working-class family. Undine finally admits her culpability to Guy: "I told everyone my family died in a fire, and I came to accept it as true. And it was true for years. Understand, Sharona had to die in a fire in order for Undine to live. At least that's what I thought" (138). Thus she utters the words that pose the possibility of her redemption, a course enacted in the final scene when she gives birth. By this point, Undine allows herself to be romantically involved with working-class Guy, reunites with her working-class family, and accepts that she made a mistake in trying to distance herself from her past. At first she hesitates to inhale so she can exhale and deliver her baby, for fear that she will be a terrible mother. But surrounded by Guy and her family, Undine takes the breath that also delivers promise of a new Undine.

With Undine's re-education and change in perspective, the play redeems the status seeker to the point at which she accepts herself as part of a working-class community. Not surprisingly, because of how often these character types appear as a dyad, there is an artist figure in the play, one who remains perpetually conflicted. Undine's brother, Flow, has been working on an epic poem about

the African American folk trickster hero Brer Rabbit. Usually the artist is at
odds with the status seeker, and in this play he bickers with his sister after she
returns home, refusing to call her by her new name because he cannot understand why she would want to change a "beautiful African name to a European
brand" (100). Just as he does not understand Undine's self-fabrication, Undine
does not understand his interest in "fabulating," a word that frequently reoc-
curs in Flow's poem. He explains that in his poem "I am using Brer Rabbit,
classic trickster, as means to express the dilemma faced by cultural stereotyping
and the role it plays in the oppression on one hand and the liberation of the
neo-Afric (to coin a phrase) individual, on the other. We at once reject and
embrace—" (97). But Undine's voiceover, directed at the audience, interrupts:

Flow was never the same after his tour of Desert Storm. I know it's a cliché, but something did happen to him in the desert. Military school, a year at West Point, the Green
Berets and finally a security guard at Walgreen's. He couldn't ever reconcile his love of
the uniform with his quest for personal freedom. Hence the poem. (97)

Undine attributes his interests in cultural criticism to post-traumatic stress
disorder, rationalizing that his experience in the war and his subsequent downward mobility must have left him permanently confused. But we know she
is a terrible reader (she was inspired by Wharton's novel about a perpetually
dissatisfied social climber rather than cautioned by it), so hers is an unreliable interpretation. She also does not recognize that she has just experienced
a similar trajectory of downward mobility that has left her confused about her
love for the system—the equivalent of a uniform—and her idealization of self-
making and supposed freedom.

Her comment registers the tension at the heart of most upward mobility
narratives—how to be part of the system and yet an individual. Furthermore,
in ethnic upward mobility narratives, being part of the system is often seen as
in conflict with being part of an ethnic community. In the play, this tension
is resolved in so far as Undine is redeemed when she has nothing left to lose
but everything to gain and gain is equated with reuniting with her working-
class family. But there is an unresolved tension, mainly, the fact that most of
the characters with whom she interacts are Black guards who make their living protecting the resources of big business. Flow is a security guard and so
are Undine's parents and Guy. Aside from her grandmother, her working-class

community is composed of security guards. Being part of the system as a guard, private or public, offers a stable job, and for many people of color, these systemic jobs enable class security. It ensures that they will be part of the working or middle class and not the "underclass" that Undine so feared. Thus the play includes characters whose occupations involve guarding neoliberal commerce that continues to disenfranchise people of color but does not center the story on them even as it marks how prevalent this position is. Characters do express desires for other kinds of work: Guy aspires to be a firefighter and Flow wants to be a poet, though the play implies that the attainment of these alternative professions will be a challenge for both of them, signaled by Guy's documented history of drug abuse and charges for possession and Flow's inability to complete the poem he has been working on for over fourteen years.

That Flow cannot find the words to finish his poem becomes part of the play's message about cultural types. Amidst his family, Flow spontaneously recites,

This ain't the beginnin' you wuz
expectin'

[ . . . ]

It ain't a holler or a song.
It ain't no geechie folk yawn.
It ain't a road that been tread,
With a stained rag around the head.
It all about a rabbit,
Or it ain't.

It ain't a myth that so old,
That it been whole-saled and
re-sold.
It ain't a Bible lover's tale,
Or a preacher's parting wail. (130–131)

The beginning stanzas indicate that the poem is not delivering forms ("holler or a song," "folk yawn," "myth that so old," "Bible lover's tale," "preacher's parting wail") or types and images ("stained rag around the head," "Bible lover," "preacher") that will offer familiar moral lessons. It tells us instead that

"It all about a rabbit, / Or it ain't," a refrain repeated three times before the final stanzas:

'Cuz.

It that ghetto paradox,
When we rabbit and we fox,
And we basking in the blight
Though we really wanna fight.

"It 'bout who we be today,
And in our fabulating way
'Bout saying that we be
Without a-pology.
It's a circle that been run
That ain't no one ever won.
It that silly rabbit grin
'Bout running from your skin,

'Cuz.

It a . . . It a . . . (131)

The paradox of being both the fox and the rabbit, hunter and the hunted, echoes the contradiction referenced by Undine in characterizing Flow's afflic- tion and which also pertains to hers: their inability to reconcile their desire to be a part of the system (because if you are not the fox you are the rabbit) and still outside of it (the rabbit as a trickster who outsmarts the fox). Yet the poem claims it is offering an alternative to the familiar folk story and moral lesson. Aimee Zygmonksi demonstrates that Nottage's trickster aesthetics come in the form of an unreliable narrator and through her satirical voice.[43] Here we also see Nottage directly invoke the trickster figure Brer Rabbit in a poem about the contradictory nature of individual and group identity that parallels the play's depiction of fractured selves and a fractured Black community along the lines of class. It values working through these contradictions via new narratives, even if they cannot be reconciled. We know they cannot be reconciled because Flow cannot finish his poem and sees it as "open-ended. A work in progress. A continuous journey" (97).

Undine's identity crisis is, in contrast, easily reconciled. The play, as a fable with a moral lesson, is not open-ended about its message with regard to the ethical course for Undine. Once she accepts and reunites with her working-class family and community, she is presented as a more authentic version of herself. By correlating her return to class origins with unity and authenticity, the play ends nostalgically. Scholars such as Nicole King, Rolland Murray, and Kenneth Warren have argued that in an era with increased class heterogeneity among African Americans, nostalgia in contemporary Black literature registers the paradox of a Black communal identity: how the contemporary calls for Black racial solidarity are a form of nostalgia that often look to the Jim Crow and civil rights eras as periods when there was a sense of a unified Black community even as the goal in those periods was to overcome the conditions that led to the sense of a unified community in the first place.[44] Even as it values the process of creating new narratives, of "fabulating" beyond the usual cultural types, *Fabulation* reintroduces E. Franklin Frazier's critique of the "rootless" and white-emulating Black bourgeois and imagines a scenario by which the rootless can come back to more secure ground. It is not back to a historical era of Black disenfranchisement, but to a class state, in which a lack of resources strengthens communal ties. Nottage's play ultimately re-envisions Black unity based on working-class struggle. One could argue that this is not a viable model for communal solidarity, if one has to lose it all in order to attain some elusive sense of authenticity and communal ties. But, arguably, the appeal of upward mobility narratives in depicting financial rises that lead to moral descents and the inverse of that trajectory is that they do the social work of imagining and playing out these paths so we do not have to experience them ourselves. In this sense, there is safety and appeasement in the genre's didactic function.

While Monk and Undine do not see anything productive about having to contend with the tax placed on Black upward mobility, *Erasure* and *Fabulation* say otherwise. In a cautionary tale of a cultural producer who sells out, Monk's failure in negating the racialized class fantasy underscores that fantasy's commercial and ideological power. And where *Erasure* ends, *Fabulation* begins. Monk ends as a sellout but Undine begins as one, and thus her story offers a different message about what to do with the possessive investment in blackness. Both texts suggest that class-inflected racial stereotypes cannot be dispelled through individual actions, whether one tries to parody them or run away from them. But *Fabulation* goes a step further in showing that they can lead to class prejudices, which is the real cost of a belief in "self-making." By reintegrating Undine into communal wholeness, the play posits redemption. In the next chapter, I continue to explore representations of sellouts who are "redeemed" in the service of pressing political issues.

# CHAPTER 6

# SWITCHED ALLEGIANCES

> If certain forms of inaction are seen as failures to pay racial dues, so, too, are certain forms of action.
>
> Randall Kennedy, *Sellout*[1]

## THE POLITICS OF SELLOUT REDEMPTION NARRATIVES

At the end of Américo Paredes's novel *George Washington Gómez*, the eponymous Mexican American protagonist returns to his Texas hometown college-educated, married, and employed. As the prophesized "leader of his people," George is welcomed back by his family and friends, who hope that he will run for office and overthrow the existing racist political machine.[2] George, however, is not the man they think he is. Serving as a U.S. counterintelligence officer, he has, in fact, been sent to the border to spy on those very same friends for possible seditious activity. In disappointment and anger that the boy they so admired has turned into a man who ridicules their efforts to elect Mexicans into office, one of George's friends calls him a "*Vendido sanavabiche*" (son of a bitch sellout), capturing in brief the sentiment that shifts this upward mobility narrative into the territory of the sellout narrative.

Arguing that there is an egalitarian impulse in upward mobility narratives, Bruce Robbins posits that "When upward mobility goes wrong," it ignores inequality and complicity in order to highlight individual success: "Founded on an initial injustice or deprivation, the genre always risks allowing the screen to be filled by the challenges to be overcome and the joy of overcoming them."[3]

Through George's individualist-minded ascension, *George Washington Gómez* emblematizes upward mobility gone wrong. Spanning the years from 1915 to the 1940s and portraying an ethnic minority who switches allegiances in favor of the U.S. legal system and against his community of origin, the novel plays out an ethnic group's fear of assimilation and its potentially obliterating effects on one's cultural attachments and empathy for the disenfranchised. In an interview conducted fifty years after the novel was written, Américo Paredes was asked what changes he had seen in Mexican American culture from his childhood to the present, and he replied that while in 1990 youth was more *despierto* (awake), he hoped that "most of our young people can become acculturated because they need to. But without becoming completely assimilated."[4] By making a distinction between acculturation and assimilation, Paredes proposes a scenario in which one can learn the culture of the dominant group out of necessity, without being enticed into identifying against a marginalized identity. In Paredes's novel, George as border agent cannot make this distinction. No longer the embodiment of promise to come, George trades in his cultural ties to make sure others do not transgress the legal and social status quo.

In the postmillennium, representations of the Mexican American Border Patrol figure as sellout emerged in audiovisual form, and they hinge on the premise that upward mobility gone wrong can be righted. *The Gatekeeper* and *Machete* are films depicting the plight of the undocumented and the exploitive economies enabled by immigration policy.[5] *Sleep Dealer*, meanwhile, is set across the border to portray the guarding of transnational capital against an insurgent Mexican working class.[6] All three films feature border-patrolling characters who enjoy the status and privileges granted by American citizenship and show how domestic upward mobility is enabled by a U.S. foreign policy that needs individuals to guard the country's political and business interests. Since these assimilated middle-class Mexican American characters are unlikable and are pitted against highly sympathetic working-class and undocumented characters, these films start out as sellout narratives, in which characters take part in cautionary tales to warn against those who have turned their backs on their ethnic origins and who, more dangerously, now work with those in power against those without it. Unlike Paredes's novel, however, these films take as their starting point an already assumed entrance into the middle class. These characterizations have historical significance: they represent a Latina/o middle-class subjectivity that has already formed and are interrogating what that means for collectivist politics. The question becomes not "What if upward mobility has the effect of diminishing your cultural ties?" but "Given that upward mobility can entice you into identifying with those in power, will you still come to the aid of those without it?" In other words, in times of crisis, can and will you switch your allegiances?

As discussed in the previous chapters, identity groups police boundaries through narratives that demarcate insiders and outsiders. Outsiders are those who threaten the interests, the values, and, in these films, the safety of members in the group. Sellout narratives are one means by which outsiders are made clear, and the minority law enforcement official is represented in these films as a sellout par excellence, upholding a repressive order for his or her own gain. However, rather than completely excising the sellout, leaving him or her to remain on the outskirts to stand in for definitive betrayal, these films modify the sellout narrative to work toward reintegration. In analyzing these maneuvers, I situate *The Gatekeeper*, *Machete*, and *Sleep Dealer* within the tradition of Chicana/o film, whose project, film scholar Rosa Linda Fregoso argues, "may succinctly be summed up as the documentation of social reality through oppositional forms of knowledge about Chicanos."[7] I contend that these films portray a middle-class oppositional politics through the inclusion of character types that allow for filmic interpretations about the ethically charged nature of the insider/outsider—the insider who knows the community intimately, but who is an outsider by profession.

These films exemplify how ethnic cultural production often reveals that "community" cannot be assumed, given the vast array of experiences and ideological outlooks that exist within racialized ethnic groups. However, cultural production can try to forge affective bonds among diverse populations, and these films model how contemporary Latina/o cultural production is endeavoring to represent and shape the belief of a shared group consciousness when it comes to immigration as an issue that transcends the divisions of social class. As Randy Ontiveros argues, "The immigrant rights struggle—the most urgent area of contemporary Chicano/a politics—requires both legislative and cultural strategies, which is to say there must be a reforming of the imagination before there can be meaningful political reform."[8] All three films feature Mexican American actors portraying middle-class Mexican American characters who face ethical conflicts regarding their positions as law enforcers and who have the potential to marshal their middle-class cultural capital to help those in need. Dramatizing scenarios in which the Border Patrol agents switch allegiances, these movies reveal and resolve intra-ethnic tensions through characters that at first keep guard against coethnics and then disregard previously held beliefs to come to their aid. I demonstrate how the sellout narrative, while traditionally serving as a cautionary tale, turns into a narrative of redemption in these films to dramatize political awakening and group solidarity. After detailing how and why this transformation occurs in Latina/o films, I end the chapter by examining analogous representations of Black police officers in film. By putting these representations in conversation with each other, we can see how the structural position and discursive role of the minority law enforcement agent is similar across these two ethnic groups, and can better understand why there are differences in their filmic manifestations.

## PATROLLING TERRITORIAL AND RACIAL BORDERS

Immigration films featuring Mexican American Border Patrol agents reflect a relatively new phenomenon—that the majority of Border Patrol agents are now Latina/o. In her comprehensive account of the Border Patrol's history, Kelly Lytle Hernandez recounts how the Border Patrol used to be a vocation predominantly occupied by whites. According to Lytle Hernandez, in its establishment in 1924 and into the 1950s, the Border Patrol's units were composed of an "Anglo-American working class, who often used law enforcement as a strategy of economic survival and social uplift."[9] Entering positions of authority was also a means for these men to "shore up their tentative claims upon whiteness,"[10] claims that could be weakened if they otherwise worked in a heavily racialized agricultural sector. By distancing themselves from Mexicans, patrollers could assure themselves of an elevated social status even if they were not landowners themselves. The job, in turn, became a project of patrolling physical borders as well as racial ones.

During this time, the job also had a unique appeal for middle- and upper-class Mexican Americans by offering them access to whiteness. Historian Neil Foley explains how in the early twentieth century, "Mexicans walked the color line. Heavily recruited by growers throughout the Southwest, Mexicans were represented variously as nonwhite 'mongrels' who polluted the Anglo-Saxon racial stock and as almost white laborers who worked in unskilled occupations shunned by most whites. . . . [Therefore] growing numbers of Mexican Americans sought acceptance within the ranks of the American working class by insisting on their status as whites."[11] However, even though lighter-skinned and wealthier Mexicans could be considered white, Lytle Hernandez points out that "the class-based flexibility in the application of racial segregation could be unpredictable."[12] Because class and race were often conflated and the majority of Mexicans and Mexican Americans were part of the working poor, even middle- and upper-class Mexican Americans were at risk of being perceived as lower class and therefore discriminated against. Citing official organization documents and letters from branch leaders, Lytle Hernandez demonstrates that Mexican American civil rights organizations like the League of United Latin American Citizens and the American GI Forum supported Border Patrol endeavors throughout the 1930s and 1950s out of a fear that Mexican immigrants were halting their social progress.

Serving as a means of social authority, enforcement, and uplift, the U.S. Border Patrol has attracted more and more Mexican Americans over the years, facilitated by an increase in the Border Patrol's budget after 1965. While in 1929 rosters listed only six men with Spanish surnames, by 2008 52 percent of the officers were Latina/o.[13] If one considers that this is more than three times the percentage of Latina/os in the United States, this data is striking indeed.[14] But it is not surprising, given that the Border Patrol implements initiatives to recruit and retain Latina/os. The U.S. Customs and Border Protection (CBP) *Fiscal Year 2010 Annual Report on Hispanic Employment* boasts success rates of youth educational programs; outreach and mentoring programs; and advertising campaigns using billboards, magazine spreads, and sponsorship of job fairs at community events.[15] The CBP's website itself touts the job as one offering good pay, room for advancement, and excellent benefits.[16] Clearly invested in recruiting a Latina/o workforce, the CBP's efforts paid off, as the 2010 report states that the percentage of Latina/o Border Patrol officers at the middle officer level (grades 10–11) was at 54.43 percent.

The job of Border Patrol agent for Latina/os is fraught with moral tensions shaped by public discourse around increasing immigration enforcement. On one hand, as cultural insiders, Mexican American Border Patrol agents have certain desirable vocational traits. A 2008 *Houston Chronicle* article describes the advantages Mexican American recruits have in their linguistic and cultural fluency and knowledge of local terrain.[17] On the other hand, these same qualities also make their position as insiders/outsiders subject to vocal opposition, as another article, published in the *New York Times*, lays bare. "Hispanic Agents Face Hurdles on Border Patrol" quotes officers facing criticism from family and community members for the kind of work they do, and mentions that they often hear pleas from border-crossing migrants who try to appeal to them through ethnic ties.[18] A seventeen-year veteran quoted in a 1993 *Los Angeles Times* article sums up the pressure agents feel to prove their allegiance to the force by showing toughness: "For Hispanics, there's no in between. You're either a hard-ass or a bleeding heart."[19]

At issue is the question of whether one should be loyal to one's country or to one's ethnicity. In the past, the Border Patrol itself demonstrated skepticism when it came to trusting Mexican Americans as agents. A *New York Times* article quotes historian Leon C. Metz's explanation that the rise in Latina/o agents demonstrates a shift in the Border Patrol's perception of Latina/os: "There was some fear that if you assigned people who speak Spanish and whose ancestors came from Mexico to the border, they would be sympathetic to those they should be apprehending."[20] Notwithstanding the agency's developed faith in Latina/o agents, the issue of trust is still mulled over in the popular sector. A 2010 Yahoo! Answers thread attempts to respond to the question "How does Mexico and her people feel about Mexicans working for the Border Patrol arresting Mexicans?" while the tongue-in-cheek advice column "Ask the Mexican" replies to a letter printed that same year in the *Dallas Observer* asking, "Are Mexican-American Border Patrol Agents Traitors?"[21] A concern with the implications and ethics of this particular vocation for Mexican Americans runs throughout these articles, web posts, and *The Gatekeeper* and *Machete*. The films centralize these ethical challenges by depicting Mexican Americans as agents of U.S. law enforcement who are thus situated as possible agents of repression against people sharing their ethnic identity, and who have learned to profile, arrest, and deport such people.

## OPERATION TRANSFORM *THE GATEKEEPER*

Produced with a $200,000 budget, *The Gatekeeper* focuses on the experiences of Adam Fields, a Mexican-hating Border Patrol agent who is half Mexican himself (Figures 3 and 4). He executes a plan to pose as an undocumented Mexican

FIGURES 3 AND 4. Agent Adam Fields on patrol and standing over his victim. Source: *The Gatekeeper*, directed by John Carlos Frey (Screen Media, 2002).

with a hidden camera to reveal how immigrants are crossing the border, but when his hired coyote leaves him indentured as part of a drug-producing labor site, he is affected by the suffering and deaths he witnesses and starts to question his long-held animosity toward Mexicans. At the conclusion of the film, Fields is given the opportunity to destroy the labor site and mourn the dead, an ending that implies he has had a change of heart and has developed compassion toward Mexicans. All the characters in the film speak in English, and it requires a suspension of disbelief to maintain that Fields is never suspected of being a non-immigrant. Despite its flaws, the film offers a unique angle on the immigration experience from two points of view: the undocumented Mexican and the assimilated Mexican American.[22]

The film's title references Operation Gatekeeper, the controversial immigration measure, and gatekeeping, the position of power preventing others from gaining admittance. The first meaning is most obvious in the film, which features writer, director, and producer John Carlos Frey in the role of Agent Fields, who takes extreme measures to halt migrants from crossing over. As Douglas Massey, Jorge Durand, and Nolan Malone's *Beyond Smoke and Mirrors* explains, after the 1986 Immigration Reform and Control Act, there was a marked change in U.S. border strategy.[23] Whereas previous attempts at curtailing migration were made through apprehensions once migrants were already across the border, officers now opted for "prevention through deterrence." After the success of El Paso's Operation Hold-the-Line in 1993, which had patrol officers standing a few feet from the border and guarding frequently trafficked areas, Operation Gatekeeper was launched in San Diego in 1994. Operation Gatekeeper included "the installation of high-intensity floodlights to illuminate the border day and night, as well as an eight-foot steel fence along fourteen miles of border from the Pacific Ocean to the foothills of the Coast Ranges."[24] In addition to the officers stationed near the border, a "new array of sophisticated hardware (motion detectors, infrared scopes, trip wires) was deployed in the no-man's land it fronted."[25] The film depicts the effects of this new border strategy, which inevitably led migrants into less trafficked and more dangerous crossing points, but it does not focus on the perils of crossing over mountainous areas or desert lands. Instead it presents the militarization of the border as a major contributing factor to the criminalized underground economy that arose around coyotes and drug smuggling, leaving Mexican migrants at the mercy of both.

The second meaning of the title is best understood if one considers the power that gatekeepers have in society at large, in any sector in which access to resources is dependent on intermediary figures who can deny or grant approval. The film coalesces these two meanings with an added twist: Agent Fields is not only a Border Patrol officer—he is a middle-class Mexican American who is trying to prevent others from attaining the same rights that he himself enjoys. Considered in this light, the title signals broad social concerns over federally sanctioned immigration policies and also hints at intra-ethnic tensions, manifested through Fields's position as someone who can deny other Mexicans entry into the United States. These intra-ethnic tensions are based in both class and citizenship status, with the former expressed through animosity toward those without citizenship.

Fields's political involvement with the immigration issue is personally motivated. He does not identify as Mexican American, not because his ethnicity is no longer relevant for him, but because he has actively worked to sever ties with it. Ironically though, his denial of his background as well as his shame and anger at his Mexican mother and his upbringing are so consuming that his choice of vocation and subsequent actions are directly motivated by his inability to stop thinking about Mexicans and his own Mexican identity. While Fields as gatekeeper tries to guard the U.S. Mexican Border, he is also a status seeker trying to guard himself against any closeness to other Mexicans.

Ever on the offensive lest these ties be reinforced, Fields shows how guarded he is in a scene in which, after a ten-year absence, he visits his mother on her deathbed. His rage rises to the surface when a caretaker gives him the money that his mother had saved up for him. He renounces the gift as a bribe, displaying his disgust with his mother's former life as a prostitute; he insinuates she may not have even known the identity of his father. He begins to tear through the cabinets, searching for an alternative inheritance: the sugar packets his mother idiosyncratically stole from restaurants over the years. Faced with another shameful aspect of his upbringing, he flings the bulging bags of "damn Mexican sugar packets" onto the floor before proceeding to break the "garage-sale dishes." When the women in the house attempt to stop him, he screams out, "No one lay a fucking brown finger on me, comprende!" The shot angles show the effect his words have on the women and then what he looks like from their point-of view (Figures 5 and 6) before he runs out of the house, asking the viewer to identify with the receivers of the words rather than the utterer

FIGURES 5 AND 6. Agent Fields warns the Mexican women to not lay a brown finger on him. Source: *The Gatekeeper*, directed by John Carlos Frey (Screen Media, 2002).

of them. This scene also illustrates that even as Fields attempts to reject those who speak his native tongue, the irruption of Spanish into his speech points to the inescapability of his past.

Fields essentially criminalizes his Mexican mother, who becomes a symbol of all Mexicans whom he sees as part of the "invasion." By labeling his mother's gift a bribe, he renders it an illicit transaction rather than a passing down of a lifetime of savings. Very starkly, this scene contrasts with the scenario that occurs in the dream state at the end of *George Washington Gómez*. In the dream, the assimilated George envisions himself as a revolutionary Mexican leading others in battle in the war against Texas, a dream that Ramón Saldívar reads as a return of the repressed that arises "to offer an alternative ideology and different self-formation."[26] In *The Gatekeeper*, however, Agent Fields does not in his waking or dream life attempt to work out his antagonism toward Mexicans or try to reintegrate his Mexican heritage. While George's unconscious tries to offer him a different sense of self, one that leads others in protecting Mexican land against Anglo invaders, Fields identifies as a white man on land being invaded by Mexicans. He refuses to be bought by what he sees as his mother's "bribe" because he has sold out his heritage long before—for a badge, a rifle, and the ability to distance himself from all Mexicans.

That his anger toward his upbringing stems from his anger toward his Mexican mother while his white father is never blamed parallels the scapegoating of the brown mother in the Malinche myth propagated by Octavio Paz. In his essay "Sons of Malinche," Paz famously drew out the correlation between the maternal signification of Malinche, the indigenous translator and concubine of Hernán Cortés, and the phrase "la chingada," which means the "fucked one."[27] Representing passivity, violation, and cultural betrayal, Malinche becomes, Paz argues, part of the Mexican psyche that has not reconciled its hybrid origins:

When we shout "¡Viva México, hijos de la chingada!" we express our desire to live closed off from the outside world and, above all, from the past. In this shout we condemn our origins and deny our hybridism. The strange permanence of Cortés and La Malinche in the Mexican's imagination and sensibilities reveals that they are something more than historical figures: they are symbols of a secret conflict that we have still not resolved. When he repudiates La Malinche, the Mexican Eve . . . the Mexican breaks his ties with the past, renounces his origins, and lives in isolation and solitude.[28]

Norma Alarcón points out that in "Paz's figurations illegitimacy predicated the Mexican founding order," while Sandra M. Cypess argues that "Paz seems to imply that until La Malinche is somehow integrated within the totality of the Mexican psyche and is no longer a figure to repudiate, the Mexican will not develop to his fullest potential, but remain an orphan, a wandering soul in the labyrinth of solitude."[29] As if providing an updated version of Paz's paradigm, one that restarts the origin myth on U.S. soil for the biracial Mexican American, *The Gatekeeper* posits illegitimacy and the mother's cultural signification as integral to the foundational subjectivity of the alienated Mexican American who is trying to break with his past and deny his origins. Like his namesake, Adam Fields feels betrayed by a Mexican Eve. The film suggests that if Agent Fields would only accept his brown mother, and consequently his own brownness, he would cease to be tormented and would achieve wholeness.

Foregrounding this psychic conflict that occurs within Fields, the film employs his vocation to explore the premise of a self-loathing Mexican American even as it is careful not to condemn the Border Patrol itself. It avoids vilifying the entire agency by depicting Fields as a rogue officer who teams up with a group of vigilantes known as the National Patrol. The film's opening scene shows Fields not only patrolling the border but also deliberately instigating conflict in conjunction with the National Patrol, which also has a radio show on its ironically acronymed channel, NPR ("National Patrol Radio"). The film opens in green night-vision light, and the first image we see is through an infrared video camera, filming twinkling lights from cars in the distance. As the camera focuses, we see undocumented Mexican men attempting to cross the border. A voiceover welcomes us to National Patrol Radio, claiming to "defend America from the Mexican invasion." Slowly, as the film cuts from an image of the eye doing the viewing to a mouth doing the speaking, it becomes apparent that the man (identified moments later as Fields) who is holding the video camera is also the one who has called in to the radio station, asking why the station continues to condemn Mexicans. He then lauds Mexican and Aztec historical accomplishments, setting up the radio talk show host to provide "facts" as a rebuttal. The radio host leads up to the declaration that today's Mexicans are the offspring of "cannibalistic savages bred with greedy imperialists" and argues that instead of "defending a lost civilization" the caller should be defending America because it is under threat: "You are becoming the conquered civilization. You are being invaded by a foreign power and you will be forced to eat beans and tortillas for the rest of your life." Fields mock-surrenders the argument saying, "I see your point. I see your point." This scene stages and also foreshadows a series of reversals. First is the radio talk show host's reversal of the imperial narrative to portray a United States under threat. Second is Fields's feigned reversal of opinion. These pretenses prefigure the actual reversals of opinion and more repetitions of scenarios and dialogue in the film.

As a sellout redemption narrative, the film ends with Fields undergoing a change in consciousness. The strategies employed to underscore this change include repetitions (both in plot and in dialogue) and scenes drawing parallels between Fields and Mexican migrants once Fields directly interacts with them. Not content to just engage in inflammatory rhetoric, provide video footage of crossing Mexicans, and shoot directly at Mexicans (right after the phone call to the radio station he shoots a crossing migrant in the leg), Fields concocts a plan to obtain more revealing recordings of weaknesses along the border. With the help of the National Patrol, Fields executes a plan to go undercover as Juan Carlos Mendoza, a Mexican who hires a coyote to cross the border. Equipped with a hidden video camera, Fields intends to expose how migrants are still getting across in order to show how current patrol efforts are not enough to stop the "invasion." His plan goes awry when he witnesses his cohort of vigilantes ambushed by the smugglers, who then indenture him and a group of Mexicans into producing amphetamines once they have crossed over into the United States.

The illegal labor site's purpose in the film is twofold: to showcase how migrants can be economically exploited and how an alternative form of work simultaneously occurs within newly formed groups. It highlights the work that goes into establishing and reinforcing social ties when there is no blood kinship but there is a clear need to recognize an in-group and an out-group: in this case, the oppressed and the oppressors. Two characters in particular attempt to forge bonds with the recalcitrant Fields (whom they know as Juan Carlos from the Mexican state of Morelos): Lenora (Anne Betancourt), the elder mother figure who tends to the laborers, and José (Joe Pascual), the current on-site chemist who trains Fields to prepare the amphetamines. José also prompts a dialogue on and demonstration of ethnic fraternity. During their first training session Fields is so overcome by the fumes that José takes him down into the shed's basement for respite. There he has a private hiding space and reveals to

Fields that he has installed a bell that the outside guard presses to let him know if the boss is coming. A surprised Fields asks, "the guard?" to which José explains, "Somos hermanos. It doesn't matter if he's the one with the gun. We're all familia right? If we don't take care of each other, then . . ." He shrugs. His rhetoric of familial ties puts forth an alternative perspective of the relationship between the guard and the guarded, one that overrides any opposition between them when it comes to surviving against a nonfamilial force.

While at first Fields ignores any attempts at camaraderie and advice from the other Mexicans in the labor camp, he gradually begins to develop an empathetic connection to them. When he is outside getting fresh air in relief from the fumes, he makes a break for freedom but is quickly apprehended and brought back to the campsite. In between scenes of him running and the scene of his return to the campsite as a hostage, the film cross-cuts to a scene of the other female at the site, a young mother named Eva (Michelle Agnew) being raped by the boss after he assaults her while she is doing housework. By interjecting the rape scene of Eva between scenes of Fields's escape and capture, the film correlates the exploitation of the men to that of the women and conveys the message that at this point in the film, there is no escape from either situation. To underscore this point, Eva is traumatized and Fields literally becomes immobile. After he is brought back to the campsite, the boss makes him translate to the group, stating that because he tried to run none of them will get paid for the week. In addition, the boss's sidekick makes him translate that he is a stupid Mexican and that to ensure he does not try to escape again he will take a bullet in the leg. This prompts a close-up of José, begging for leniency on his behalf, and while the boss relents, his henchman still shoots Fields anyway. A comeuppance for his earlier callous treatment of the Mexican migrant whom he shot in the leg at the beginning of the film, this repeated instance of punishment for an unjust transgression is one of the ways in which *The Gatekeeper* reiterates the connection between Fields and the other Mexicans.

This scene is then the catalyst for how Fields subsequently comes to understand himself in relation to the others, what political scientist Michael C. Dawson has called "linked fate."[30] Dawson developed the concept of linked fate as the "belief that one's fate is linked to that of the racial group" by studying a cross-section of African Americans.[31] Asking whether race for African Americans was still a salient factor influencing their political outlooks even

when they moved up the U.S. class structure, Dawson found that they still perceived their self-interests as bound up with group interests due to their shared
historical memory of slavery and economic subordination. Scholars have tested
the theory of linked fate on Latina/o groups to see whether the concept has
cross-ethnic applicability. From their study of the pan-Latina/o 2006 National
Latino Survey, political scientists Gabriel R. Sanchez and Natalie Masuoka
found that Latina/os do express a belief in linked fate, but they contend that it
may be generationally and class bound, tied to the experience of immigration
and social marginality. They found that in contrast to Dawson's findings, class
status does influence Latina/os' perception of linked fate, with those having
"lower levels of income [being] more likely to believe that their status is tied
to that of other Latinos."[32] Furthermore, they argue that "the experience of
social marginalization is key to the formation of linked fate," and one of the
most common experiences of social marginalization is a shared experience of
immigration.[33] The further Latina/os get from the immigrant generation and
the more assimilated they get, the weaker their sense of linked fate.

In *The Gatekeeper*, a sense of linked fate is forged when Fields directly experiences the social marginalization that the other immigrants endure. Moreover,
what happens to him happens to them, and vice versa. His inflicted punishment,
which affects them all, makes him feel directly obligated to them financially for
their loss of a week's pay and grateful for their help in tending to his leg. Even
though he has sought to curtail the mobility of Mexicans like them, he's now
dependent on them for his own mobility. However, for all that Fields and the
other Mexicans come to share in their relative servitude and helplessness, they
have distinct ideological perspectives on agency. After he is forced to go back
to work a day after having been shot, Fields has an exchange with José in which
José, noticing how upset and disengaged Fields is with the work, tells him,

You think I like it? You have to learn to live with what life gives you. Oye, Juan, you
can make a lot of money here. My son can now go to school. My wife has enough
money to feed him. You have to do what you can for your family. Then, then it's
not so bad. . . . My life . . . I know my place. Not like the Americans. They always
want something more. Verdad? They're always blaming their mother, or blaming their
father. Blaming the job, blaming the government. They're always trying to, to win.
Always trying to prove something. Me? I know my place.

José's perspective is clear—he is willing to sacrifice himself for the betterment of his family. This is a stance that Fields has never understood, as his hatred for his mother's actions prevented him from seeing them as sacrificial acts. In order to reverse his position on this point, the film repeats the mother and son scenario through Eva and her son, Carlos. After Eva is raped and Fields has been shot, he is lying nearby in a painful haze when he overhears Eva crying to Lenora that she worries what Carlos will think when he finds out his mother is a "whore." While later in the film Fields tells Eva that her son will never understand, by the end of the film, Fields has witnessed enough abuse and holds Carlos's hand at Eva's gravesite after she has been killed by the boss, implying that he now understands the costs of attempting to cross and raise children on the other side of the border.

Along with José's self-expressed martyrdom, the film presents Lenora's acceptance of her circumstances and disengagement with external wrongs. Once a dreamer who hoped for a life as an actress, Lenora tells Fields that now that she's older and lives in America, she has accepted that she will never fulfill her dreams. She advises, "Your life is not about making right what is wrong. It is better lived if you make who you are right. I'm with my family, my people. It doesn't matter what happens during the day. My God will always bless me in the morning and put me to rest at night." Both she and José advise Fields to accept things as they are and to disregard any inner turmoil. So accepting of their own oppression, they do not fight back against their oppressors and they reconcile their linked fate as one of indisputable economic and social subordination. In one sense, their views can be seen as pacifist and precluding of social change. In another sense, their fortitude in making the best of their circumstances speaks to their resilience.

Rather than deliver a scene in which Fields or the Mexicans triumph over their capturers, the film ends with Fields put on the defensive once the boss finds out who he really is, with José dead from toxic poisoning and with Eva killed by the camp boss for her treason in notifying Fields that the Border Patrol is looking for him. Fields is at least able to save Eva's body from the explosion that destroys the work shed. The film suggests that having experienced now what it is like to really be invaded and put in the position of fearing for one's life at the hands of another, Fields has come to a full reversal of his previous thinking. This is the implication of the final scene in which he is standing over Eva's body and holding Carlos's hand (Figures 7 and 8). Though Fields once

FIGURES 7 AND 8. Agent Fields and Carlos at Eva's grave. Source: *The Gatekeeper*, directed by John Carlos Frey (Screen Media, 2002).

scorned the laying of a "brown" finger on him, in this ending the film conveys through the power of touch and linked hands their linked fate. This character who has stood for a fractured self now stands in a unified circle, while the scene zooms into a full body shot with Fields and Carlos at the center. Both now motherless sons, man and boy are left standing together, even as the film gives no hints as to what the next step for them will be, whether Carlos will become an American, or whether Fields will now identify as Mexican.

While I have discussed the film's political significance, I do not discount the film's weaknesses. I can see why Jules Brenner of *Cinema Signals* thought Frey "unexpressive" and argues that the script is "not energetic enough." Similarly, Dave Kehr from the *New York Times* considers the script "stagnant" after the characters reach the labor camp.[34] The lack of emotion from Frey and the lack of action from the characters all leave more to be desired, and though Fields has a change of heart, the script does not allow him to demonstrate a change of action. At the end of the film he is only capable of reaction. This is a sellout redemption narrative played out only to the point at which we can witness the buildup of empathetic connection and the circumstances creating perceptions of linked fate but not the subsequent portrayal of what that would mean for Fields as a Border Patrol agent. He has been too guarded with his feelings to give us any indication as to what he would do next, now that he has had the experiences of Juan Carlos Mendoza.

John Carlos Frey's directorial statement, by contrast, provides a more complete narrative of transformation. Posted on his website, its opening paragraph introduces Frey's previous stance toward immigrants by describing his upbringing along the border. Born in Mexico but having a European American last name (his father is Swiss), Frey grew up in San Diego and tells us he "was raised with mostly 'Anglo' friends." He further relates, "I saw how Latinos were discriminated against in school and the media, and wanted to fit in. I didn't want to be from Tijuana, didn't want to be a Mexican immigrant." The next paragraph then explains what prompted his political awakening:

But as I witnessed on a nightly basis, the influx of hopeful migrants chased and hunted by border patrol vehicles and helicopters, a transformation had begun. With few stories about the border and the people who crossed it portrayed in film, I decided to write a screenplay about illegal immigration. While compiling the staggering facts and accounts of snobbery, misery, and death the desperate migrants faced, I grew personally affected. I learned to have respect for those who made the journey north to America. What must it be like to leave your family, your language, your heritage and your country for a menial job. . . . My compassion grew and my immature shame of my heritage and ethnicity diminished, and as I learned more about "my people" the more I was determined to complete the film.[35]

Delivering an account of shame turned into compassion, the paragraph culminates with a self-assessment: "These illegal aliens have taught me about myself. I have learned to embrace my culture, my heritage and place of birth. . . . My plan was to elevate my career, but the result has been a complete transformation and elevation of my personal perspective." Revealing that the film was born out of opportunism and the use of working poor immigrants in the process of self-identification, Frey's directorial statement creates a narrative of a status seeker transformed by the creative process and frames his story as one that goes from cultural denial and distancing to compassion and political involvement. While the film draws out a fantasy of switched allegiances, this statement portrays Frey's life trajectory as one that employed that fantasy to work through his own process of cultural realignment.

Together the director's statement and the final film product present narratives of transformation through empathetic connection. Bearing witness, acknowledging similarities or highlighting them, Fields and Frey mark attempts at articulating and representing how the development of linked fate for Latina/os entails identification with the undocumented immigration experience. While scholarship argues that the more assimilated Latina/os are, the weaker their sense of linked fate, *The Gatekeeper* imagines a scenario in which an assimilated ethnic gets access to immigrant experiences and gains empathy from the encounter. *The Gatekeeper* depicts immigration as an issue that, because of its ethical repercussions, has the potential to affect anyone irrespective of class differences.

## *MACHETE*'S ALLIES

*Machete* was released in September 2010 after months of rumors of its potential to incite a "race war." A fake trailer, leaked on May 5, 2010, through the website *Ain't It Cool News*, began with star Danny Trejo gruffly announcing,

"This is Machete with a special Cinco de Mayo message . . . to Arizona." Released just as the controversy over Arizona's SB1070 bill was coming to a head, the trailer showed images of Machete as a vengeful Mexican hit man hired to kill an anti-immigration senator, white characters spouting insults about Mexican immigrants, and even a scene in which Machete stands Moses-like in front of a group of Mexicans as they all raise their machetes in solidarity. The trailer, a leaked version of an early script, and then the film itself drew criticism from Internet talk show host Alex Jones, who categorized the film as the "equivalent of a Hispanic Birth of a Nation" since it "paints whites as all a bunch of murdering racists that are trying to kill Hispanic children and murder Catholic priests and crucify them" and ultimately called it "unspeakably evil."[36] Similarly, John Nolte of the conservative website *Big Hollywood* deemed the film "Dull, Convoluted, Racist and Anti-American" in that it depicts a revolutionary uprising occurring among Mexicans against Americans.[37] Other critics dismissed these nativist cries of racism and their warnings of violent outcomes, pointing to how the film mimics the conventions found in 1970s exploitation films, inasmuch as it celebrates the grindhouse genre with "bloody, near-cartoonish violence, a ludicrous plot, scenery-chewing performances and hammy dialogue."[38] Positive reviews pronounced the movie to be "self-aware, flashy and fun" (*New York Post*), "gleefully inflammatory" (*New York Times*), and full of "playful, pointed irony" (*The Boston Globe*).[39] Views of the film consequently ranged from those that projected righteous anger to others appraising the film as part of a highly stylized tradition, offering either ideological or formal critiques.

*Machete* was written by Texas native Robert Rodriguez and his cousin Alvaro Rodriguez and directed by Robert Rodriguez and Ethan Maniquis.[40] As noted, the film stars Danny Trejo as the title character, a socially conscious ex-Mexican Federale with vengeance driving him to punish those who have double-crossed him. This includes Rogelio Torrez (Steven Segal), leader of a Mexican drug cartel (who in the opening scene decapitates Machete's wife right in front of him) and a corrupt U.S. campaign advisor named Michael Booth (Jeff Fahey). After Machete migrates to Texas seeking work as a day laborer, he is approached by Booth, who is advisor to Senator McLaughlin (Robert De Niro), a politician seeking reelection through an anti-immigration platform. Posing as a businessman concerned about the effects of tighter border security

on the state's economy and appealing to Machete's Mexican heritage, Booth
hires Machete to shoot the senator, in hopes of garnering the senator sympathy votes and a pretext to enact more stringent immigration laws. Booth convinces Machete to shoot the senator for the "good of both our people." When
Machete learns of Booth's true identity, he is spurred to exact revenge, getting
help along the way from Luz (Michelle Rodriguez), a young Chicana running
a taco truck at a day laborer site. Luz heads an underground support network
for migrants using the code name of Shé. On both their tails is Agent Sartana
Rivera (Jessica Alba), a member of Immigration and Customs Enforcement
(ICE), otherwise known as "la migra," as she threateningly says to Machete at
one point in the film (Figure 9).

While the film's protagonist is Machete, its resolution exposing a corrupt
political ring would not be possible without the supporting character Rivera.
By including scenes in which she is pitted against the network aiding undocumented immigrants, the film spotlights Rivera's role as foe and sellout. Like
Agent Fields in *The Gatekeeper*, the first time Agent Rivera appears on screen
she is using a camera to document the undocumented, putting them at risk of
deportation. By including scenes of these border agents using cameras, the films
present their ideological antitheses: in contrast to these agents, the films are
documenting the people that exploit the undocumented. After Rivera finishes

FIGURE 9. Agent Sartana Rivera. Source: *Machete*, directed by Robert Rodriguez and
Ethan Maniquis (Twentieth Century Fox, 2010).

imprinting them on record, she saunters over to the taco truck, with the day laborers scattering as she nears. Luz and Rivera then have the following exchange:

Luz: You think what you do is right? Taking your brothers and sisters in? Deporting
    them back to their own personal hells?
Rivera: It's the law.
Luz: There are many laws.
Rivera: There sure are. Immigration fraud, aiding an illegal entry, unsanitary food
    prep. But you wouldn't know anything about that, would you? Can I get my tacos?

As a character who disregards accusations of ethnic betrayal, in this instance referenced through imagined familial relationships, Rivera is posed as the antithesis to Luz. This scene of them coming face to face was not, however, included in an earlier, undated script.[41] This initial friction helps convey the fact that two members of the same ethnic group can hold opposite political views, establishing Rivera as someone who is not sympathetic toward Mexicans and as someone who has the potential to derail the efforts of the migrant network.

Tough like Luz, Rivera is also ambitious, a trait often exercised at the expense of the undocumented. At one point Rivera describes to Machete how she made her way up the agency ladder from translator to agent in charge of investigations as evidence of how well the system works in the United States. Her class status is also highlighted by a still shot of her house, a distinctly modern and well-kept two-story home with a retro car in the driveway. The scene then cuts to the inside of her living room, which is decorated in pinks and reds. There are certificates mounted on the wall: subtle signals of her professional accomplishments. Rivera is working out to a Wii; a close-up of the video game shows a shirtless, big-muscled caricature of a border-crossing figure named "Tequila." The video game background depicts cacti, a van, and a trailer. The bottom of screen reads "Tequila vs. Sartana." And after delivering a few punches, Rivera knocks Tequila out, right before receiving a phone call from her boss telling her to start looking for Machete. By providing a glimpse of Rivera's home, exterior and interior, the film establishes the following: she makes a good living; she enjoys independence; and while her profession entails that she track down and deport the undocumented, she also plays at defeating border crossers. That is, her profession is not just a job to her: it is also part of her off-the-clock identity. Even during her lunch break she engages in an activity in which she can fight and get satisfaction from beating her Mexican opponents.

However, by the climactic scene in which Machete and the Mexicans take up arms against the vigilantes, Rivera has switched sides and is now fighting with the Mexicans and not against them. Leading up to this point, she has passed up several opportunities to sell them out in fulfillment of her job description. First, she learns of the network's extensive reach at Shé's headquarters, where Luz shows her their stockpile of arms but also photos of all the migrants who cannot be accounted for due to the vigilantes. Luz explains what the network is composed of: "All types. All races. Lawyers. Priests. Doctors. Homeboys. That's why they call it the network. The way we see it people risked everything to get here. But the system doesn't work. It's broken. So we created our own." Painting a multitiered portrait of the underground movement, which crosses race, ethnicity, and class, her words and the images of the missing migrants are sufficient to sway Rivera. When one of the members asks her, "So Migra, gonna burn us, huh? Turn us all in?" Rivera replies, "No. I'm going to walk away and pretend I didn't see any of this." Actively ignoring incriminating evidence of the network, she leaves and allows them to continue their work. Here she is not directly helping in their cause, but she is not hurting them either.

Her real change of action occurs when she defies her boss's orders and joins Machete in bringing down Booth, Senator McLaughlin, the vigilantes, and Rogelio Torrez. Machete gives her video evidence of how all four are working together to create a border that can be controlled by politicians and the drug cartels, and she reveals this all to her boss. Expressing incredulity, her commander urges her, "Listen to yourself. This man is an illegal alien. Illegal. As in against the law." At this point, after being exposed to evidence in support of the underground Mexican network and against the politico-drug cartel-vigilante network, Rivera makes this distinction: "Well there's the law, and then there's what's right. I'm going to do what's right." She then delivers the footage to a Spanish-language news station, a pivotal action that brings the conspiracy to light and leads to the dissolution of the more powerful network depicted in the film.

Rivera's trajectory toward political transformation does not stop or just revolve around ignoring and disseminating information. She assumes a leadership stance when the film gives her the opportunity to rally the Mexican laborers to Machete's cause. At first the Mexicans dismiss her pleas to help her, not trusting the agent who has been keeping tabs on them all. But suddenly Rivera jumps onto the hood of a car and yells,

Listen to me! Yes, I am a woman of the law. And there are lots of laws. But if they don't offer us justice, then they aren't laws! They are just lines drawn in the sand by men who will stand on your back for power and glory. Men who deserve to be cut down. It is time to erase their mierda lines and show these cabrones the meaning of true law. We didn't cross the border, the border crossed us!

Throwing in Spanish and finishing the speech by waving her fist in the air, Rivera has riled up her audience to the point at which they all join her in shouting, "Viva Machete!" With her striking a militant pose and repeating Luz's message about a broken system, the transformation from sellout to ally is complete. This figure of cultural betrayal now becomes the one expressing ethnic nationalism, and a member of the legal system charged with keeping order now mouths the rhetoric of violent resistance.

Notwithstanding the important role Sartana Rivera plays in the movie, her character was not included in earlier versions of the script. There was a similar character, but her name was Elektra Rivers and she was not designated as a Latina; furthermore, her most distinctive characteristic was that of having a promiscuous identical twin. While there is no official statement about the differences between the original script, which is readily available on the Internet, and the final filmed product, Alba has stated that she had a hand in revising her role. Though news items just report her efforts to make her character less sexualized, it is also possible that she had a hand in the politicization of her character.[42] In *Machete*, Alba chooses to play a character who appears to have sold out her community for career opportunities, a character who is also capable of changing her mind, and as a result assumes a more prominent place in the narrative.

In a real-life parallel, Alba was accused of being a sellout after reports emerged citing she had uttered culturally derogatory remarks such as "Mexicans spread all their seeds," "My grandfather tried to forget his Mexican roots," and "As a third-generation American, I feel as if I have finally cut loose."[43] To address these rumors, Alba gave an interview to *Latina* magazine in March 2008, which also recounted that reporters at the 2003 Annual Latin Grammy Awards shunned her for not speaking Spanish. The article stresses that Alba is in fact proud of being Latina even though her grandparents and parents tried hard to assimilate. "Whatever it takes, Alba is determined to give her children the cultural connection she yearned for as a child," the magazine reports. An adamant and pregnant Alba is even quoted as stating, "I'm excited for my baby to be brown. I just have to believe the dark gene is going to survive."[44] Whether or not the decision to play Sartana Rivera was a strategic move on her part to rehabilitate her image as a Latina actress, it is clear that Alba has known first-hand the advantages of assimilation but also the pressure to not come across as removed from Latina/os.

The film, in turn, is strategic in its use of Alba's character because it uses her position to make a commentary about the necessity of cross-class ethnic alliances. Machete, who is consistently socially conscious and vengeful, remains static as Rivera transforms. The film also employs her as a necessary component of the triangulated relationship that allegorizes the confluence of forces enabling exposure and retribution to occur in the film. In a film about the absurdities of prejudice toward the undocumented and the injustice of betrayal, the finale hits home the film's political messages after the villains have been documented and the betrayers have been punished or have reversed their politics. The women in the film, who complete a symbolic and romantic relationship with Machete, make these ends possible. Both Rivera and Luz have sexual relations with Machete, driven by desire for him and for justice. Machete's looks, unconventional in Hollywood, make him an unlikely romantic hero but play a role in how he appears as a formidable physical force. Luz, as organizer and leader of Shé, is meanwhile a catalyst of network capital. Completing the symbolic trio is Rivera, whose authority and credibility enable her to act as a reliable source of information. A collaboration between all three—physical force, social networks, and institutional credibility—in other words, working within and outside the system—is what allows for the exposure and defeat of the film's villains.

The inclusion of Rivera's character also enables the film to stage a scene in which her character offers Machete legality and he refuses:

Rivera: I called in some favors. Look at this. All the right papers; a real identity. You
    could start over, be a real person. (She puts the green card in his hand.)
Machete: Why do I want to be a real person . . . when I'm already a myth?

In refusing proof of citizenship, Machete refutes the reification of papers as proof of legitimization. But he also refuses on account of having achieved mythic status, privileging the power of fantasy over fact. His denial of the papers is a denial of geopolitical boundaries and an affirmation of the power of symbolic forms. His action suggests that he would not want an ID and risk the State tracking him down with it. If his mission is to protect and inspire hope in the disenfranchised, then his existence as a narrative bestows him with a more powerful identity, one spread by word of mouth rather than one pinned down to a specific address and social security number. The offering of papers and the subsequent refusal of them also occurs in *The Gatekeeper*. After Eva learns who Fields really is, she calls him a monster and asks how he can do what he does to his own people. Needing her help to notify his superiors because she has access to the boss's fax machine, Fields promises to help her secure her papers, but Eva rejects him, not trusting his promises or his help. Since such a scenario takes place in both films, it indicates that the Border Patrol characters serve as interlocutors for the films' interrogation and repudiation of citizenship. Rivera, like Fields, is strategically situated by the film to highlight structural divisions and abuses of power.

In showcasing the ideological reversals that the Mexican American Border Patrol agents undergo, both films include scenes in which there are also reversals of traditional gender representations. At the beginning of *The Gatekeeper*, Agent Fields is a hypermasculine, modern-day, rugged individual. But by the film's end he has been softened by an increasing acknowledgment of interdependence. In the image of Fields mourning over Eva's grave and holding Carlos's hand (Figure 10), he visually assumes a surrogate mother role. In contrast, the scene portraying Agent Rivera's transformation from foe to ally in *Machete* has her adopting a traditionally masculine, militant stance (Figure 11). The films layer on an added benefit to this political realignment, correlating it to a breakdown in gender norms.

Enacting visual representations that push against boundaries of gender and ethnic identity, the two actors that play these transgressing Border Patrol agents also share racial backgrounds that resist homogenizing impulses. Both Jessica Alba and John Carlos Frey have mixed Mexican and European ancestry and have played nonLatina/o characters in other films and television projects. The

FIGURES 10 AND 11. Agents post-transformations. Sources: *The Gatekeeper*, directed by John Carlos Frey (Screen Media, 2002), and *Machete*, directed by Robert Rodriguez and Ethan Maniquis (Twentieth Century Fox, 2010).

fact that they can "pass" as nonLatina/os makes their embodiment of cultural betrayal even more interesting, as mixed racial and cultural identity stands as the subtext of their on-screen presence. This mixed identity has potentially facilitated their careers in the entertainment industry and has surfaced in their adult lives as something they needed to reconcile in order to identify and, in Alba's case, to be identified with the Latina/o community. Underlying these films, therefore, is the unspoken relationship between mixed race and social mobility: that the former (specifically, light skin or features perceived to be white) enables the latter. In the two films, the mixed-race characters embody how these privileged socioeconomic positions could translate into political convictions that put them at odds with disadvantaged racialized ethnic communities. But they also appear in narratives that work to counter these effects. In analyzing the discourse around Black-white mixed-race identity, Michele Elam demonstrates that mixed-race postmillennial artists and writers have interrogated racial boundaries to unsettle and expand the significations of Blackness.[45] These films, too, try to challenge narrow perceptions of Latina/o identity by featuring mixed-race characters who ultimately do not stand in for cultural betrayal, yet simultaneously they rely on that associative link to highlight ideological transformations.

Despite these similarities, there is a major difference in the depictions of the male Border Patrol agent in *The Gatekeeper* and the female agent in *Machete*, stemming from their racial portrayals. Even though it is well-known that Alba is mixed race, Sartana Rivera is identified only as being of Mexican descent. By contrast, the fact that Frey's Adam Fields is mixed becomes one of his defining characteristics. This difference affects how the two Border Patrol agents play out their roles as cultural betrayers. Fields serves as the protagonist of his film, while Rivera is a supporting character; Fields is given the narrative space to reveal a psychological backstory and a deep interiority, while Rivera is not. Rivera's lack of interiority does not discount that she is a strong female, since her character follows the trend of how women are depicted in the film more generally. Robert Rodriguez, like his friend and collaborator Quentin Tarantino, is a fan of representing strong-willed women, equipped with guns and having the ability to use them. However, the women in *Machete* are limited not by their ability to use force but by their lack of nuance.

In *Machete*, nuance is bestowed on the titular character through both a backstory (the flashback of his wife killed by the drug cartel) and symbolic

status. He claims the latter by rejecting citizenship in favor of mythic standing. By contrast, the female character in the film who could also claim mythic
status rejects it. In one scene, Machete asks Luz if she is Shé, the purported
mythic leader of the underground migrant network. Luz denies that she is Shé
and instead asserts that Shé is everywhere. On one hand, by rejecting the label
she is disavowing individualist grandeur in favor of collective politics. On the
other hand, Machete's acceptance of mythic status does not detract from his
role in working on behalf of a collective. Luz's flatlining into a self-abnegating
female activist aligns with how Rivera as Border Patrol agent is circumscribed
psychologically. Even though one of the most obvious differences between *The
Gatekeeper* and *Machete* is in the gender of the Border Patrol agent, they share
the similarity of denying female characters symbolic or psychological complexity. Staging ideological realignments to deliver messages of cross-class politics,
the films nevertheless fluctuate between interrogating gender roles and adhering
to traditional filmic practices that privilege male-centered storylines in which
male characters have depth and nuance.

## CROSSING INVISIBLE BORDERS IN *SLEEP DEALER*

A futuristic sci-fi drama with unmistakable similarities to the two films just discussed, *Sleep Dealer* was directed by Alex Rivera and written by Rivera and David
Riker. It portrays Mexican American Rudy Ramirez (Jacob Vargas) switching
allegiances to redress wrongs he helped perpetuate against Mexicans. Ramirez
is a rookie drone pilot hired by Del Rio Water Inc. to inflict an attack on perceived "aqua terrorists" in a Mexican small town (Figure 12). The corporation
closely guards the dam that prevents any Santa Ana Del Rio residents from accessing river water without paying high amounts for it. Rudy is not a Border
Patrol agent in the way Fields and Sartana Rivera are—he is not commissioned
to keep immigrants from crossing the border. But he is still part of border-
policing endeavors. It is not explicit whether he is a U.S. soldier or working
solely for U.S.-based companies. Javier Duran argues that this ambiguity reveals

the blurring of lines between the state and global capital. Rudy is supposed to be a
U.S. armed forces soldier. He is in fact following a family tradition by joining the Air
Force. On the other hand, the film talks about "security forces" that guard private
companies' resources. When Rudy is called into action he is responding to an alert

FIGURE 12. Agent Rudy Ramirez. Source: *Sleep Dealer*, directed by Alex Rivera (Maya Entertainment, 2008).

sent from Del Rio Water Inc. . . . [I]t is never clear if these forces are U.S. nation-state forces or private guards.[46]

A kind of Border Patrol agent of the future, Rudy is critically central to this dystopic film, which plays out an extreme version of a world where people are, as Alex Rivera has stated, "connected by technology but divided by borders."[47] Tasked to maintain the border between private transnational capital and insurgent Mexican forces, Rudy completes his task but is driven by guilt to cross geographical and class borders in order to make amends. As a result, just as we see in *The Gatekeeper* and *Machete*, the gatekeeper figure undergoes this trajectory: inflicting injury on Mexicans, securing access to the (im)migrant experience, and then switching allegiances.

Rudy's drone attack ends up leading to the death of a Mexican farmer and the birth of an oppositional consciousness, his own and that of the farmer's son, protagonist Memo Cruz (Luis Fernando Peña). The night before, Memo had accidentally intercepted Del Rio Inc. communication frequencies while tinkering with his radios, trying to listen to conversations from the north as a way to escape the humdrum of rural life. The next day he and his brother watch live news coverage of the drone strike as it zooms in on the building where their father is. They run to warn him, but it is too late. After a slight hesitation, Rudy fires the missile that kills Memo's father. The father's death is then the catalyst for Memo's migration to Tijuana in search of work and for the portrayal of the film's main conceit—the use of "node workers" in the futuristic global economy. So called because they are laborers whose limbs have been inserted with nodes, they find work in the "sleep dealers," the factories along the border where they hook their nodes up to machines that then use their life energy to operate robots across the border. As a system enabling the migration of labor flow without actual laboring bodies, this economic future is made possible, asserts Lysa Rivera, by a "dying indigenous working class—by people like [Memo's] father."[48] Disconnected from his family and his family from egalitarian agrarian practices, Memo is then forced into an economic system that will use his labor until he connects with, of all people, Rudy and also another character, Luz (Leonor Varela).

In *Sleep Dealer*, as in *The Gatekeeper*, undercover undertakings are the means by which assimilated Mexican American characters gain insight into the experiences of people they would otherwise not come into contact with due to geographical, generational (as in generations removed from the immigrant experience), and class distances. Luz turns out to be the means by which Rudy gains access to Memo's migrant experiences, going undercover by hiding the fact that she is offering her interactions with Memo for sale. She is an aspiring journalist who makes her living by uploading her memories like blog entries, which viewers can access for a fee. She meets Memo on the bus ride to Tijuana and gets romantically involved with him while also uploading memories of him for purchase. It is revealed that the individual who has been commissioning her to attain more info from Memo is Rudy. He wants to know why Memo left Santa Ana, and when he finds out, he is wracked with guilt over his role in the drone strike. In *The Gatekeeper*, we saw how Agent Fields gained insight into the causes of and experiences of immigration by directly interacting with Mexican immigrants when he was undercover. By impersonating an undocumented immigrant, he engaged in class passing, a narrative scenario that has been critiqued for masking structural class divisions through a superficial cross-class awareness. Eric Schocket, for example, has argued that in late nineteenth- and early twentieth-century literature, white middle-class characters dressed up as part of the poor out of curiosity and to show that, despite class differences, they shared a common humanity. Schocket points out that these works convey that "difference can be effectively assimilated through sartorial means alone."[49] However, neither *The Gatekeeper* nor the other films communicate that bridging class differences would be so easy. *The Gatekeeper* shows that Fields has to actually experience what the immigrants experience before he starts to understand their linked fate. It is not a matter of just dressing like an immigrant, he has to work, have his mobility constrained, and suffer like the others at the labor camp. Even then, the fact that he has American citizenship and will have rights and access to resources that the others do not make it impossible to ignore the structural hierarchies dividing them. In *Sleep Dealer*, Rudy tries to bridge the distance between him and Memo when he acknowledges the geopolitical barriers between them. The film does not erase these differences; rather, it foregrounds them in order to impart a message about the value of transnational alliances.

What we then see in this film, which we do not see in the others, is a verbal confession of complicity. When Fields and Sartana Rivera gain ethical sensitivity, they act accordingly to bring down either the site of oppression (Fields and the labor camp) or the perpetrators of oppression (Rivera and the political network), which signals rather than states their regret over their previous politics. But *Sleep Dealer* stages an actual encounter between the Mexican American and the Mexican he has injured when Rudy approaches Memo in the food market:

I want to talk to you. When I was a kid, my dad brought me here to Tijuana to visit my grandma . . . before the wall. When I was young, all I wanted . . . was to be a soldier like my parents. So I signed up. And a second later, I'm a pilot. And my first mission was in Mexico. But I didn't expect . . . to see . . ."[50]

Here Rudy acknowledges the distance between the two in revealing that he is generations removed from living in Mexico, but he tries to shorten that distance by evoking his familial tie to Mexico, a tie that was interrupted by the wall as a geopolitical construction. He also tries to explain his involvement in the mission by framing it as following in his parents' professional path, attempting to convey that he had not fully thought out what his profession would entail. Rudy's short speech, however, is not immediately understood by Memo as a statement of remorse. At hearing that Rudy was the pilot, Memo bolts out of the market in fear. Rudy catches up with Memo on a bus and finally tells him, "I was following orders. And I'm sorry." Rudy's confession admits that culpability can stem from not questioning one's involvement in an exploitive system.

Rudy's character redemption occurs when, like Fields and Rivera, he switches allegiances to care for and work with Mexicans and when he engages in a heroic destructive act. In all three films, heroism is demonstrated and narrative closure is made possible by the destruction of an exploitive force: Fields destroys the labor camp, Rivera the corrupt political network, and Rudy the dam. Notably, Rivera uses information while the two males use explosives; apparently, the ammunition the three can wield conforms to gender typing. In *Machete* and *Sleep Dealer*, the heroic act is also a product of an unlikely triangulation.

Like *Machete*, *Sleep Dealer* presents another Luz upon which this triangle hinges. As their names bespeak, both shed light on the depicted crisis by having access to information: in *Machete* Luz knows Shé's operations and in *Sleep Dealer* Luz comes to know Memo's reasons for leaving Santa Ana. The revelation of this information connects Rivera to Machete and Rudy to Memo. And just as the trio in *Machete* has symbolic significance, so does the one in *Sleep Dealer*. Luz as light links Rudy to Memo, the destroyer to the builder. Initially, Rudy destroys out of ignorance and Memo builds (radios) out of a desire for escapism and exhibits apathy toward building anything out of his family's distressed farm. His symbolic role as builder is also referenced through his job as a node worker laboring in construction. But when Memo, Luz, and Rudy form a transnational alliance to link Rudy up to the drone a second time, their union enables Rudy to destroy for productive purposes and turns Memo into a movement builder who wants to stay connected to and ameliorate the injustices along the border. Hence the final scene of the film, showing Memo growing his own *milpa* and declaring that there is a home for him on the border if "I connect. And fight."

That this transnational alliance is facilitated and contingent on Luz's involvement is significant in light of the fact that she is an artist figure, one who compiles stories about the people she meets but who also makes a living off of them and becomes conflicted about doing so when confronted by Memo. Explaining to Memo how she began her narrative project, she tells of visiting her friend's village and how she wanted to share what she had seen so she uploaded the memory and it sold. Memo begins to question the ethics of this endeavor when he asks, "She invited you to her home and you sold the memories?" Being self-reflexive here about the ethics of representing and profiting from the stories of other people, the film presents Luz and her narrative project as playing a crucial role in linking people together. She defends her stance as a connecter and mediator in explaining how she felt about her first experience traveling to her friend's village: "Going there—for me—was like crossing an invisible border. I hate that there's so much distance between people . . . The only thing nodes are good for, are to destroy that distance . . . to connect us . . . to let us see." Memo reminds her of this stance when trying to convince her that they should trust Rudy in order to destroy the dam: "Luz, think about it—remember what you told me about crossing to the other side? That's what he did. He crossed over. All we have to do is help him." The parallels between the film and Luz's function in the film become clear when we consider that both are mediating the experiences of others for political purposes. Just as Luz's mediation helps Rudy cross over to the other political side, so does Alex Rivera's film mediate to raise awareness among a viewership who could potentially cross over ideologically as well.

## IMMIGRATION PROBLEM FILMS

By portraying upward mobility as assimilation, all three films have inherited some features of what film scholar Charles Ramírez Berg has identified as the "assimilation narrative" characteristic of "Chicano social problem films."[51] Classifying Chicano social problem films as part of the social problem film genre that developed from the 1930s to the 1960s,[52] Berg outlines the assimilation narrative's conventions whereby success in the U.S. class structure translates into treason and failure as a member of an ethnic group, and failure to fully assimilate actually means moral success and collective ethnic cohesion. In other words, to succeed as an assimilated subject requires the characters in these films to adopt certain individualistic American values, such as aggression, ambition, and opportunism—values that lead to their alienation from their communities of origin. In the end, however, these films reconcile these tensions by having the protagonists fail at their individualistic endeavors, as high-profile lawyers, boxers, and so on, in order for them to reintegrate into their original communities and prove incorruptible. While such a trajectory can read as noble, Berg argues that, insofar as "these films preach class and economic stasis,"[53] they actually help reinforce the status quo that keeps ethnic people geographically and socially limited:

The best course of action is for ethnic/immigrant/class/gender Others to go home to their old ethnic neighborhood, the locus of all that is good and true. Abandoning their aspirations of mainstream integration and success, these characters can remain content in the knowledge that they have gained morality, a prize far greater than fame or fortune.[54]

Being a loyal and moral ethnic person means giving up any creative, profitable, or individualistic endeavor, which Berg reads as self-sacrificial and which glorifies passive cooperative values for ethnics.

Berg's analysis of assimilation narratives provides a useful historical comparison; the tradition being expanded in *The Gatekeeper*, *Machete*, and *Sleep Dealer* is the social problem film centered on immigration and one that rewrites the assimilation narrative, as these too are exploring what it means to assimilate at the expense of collectivist values. These films similarly reintegrate ethnic outliers to the fold, after showing how their politics are incompatible with those of their community at large. However, this reintegration is solely political and not depicted as geographical or socially limiting. Historically, this is significant since it takes into account that Latina/os are no longer circumscribed to ethnic enclaves, nor do these films espouse a return to the barrio as the only ethical course of action.

The employment of Border Patrol characters to enact fantasies of switched allegiances marks an evolution of Chicana/o cultural production in exploring oppositional politics through sellouts—characters who have traditionally not been depicted as undergoing growth. They demonstrate that the sellout redemption narrative is utilized to different ends from the traditional sellout narrative—in which characters serve as cautionary tales. The sellout redemption narrative instead uses the characteristics of those in intermediary positions—the very positions they have attained as a result of mainstream incorporation—to the advantage of their ethnic communities. Rather than deploying the sentiments of fear and disappointment of betrayal to communicate the need for political engagement, they draw on the potential for group consciousness to emerge in those that at first seem like unlikely proponents, for a reconsideration of the current legal system by those that are in key positions to speak out against it.

## POLICING ALLEGIANCES

Having looked at Latina/o films that present sellout redemption narratives, I now turn to the question of whether the same pattern emerges in representations of Black law enforcement characters. Films that represent people of color in law enforcement positions speak to a demographic class reality: government jobs, such as those in the criminal justice system and in the armed forces, have been proven avenues of class mobility for people of color because of federal injunctions against discrimination in these sectors and recruitment efforts targeting racial minorities. These are also jobs desired for providing stability and status. However, historically, status has been derived from being on the side of those doing the policing and not on the side of those being policed.

Like Latina/o Border Patrol agents to other Latina/os, Black police officers have had, or have been perceived as having, an antagonistic relationship to Black communities. For instance, one of the most popular Black films depicting urban violence, *Boyz n the Hood* (1991), showcases a scene of police cruelty toward Black men, with a Black officer doing the terrorizing. W. Marvin Dulaney's history of Black police officers in the United States helps us understand the roots of this antagonism. He recounts that the first African American police officers were part of the New Orleans city guard in the early 1800s and were able to garner an elevated status by policing other Blacks. Dulaney explains, "If the duties of citizenship required patrolling, policing, and suppressing 'black' slaves, the 'free persons of color' in New Orleans were willing to assume such tasks in order to improve their own precarious position in a society where skin color usually determined status and condition of servitude"[55] The hierarchy of power in which Black officers work, which requires an allegiance to the state and which may pit them against communities of color, continues to be a heated issue. In 2014, nationwide protests in the aftermath of Michael Brown and Eric Garner's deaths were directed at the history of violence that white officers have inflicted on Black men, but Black police officers were not exempt from criticism, as taunts of "sellout" and "Uncle Tom" at demonstrations charged Black officers with being complicit.[56] These criticisms were attempts to police allegiances, to induce Black officers into seeing their jobs as ones opposed to the collective interests of policed Black bodies. It is a catch-22, since this rhetoric accuses Black officers of being functionaries of a racist system, and yet one of the troubling facts that arose in the Michael Brown case was how few Black officers (four out of fifty-three) there were in Ferguson, Missouri, a city that is majority Black. The fraught position of Black officers is apparent in filmic practices as well, with betrayal not just an issue of ethnic solidarity, but a punishable offense.

Observing how frequently Black actors appear in law enforcement roles, journalist Wesley Morris has remarked, "If you're a black actor in Hollywood, you've probably played a cop."[57] Despite the frequency of such roles, sociologists Franklin T. Wilson and Howard Henderson found through their content analyses of films in the core cop genre from 1971 to 2011 "a disturbing 40-year trend of African American municipal police officers being depicted as either comedic fodder or sellouts to the African American community."[58] They found only four films that represent in detail the double marginality that black officers face, that show how hard it is to be accepted by either the Black community or the police force: *In Too Deep* (1999), *Shaft* (2000), *Training Day* (2001), and *Dirty* (2005). They cite *Training Day* and *Dirty* as two films that explicitly portray Black officers as sellouts, showing "officers that abuse their powers in an effort to gain status within the police force and power over the community rather than serving the community."[59] The article does not delve into the depictions of the sellouts or their outcomes, but looking at the films they name, we can see that sellouts do not fare well at all.

It appears that if Black officers are depicted as sellouts, there is no room for growth, no room for them to change their minds or motives. In *Training Day* and *Dirty*, starring Denzel Washington and Cuba Gooding Jr., respectively, the Black officers have presumably sold out twice, since they have subsumed any ethnic or professional allegiances in their pursuit of status and wealth. For these betrayals, they pay with their lives. Washington's Alonzo Harris and Gooding Jr.'s Salim Adel are not killed by Blacks or fellow officers, but their trespasses against both groups leave them in a defenseless state by the time they are killed—Harris by the Russian mafia and Adel by a Latino gang. In the newest *Shaft*, Black officer Jimmy Groves (Ruben Santiago-Hudson) betrays Shaft (Samuel L. Jackson) and his partner Detective Carmen Vasquez (Vanessa Williams). For his betrayal, he is killed by Vanessa Williams's character. Rather than redemption, Black officers depicted as sellouts remain static, as in *Boys n the Hood*, or are killed off.

The scenario of switched allegiances tends to be foreclosed for Black officers, except in one case: *The Glass Shield*, directed by Charles Burnett and based on a true story.[60] Achieving critical acclaim with *Killer of Sheep* (1977) and *To Sleep with Anger* (1990), independent Black film producer Charles Burnett teamed up with Miramax for his fourth feature film, *The Glass Shield*, so that the project would have wider distribution. It was a reportedly troubled partnership, as Miramax demanded that Burnett redo the film's ending to be less bleak and ambiguous, delayed the film's release by a year, and then showed it only in limited venues. Writing about why the film was undervalued by Miramax, film critic Jonathan Rosenbaum surmised that "what's confusing about *The Glass Shield* . . . is that it's a police procedural that refuses to play most of the Hollywood games associated with police procedurals: there's no profanity, little violence, not much humor, and just a smattering of action."[61] Although the film was produced in the mid-1990s, when movies like *Boyz n the Hood* (1991) and *Juice* (1992) had helped cement expectations for urban dramas, Amy Abugo Ongiri notes that while it is concerned with police brutality, it portrays violence "as institutional and systemic rather than spectacularized in the manner of Hollywood."[62] By breaking from expectations for police procedurals or urban dramas, Burnett's film was not a commercial success, but it offers a rare depiction of an ethically conflicted Black law enforcement character who has the chance to grow over the course of the film.

The film centers on rookie police officer John Johnson ("J.J."), played by Michael Boatman, who has just joined the all-white Edgemar Sheriff's Station in Los Angeles (Figure 13). Idealistic J.J. has always wanted to be a cop, so he shrugs off racist comments and mistreatment. In one scene, the other rookie

FIGURE 13. J.J.'s first day. Source: *The Glass Shield*, directed by Charles Burnett (Lionsgate, 1995).

in the department, Deborah Fields (Lori Petty), who experiences sexism and anti-Semitism throughout the film, jokes with J.J. about how now the station has another person to pick on. J.J. reassures her that he was picked by the commissioner's office, to which Fields laughs and replies, "We were both picked for our jobs. That and a dollar will get you on the bus." The film then traces J.J.'s transformation as he comes to ally with Fields to uncover the rampant corruption in their station.

Their alliance is prompted by J.J.'s realization that his unflinching loyalty to his fellow officers has made him complicit in the false arrest of Teddy Woods (Ice Cube), an innocent man being framed for murder. J.J.'s indoctrination into the station's racism and corruption culminates with Woods's arrest. J.J. happens to be nearby when a white officer named Bono (Don Harvey) pulls into a gas station after Woods and starts interrogating him, looking for reasons to search his car. Bono finds out that Woods has a warrant out for a traffic violation, and after threats about taking possession of his car, he gets Woods to reveal that he has his father-in-law's gun in the glove compartment. The gun is later used to frame Woods for the murder of a white woman who was in a car with her husband when two Black males allegedly attempted to rob them and shot her. At first, J.J. is proud to have been part of the team that arrested Woods, but he later learns that his police report has been altered. An earlier scene shows the commander berating J.J. for his police reports, telling him he has seen "three-year-olds who spell and use grammar better," so after the Woods arrest, another scene depicts J.J. meticulously filling out the report. When he sees that the serial number he wrote down for the gun on the report has been whited out, a new number superimposed on top, J.J. can no longer trust his fellow officers so completely. This prompts J.J. to start asking questions about a Black man who died while in police custody. An older officer reveals bits of information that J.J. and Fields piece together to unveil that some officers are blackmailing high-profile city officials so that they can get away with their excessive violence. By the end of the film, J.J. has a complete change of stance toward his fellow officers, and directly confronts them after he finds out that they have put Fields in the hospital in retaliation for her investigations (Figure 14).

Similar to *Machete* and *Sleep Dealer*, but here in a much quieter fashion and without explosives, a multiperson coalition leads to the dismantling of an oppressive force. With the help of a Black lawyer, J.J. is able to get the district

FIGURE 14. J.J. challenges the status quo. Source: *The Glass Shield*, directed by Charles Burnett (Lionsgate, 1995).

attorney to investigate the station, which leads to the prosecution of several officers and the closing down of the station. Despite an ending that suggests justice has prevailed, the film offers no glamorous resolutions when it comes to J.J. The text at the end of the film tells us that the real J.J. left the job after he was convicted of perjury during the Teddy Woods trial.

If J.J. cannot be a complete hero, it is because he switched from observer to participant when he backed up Bono in the lie Bono made up to avoid being accused of racial profiling. After hearing advice from his lawyer, Bono tells J.J. that the Woods case might be thrown out if he does not claim having just cause for interrogating Woods. He tells J.J. that he stated that he pulled Woods over for making an illegal turn. At this point J.J. has complete trust in his fellow officers, so he offers to back up the lie and declares, "I got no sympathy for lowlife scum. So uh I'll tell them he ran four or five red lights." A "Wrong Way" sign is visible in the background as they discuss Woods's imagined illegal turn—and as J.J. makes an unethical one.

The film layers its ethical arguments further through various allusions to water. The moment Bono and J.J. arrest Woods, a rendition of the Negro spiritual "Wade in the Water" can be heard faintly in the background. One popular interpretation of the song's chorus—"Wade in the water / Wade in the water, children / Wade in the water / God's gonna trouble the water"—reads the lyrics as providing coded information used by runaway slaves urging them to get into bodies of water to avoid detection. This interpretation of the song links Teddy Woods's arrest to a longer history of racial criminalization. The other interpretation of the song—that the chorus is a biblical reference encouraging an act of purification and healing—applies to the other Black male in this scene by speaking to J.J.'s involvement in criminalizing Woods.

If the teleology of the film is to get J.J. purified and redeemed for his complicity in criminalizing Woods, it underscores this message by correlating his fellow officers with allusions to leisure activities that keep them beside of or on top of water but not in it. When the station commander orders the officers not to talk to anyone about the case involving the death of the man who died in jail, an officer turns to J.J. to warn him, "Remember that, J.J. You're one of us, not a 'brother.' You know, you oughtta learn how to surf. Know what I mean?" The officer is essentially trying to police J.J.'s allegiance to his fellow officers, and J.J.'s response, "I *got* your surfboard," uttered with a pointed look, discloses that he understands and resents the insinuations of disloyalty. Later in the film, after J.J. and Fields have learned the truth about their fellow officers, we also learn that the commander enjoys deep-sea fishing when the officers celebrate his birthday and present him with a fishing rod. J.J. and Fields watch the whole scene through a window in the back room, their silhouettes visible through blinds that demarcate how much they are outsiders to this fraternal celebration. Out of the three scenes in which white officers are associated with water-based leisure activities, the one featuring one of the ringleaders of the corruption, Detective Baker (Michael Ironside), in his home, connects with the Negro spiritual in linking the present corruption with a history of racialized violence stemming from slavery. The scene reveals Baker having a conversation with his wife about a cruise her family wants to take that he resents because of the cost. After the conversation, he resumes work on his hobby; a close-up shot shows us the model ship he is painting inside a glass bottle. Here, the film offers another meaning to the title, which most directly refers to J.J.'s badge in the film's final scene when J.J.'s fiancée tells him that she "can see through that shield [because] It doesn't hide the evilness." In the case of the model ship, the glass shields but also displays, revealing Baker's work on an object laden with symbolic significance in alluding to the slave ship and the middle passage. Like the Negro spiritual, the ship references past racial violence and its continuation in the present in another form that is also systemic and sanctioned. The film thus follows J.J.'s complete immersion into the Edgemar station culture, the station that is close to the sea but not in it, and his subsequent immersion into acts that would be truly purifying and healing, even as they cost him his job.

*The Glass Shield* stands out as a rare example of a Black law enforcement character who gets redeemed, which raises the question, What factors influence the way in which Black officers depicted as sellouts remain static or get killed off instead of redeemed? One factor is narrative precedent: since the slave narrative tradition, writers have shown how the actions of traitors lead not only to a sense of betrayal, but also to the deaths of other Blacks. Another factor is that the complexity of being a racial minority who is also in law enforcement is not a story embraced by Hollywood. To centralize these stories would be to explore the effects of white supremacy and capitalism, which creates hierarchies of status and economic gain at the expense of racialized people and the poor. And, as film scholar Ed Guerrero states, "the commercial cinema system has continued to stock its productions with the themes and formulas dealing with black issues and characters that are reassuring to the sensibilities and expectations of an uneasy white audience. These filmic images tend to mediate the dysfunctions of a society unable to deal honestly with its inequalities and racial conflicts, a society that operates in profound state of racial denial on a daily basis."[63] In addition to not centralizing stories that would make mainstream audiences uneasy, the depiction of Black sellout officers killed off by other officers or other ethnic people helps to maintain the status quo by imparting the message, as Jared Sexton has stated about the movie *Training Day*, that "the police are a self-regulating institution unrelated to the interference of public scrutiny and immune to calls for reform."[64] Even if Black writers and directors want to present alternative narratives, they are restricted in what they can produce because of the racial disparity in film financing. Referring to how "white men continue to direct more than 90 percent and finance almost 100 percent of Hollywood's output," Sexton comments that "for the most part, black cinematic practice in the United States, especially if it is critical and/or independent, continues to take place beneath the radar of the major institutions of mass media and popular culture."[65] *The Glass Shield* had a Miramax partnership, but it still struggled for distribution, its complexity mirroring the complexity of life as a Black police office and too unconventional for mass distribution. If we look at the Latina/o immigration films, we see that two of the three, *The Gatekeeper* and *Sleep Dealer*, were independent films, made with low budgets and having limited exposure. While *Machete* was made with a big Hollywood budget and was commercially successful, Robert Rodriguez's film is self-referential about its status as an entertainment film. The farcical nature of the film helps diffuse its contentious scenarios. Furthermore, the fact that the immigration films are set along the border might make them less of a felt-threat, as opposed to depictions of Black officers critiquing the status quo, which could be set in any city.

In short, sellout redemption narratives—which feature middle-class characters of color rejecting mainstream views—tend not to be depicted in mainstream movies because they turn attention onto the economic and social structures that necessitate those views for maintenance. Instead of completely vilifying individuals who have "sold out," these films task us to examine the ideologies that produced these individuals, shifting critique away from the individual to broader systemic patterns. These films also contend with the realities of class and ideological heterogeneity within racialized ethnic populations. Rather than reject characters who stand in for assimilation, the immigration films face the reality that Latina/os can be generationally removed from the immigration or working-class experience and represent assimilated Latina/os reintegrated into an affective community for political purposes. While *The Gatekeeper* represents violence toward ethnics as driven by self-loathing and personal animosity, *Machete*, *Sleep Dealer*, and *The Glass Shield* explore a scenario possibly more representative of why people in intermediary positions act as gatekeepers: they are just doing their jobs. Showing how a lack of awareness and naïveté have effects as dangerous as overt racial animosity, these films foreground scenes of awareness and participate in creating awareness themselves. They visualize gatekeepers becoming mediators to redirect what and who gets policed.

# EPILOGUE

Upward mobility narratives remain a popular genre laden with values about the best way to be and act in the world, which is why it is vital that we examine them. This study analyzed various representations of upward mobility from the 1940s to the 2000s, when existing disparities and opening opportunities led to proliferous African American and Mexican American texts reflecting and testing ways of self- and communally identifying, disseminating knowledge about inequalities, and addressing communities in need. In how these texts depict and model ways of dealing with socioeconomic tensions, they contribute to what sociologists call the "minority culture of mobility." I argue that the *tax* on upward mobility, which registers the saliency of race and ethnicity, is a catalyst for this cultural production. Moreover, this tax manifests as a formal feature of texts through allegorical pathways of social incorporation: status seekers, gatekeepers, mediators, and conflicted artists. They exemplify ways of dealing with race and class and dramatize how economic and social group boundaries are formed, reinforced, or permeated.

The status seeker allegorizes the desire for dominant group membership. Because markers of difference can prevent economic and social mobility, historically there have been incentives to distance oneself from racialized peoples, the poor, and immigrants. In many ethnic upward mobility narratives, status seekers are not just social climbers, they are marked by the group's history of racialization and the resulting socioeconomic effects. Their aspirations are driven by desires to not have a denigrated, pathologized, or criminalized status. The Black Bostonians in *The Living Is Easy* distance themselves from poorer and dark-skinned Blacks and recent arrivals; Undine in *Fabulation* pretends her working-class family died in a fire; Memo in *My Family* and Agent Fields in *The Gatekeeper* identify against the immigrant generation, and Richard Rodriguez insists he is not a minority in *Hunger of Memory*. Status seekers might be critiqued within and outside the text for upholding values that create intragroup divisions created by colorism, materialism, xenophobia, and elitism; however, they represent proven paths of social incorporation into spheres of power and financial gain. Thus texts might be critical of these endeavors or exhibit ambivalence about the tactics taken by individuals and communities. Furthermore, just as characters can seek an elevated status, so can texts themselves, as we saw with mass-market depictions of a racialized ethnic middle class in *George Lopez* and *black-ish*. Articulations of status panic occur when characters fear reduced status due to dominant perceptions of the racialized group. These moments exemplify how the text as a whole is attempting to counter class-inflected connotations of race and ethnicity that can be reinforced by the mainstream and by the ethnic group.

Since criteria for inclusion can entail limiting or barring others from accessing the same resources, status seekers may correlate with gatekeepers. The criteria for inclusivity can be explicit, as embodied through the Border Patrol agents who guard national boundaries, or implicit, as internalized by characters who adhere to codes of conduct and values that deem certain people more worthy or acceptable. The Barbadian Association in *Brown Girl, Brownstones* is portrayed as gatekeeping in the latter manner by barring African Americans and discouraging members from pursuing nonprofessional vocational paths. Because people of color can benefit from working against other people of color, portrayals of middle-class ethnics as gatekeeping sellouts and/or suffering from false consciousness have been integral to the formations of politically conscious ethnic identities. Any group formed for collective action necessitates policing mechanisms to maintain group boundaries, which is why gatekeeping can come from within the group as well. Dre comically embodies an ethnic gatekeeper in *black-ish*; throughout the series, he tries to reinforce the idea that Black culture is working-class culture, yet his family continuously resists his definitions of Black authenticity.

In contrast to status seekers and gatekeepers, mediators model ways of working between groups. Because giving back to a racial-ethnic collective could be enabled through education, one's vocation, or institutional affiliation, many postwar texts grapple with ways of reinterpreting upward mobility and middle-class status to break from the reward system of white supremacy and American individualism. Texts that portray mediators suggest that class mobility can be employed to the benefit of the racialized ethnic group, though texts might endorse radically different ways of being a mediator. *The Spook Who Sat by the Door* proposes that middle-class status can be used strategically to enact revolutionary upheaval, while *Sons of Darkness, Sons of Light* ultimately endorses institutional reform rather than armed insurgency. The ethical impulse in much of ethnic cultural production translates into frequent depictions of mediators at different stages of awareness, as evident through thirteen-year-old Estrella in *Under the Feet of Jesus*, who is just starting to come into political consciousness. It is also worth considering texts that do not fashion mediators, and here I bring up the example of the short-lived ABC sitcom *Cristela*, which premiered in the 2014–2015 season but did not make it to a second season. It featured the Mexican American comedian Cristela Alonzo playing an aspiring lawyer living with her sister-in-law's family while she interns at a law firm. In one episode she is asked to help out on the defense case of a landlord who will not rent to minorities.[1] When her sister asks her why she "would work so hard to help out someone like that?" Cristela answers, "I'm not. I'm working hard for someone like me," explaining that her boss will be picking one of the interns to sit with counsel during the trial and she wants to be that person. No one presses her on that comment, and the show does not suggest she is torn about helping to defend a racist if it means personal advancement. As Mexican American lawyers, she and Acosta's Brown Buffalo are not only generations and genres apart, but apart also in how much they feel accountable to contest racial and class inequities.

Texts may posit artists as mediators, ones who filter and offer stories or perspectives that have been censored or devalued because of hierarchies of knowledge and power. The economic realities of being an artist—the fact that artists are more likely to come from higher-income households and yet the imperative many artistic works express in critiquing economic striving—can lead to portrayals of conflicted artists. Selina in *Brown Girl, Brownstones* and Willie in *Linden Hills* exhibit aesthetic inclinations that channel critiques against status seeking and materialism, yet they are also from marginalized communities; the texts render them conflicted given that the artistic path is uncertain, as is the best way to achieve collective gains. The underrepresentation of people of color in multiple realms is a source of conflict in *The Revolt of the Cockroach People*, which depicts an artist who wants to represent an ethnic community through writing but is needed as a legal mediator as well. Moreover, he faces accusations of selling out for wanting to write a book and profit from the Chicano movement struggle. Because ethnic artists can be symbolically and structurally between groups, this positionality can be framed as either an opportunity, a source of anxiety, or a burden, sometimes all three. Serving as an artistic mediator can enable an artist to raise awareness about inequalities, as *The House on Mango Street* embraces. But texts that leave their protagonists in the state of youth can also circumnavigate the kinds of contradictions that can stem from class mobility for an ethnic artist and mediator, including profiting by depicting poverty, exerting a public voice by depicting the "voiceless," and gaining representative status because of underrepresentation. Sandra Cisneros's book of autobiographical essays brings up the "paradox for a working-class writer" in expressing "that we are never more exiled from our real homes, from the blood kin we have honored in our pages, than when we have drifted away from them on that little white raft called the page."[2] In another vein, *Erasure*'s Monk chafes against being a racial representative but is still willing to sell out to industries capitalizing on ideas about racialized culture. Race and ethnicity can be a source of currency, and artists earn symbolic and material wages for appealing to ethnic group concerns and/or market tastes, but—to return to a central metaphor in this book—these wages are taxed; the tax informs narrative choices and also gets expressed through assessments of the status of the art through language, such as *authenticity, universality, selling out.*

Artists and mediators can get juxtaposed to status seekers and gatekeepers, or texts can dramatize ways in which the latter can transform into the former. Such maneuvers signal how upward mobility narratives imagine scenarios that might mitigate the effects of intragroup class and ideological divisions. As Crystal Parikh argues, depictions of "Betrayals . . . can perform a cultural critique of the social conditions by which the minority subject comes into being and of the possibilities for agency and transformation available to that subject once it has come into being."[3] In ethnic upward mobility narratives betrayals can enact stories of redemption or caution. With the possibility that socioeconomic gain might influence a person's belief in linked fate and commitment to solidarity, past and contemporary ethnic texts do the discursive work of reintegration or excision: transforming or punishing those who have opted for individualist versus collectivist politics.

Texts can also show us how individuals embody multiple types, troubling assumptions that one pathway is more pure or uncompromised than the others. Arnold Rampersad's biography of Ralph Ellison is a striking example.[4] The portrait of Ellison that emerges is of an individual who was honest about his intense desire for status. He strived for universal acclaim and relished the perks that came with increased fame and money after the publication of *Invisible Man* in 1952. Indeed, he saw his status as a way to be a mediator of race relations in that "he believed that his art, and the prestige that came with it, was to be his main contribution [in the civil rights movement]. As the walls of segregation fell, he also saw himself bringing a refined Negro presence to places of power hitherto reserved for whites."[5] However, rather than transform spaces that were historically exclusionary, he accepted and upheld group boundaries, doing little to admit other Blacks or women, even when he was encouraged to do so. He enjoyed being the only Black person in elite spaces, whether it was a social club, a fellowship, or a philanthropic board. Rampersad writes that he was "the token Negro. He seemed proud of that fact. He saw himself as eminently qualified for these positions, as indeed he was, but he also believed that very few other blacks were. He was gatekeeper to both blacks and whites."[6] Upward mobility narratives often have a morality tale embedded in them, and in Rampersad's account, the outcome of Ellison's status seeking and gatekeeping becomes clear in the tortured relationship Ellison had with his second novel, which he worked on for forty years and which was published posthumously as *Juneteenth* in 1999. Rampersad assesses that "As a novelist, he had lost his way. And he had done so in proportion to his distancing of himself from his fellow blacks."[7] He quotes Toni Morrison, who offers a parallel view that it was this distancing and the internalization of racism that severely affected his art: "One contrasts the largeness of *Invisible Man* with its broad canvas and its wide range of effects, of insight, with the narrowness of his public encounters with blacks. The contemporary world of late twentieth-century African Americans was largely inaccessible, or simply uninteresting to him as a creator of fiction. For him, in essence, the eye, the gaze of the beholder remained white."[8] Ellison profited symbolically and materially from white approval and the Black Power movement, though he distanced himself from the latter. Even as his book sales and speaking engagement invitations increased as a result of the Black liberation struggle, he did not want to affiliate with overt political action, so invested was he in the reward system of the status quo. In how the social field was changing, yet his habitus did not, his conflict could be read as one of hysteresis, with Rampersad's biography chronicling the increasing temporal disconnect. One of the contributions of ethnic upward mobility narratives is that they enable us to see how cultural producers and characters make sense of the social and economic hierarchies that inform lives, politics, and art.

I end with a final textual example that reveals how necessary it is to understand the ideological work that ethnic upward mobility narratives do by briefly discussing the 2006 film *The Pursuit of Happyness*. If Benjamin Franklin and Horatio Alger cowrote a contemporary rags-to-riches screenplay about a man's rise from lowly origins to stock broker success, it may have looked a lot like this film.[9] Jeffrey Decker has argued that from the twentieth century onward, narratives about self-making moved away from the cultivation of moral "character" as exemplified in writings by Franklin and Alger to narratives about "personality" and outward markers of the self.[10] While another contemporary film about the finance world, *The Wolf of Wall Street* (2013), fits Decker's paradigm by offering an example of a protagonist in need of character cultivation through the rise and fall of a personality-rich but morally poor stockbroker, *The Pursuit of Happyness* helped extend the tradition of character-based narratives of success into the twenty-first century with a Black protagonist fortifying his character through self-discipline, hard work, and education. Directed by Gabriele Muccino and starring Will Smith, this box office hit was released the same year as Chris Gardner's memoir of the same name. It is no surprise when a film differs from the book version of accounts, but considering the two in relation to one another in this case reveals the extent of and significance of the film's post-race fantasy about class mobility—the countercurrent to all the texts analyzed in this book.

In the film, Chris (hereafter I refer to the protagonist of the film as Chris and the real-life person as Gardner) is a struggling salesman peddling medical devices in San Francisco during the 1980s and trying to support his family. After spotting a red Ferrari he admires and striking up a conversation with its owner to ask him what he does for a living, he is inspired to become a stockbroker. His wife, Linda (Thandie Newton), however, is unsupportive of his chasing another dream after his current entrepreneurial one has left them in dire financial straits. She ends up leaving Chris and their five-year-old son, Christopher Jr. (Jayden Smith). Chris takes an internship at a stockbrokerage in hopes of landing a permanent position, and the drama increases as he tries to balance his intense internship training, selling medical devices to pay rent, and taking care of his son, all on his own. At his lowest point, he and his son end up homeless and find shelter in a subway bathroom. As a result of his determination and hard work, however, Chris stands out as an exemplary intern, and by the end of the film earns a job as a stockbroker. The film takes creative license with only a short slice from Gardner's life. The memoir, on the other hand, traces his upbringing in Milwaukee during the 1950s and 1960s, his stint in the Navy after high school working as a medic in North Carolina, his journey to San Francisco to join a medical research laboratory, his job selling medical equipment, and then his success in the finance world first in San Francisco and then New York, which culminates in the establishment of his own brokerage firm in Chicago, Gardner Rich & Co., in 1987.[11]

As part of its fictionalization, the film makes Chris into a post-race hero who never experiences racial conflict. If it is Chris's inner character that counts, his appearance is an issue only when he temporarily shows signs of not fitting in with the white-collar environment he hopes to enter, not because of his skin color but because of his sartorial situation. In the pivotal interview scene in which Chris meets with the partners at the investment firm to try out for a spot in their internship program, he has to wear the same clothes he had on the night before—when he was arrested for unpaid parking tickets while painting his apartment. Arriving without a suit and tie and in paint-splattered pants, Chris still manages to win over his interviewers with his quick wit, references to his honesty, and work ethic. The memoir, which covers Gardner's entire life, shares his experiences with racism in various institutional settings, from high school, which he recalls "treating [him] like a dangerous Black Panther outlaw," to the bigotry he encountered as a medical researcher in San Francisco from a supervisor who freely made racist comments and interns who did not like taking orders from him, to the prejudice that made it difficult for him to sell stocks in person.[12] Gardner shares that what largely contributed to his success as a stockbroker was the fact that he conducted most of his business on the phone, which he describes as his "color shield," because no one could tell he was Black on the phone.[13]

Rather than social conflicts, the film underscores that Chris's main conflicts are economic. Since in the film Chris is on a hero's quest to defeat poverty, his antagonist is no concrete entity but, rather, value systems that imperil the pursuit of money. These value systems are embodied in the form of two different "hippies," an elderly man and a young female, who each steal his medical devices, and the IRS, which seizes funds from his bank account to pay owed taxes. Without scanners to sell and with his savings confiscated, Chris spirals into poverty and homelessness. These entities threaten to derail his membership in the corporate sphere, but they signal more potent threats to capitalism, with the freeloading hippies standing in for anticonsumerism and taxes infringing on the accumulation of capital. In contrast, the memoir is much more celebratory of counterculture, with Gardner stating that he imagines himself to have been "the first and youngest black hippie in America" because in high school he "blended the Black & Proud look with hippie garb," a combination that served as his liberation from the internalization of racism manifesting in dress codes and colorism.[14] Moreover, while the film is very anti-tax, it also does not dramatize the social and psychic taxes we have seen in ethnic upward mobility narratives because Chris is not treated differently on account of his race, nor is he concerned about a racialized collective.

As a post-race hero, Chris cannot have meaningful ties to a racialized community. To cast Chris's individualism as virtuous, the film makes certain that he has no family or friends on whom he can rely for social or economic support. "Linda" is a composite of Gardner's first wife and the woman he had an affair with—the mother of his son. Linda is depicted as a bad wife and mother for not supporting Chris and for abandoning her family. The only friend and other adult Black male represented in the film is shown solely in scenes in which he and Chris are arguing over the money he owes Chris, which he fails to pay back. In the memoir, Gardner's ties to a Black community are deep and extensive. As a genre, memoir allows for a fuller account of an individual's history in relation to a family and society. However, film biopics can, even if condensed, offer representations that historically and socially contextualize a life history. In depicting only a short period from Gardner's life, and by limiting his contact to African Americans to his estranged, critical wife and unreliable friend, the film renders him unattached to a sense of a Black community. In watching the film, one would not know the communal parenting upbringing that Gardner had through extended family members and neighbors, or the impact that Black athletes, musicians, and activists had on Gardner's sense of self, or that he started his future investment firm with the goal of investing the monies of African Americans. As Gardner puts it, he wanted to invest for people like Quincy Jones, Michael Jordan, and Oprah, and also "on behalf of black institutions, black banks, black insurance companies, black entrepreneurs and executives, black foundations" to promote "minority ownership and prosperity."[15] Gardner communicates these plans as part of his philosophy of "conscious capitalism," a combination of philanthropy and facilitating investment growth in public sectors.[16]

In essence, he portrays himself as a mediator for a collectivist-oriented, rather than individualist, capitalism, a way he has made sense of, and has been able to reconcile his role in an economic system stratified by race as well as class. And since he sees his structural role as benefiting a racialized collective, he does not have a fraught relationship to institutions as do Freeman, Browning, and Brown Buffalo—the protagonists of 1960s and 1970s novels discussed in Chapter 2. But he comes from the next generation, and he serves as an example of someone who grew up with Black Power ideology and has attempted to translate it in an area he knows and in which he has been successful. This is reflected in the way he frames his success story as one that ends with his ability to contribute to an actual Black empowerment project, the building up of post-Apartheid South Africa, through his knowledge of finance. In the epilogue, he recounts his meeting with Nelson Mandela in 2004, in which he tells Mandela how South Africa can best invest for its future: "This is my opportunity to use everything that I've learned in twenty-five years of working Wall Street and capital markets to help make a difference in the world for people that look like me."[17] Through the film's portrayal of a dehistoricized individual to make the film not about "race," one would not get the sense that Chris sees himself as part of a global racialized collective.

It makes sense, therefore, that while the memoir builds up to the depiction of a mediator, the film, participating in neoliberal subject-making, does not represent any of the recognizable character types that appear in ethnic upward mobility narratives: in a post-race world, there is no need for symbolic figures to work through class-inflected racial tensions. If Chris's interest in stockbroking is sparked by a status symbol sports car, status seeking is not a dominant trait that is played out since overcoming poverty becomes Chris's main goal in the film. There are also no alternative pathways to upward mobility or strategies for negotiating relationships to others—no mediators, conflicted artists, or gatekeepers. There is no need for them in the society represented in the film since the gate is open as long as Chris works to get through it. Yet the histories of African American and Mexican American cultural production indicate that in a society stratified by race and class, there has been a need to imagine ways of working through and against existing hierarchies.

These narratives depict upward ascent, but we can more productively read them as stories about moving *into*—into new groups and social fields. Many of the narratives examined throughout the book explore what happens during the process and after this move. Do individuals uphold the values of the status quo? Make it even harder for others to follow their path? Or, once inside, do they transform the field? In which ways, and to what degree? We can also read these as narratives of return; since Blacks and Latina/os have less intergenerational wealth than whites, and since upward mobility is barred for most, downward mobility is ever a possibility, as is the potential for individuals to identify with the economically and socially oppressed rather than with hegemonic interests. We have upward mobility narratives that endorse reform or revolution, representation or redistribution, and all are acts of imaginative and social labor. Participating in forging new identities and alliances and policing existing ones, these narratives are as much about moving into and between as they are about a return to, and a moving upward and out.

# NOTES

## INTRODUCTION

1. *The Jeffersons* was a spin-off of the show *All in the Family* (CBS 1971–1979). The Jeffersons were the neighbors of the white, working-class Bunkers from *All in the Family*.

2. "Prototype," *George Lopez*, ABC, aired on March 27, 2002. On this episode, George says he worked sixteen years on the assembly line, but in the episode "Token of Unappreciation," discussed in Chapter 4, he says it was fifteen.

3. "A Friend in Need," *The Jeffersons*, CBS, aired on January 18, 1975.

4. Lynn M. Berk, "The Great Middle American Dream Machine," *Journal of Communication* 27, no. 3 (1977): 27–31. In his analysis of the first fifty years of sitcom production, Richard Butsch found that two-thirds of sitcoms depicted middle-class families and, like Berk, argued that working-class characters tend to be depicted as inept, dysfunctional, and buffoonish. Richard Butsch, "A Half Century of Class and Gender in American TV Domestic Sitcoms," *Cercles* 8 (2003): 16–34.

5. In my employment of *race* and *ethnicity*, I refer to the distinction made by social psychologist Hazel Markus and literary scholar Paula Moya in *Doing Race*. While both terms refer to processes of categorization, ideas about race historically have been imposed on groups, sorting people "according to perceived physical and behavioral human characteristics that are often imagined to be negative, innate, and shared" (21), while ethnicity can refer to the cultural markers and practices coming from the group itself, enabling "people to identify, or be identified, with groupings of people on the basis of presumed, and usually claimed, commonalities, including several of the following: language, history, nation or region of origin, customs, religion, names, physical appearance and/or ancestry" (22). What is useful about this distinction is that it enables us to understand how "African American," "Black," "Mexican American" and "Chicano" operate as ethnic labels, with much discursive work occurring to reinforce them as sociopolitical groups in order to counter the negative effects of racialization. Hazel Rose Markus and Paula M. L. Moya, eds., *Doing Race: 21 Essays for the 21st Century*. (New York: Norton, 2010). My thinking about the dual and multiple negotiations racialized subjects make in navigating different class and ethnic contexts has been informed by scholarship on the "minority culture of mobility," particularly the work

of sociologist Jody Agius Vallejo in *Barrio to Burbs: The Making of the Mexican American Middle Class* (Stanford, CA: Stanford University Press, 2012).

6. "Former Neighbors," *The Jeffersons*, CBS, aired on March 29, 1975.

7. White supremacy is a worldwide ideological system with roots in colonialism. In the United States, racial hierarchies were institutionalized in the first three centuries of its history through laws, social policies, and cultural practices that have had lasting effects. These effects are economic, in that institutionalized racism justified the takeover of land and resources, sanctioned the exploitation of people, and prevented the accumulation and transfer of wealth over generations, and these effects are social, in that white supremacy still affects how people see and treat others, and see and treat themselves. It is important to understand how white supremacy can be internalized and reinforced by people who are racialized as nonwhite. The fiction writer Junot Díaz has said, "There's that old saying: the devil's greatest trick is that he convinced people that he doesn't exist. Well, white supremacy's greatest trick is that it has convinced people that, if it exists at all, it exists always in other people, never in us." Junot Díaz and Paula M. L. Moya, "The Search for Decolonial Love: An Interview with Junot Díaz," *Boston Review*, last modified on June 26, 2012, http://bostonreview.net/books-ideas/paula-ml-moya-decolonial-love-interview-junot-d%C3%ADaz.

8. The 1986 Immigration Reform and Control Act is also correlated to the increase of the Mexican American middle class. See Vallejo, *Barrio to Burbs,* 186.

9. "King's Dream Remains an Elusive Goal; Many Americans See Racial Disparities," Pew Research Center, last modified August 22, 2013, http://www.pewsocialtrends.org/2013/08/22/chapter-3-demographic-economic-data-by-race.

10. Rakesh Kochhar, Richard Fry, and Paul Taylor, "Wealth Gaps Rise to Record Highs Between Whites, Blacks, Hispanics: Twenty-to-One," Pew Social Trends, last modified July 26, 2011, http://www.pewsocialtrends.org/2011/07/26/wealth-gaps-rise-to-record-highs-between-whites-blacks-hispanics.

11. The "stop and frisk" law enables police officers to stop individuals in order to interrogate and frisk them for weapons. Disproportionally targeting Black and Latino males (in 2012, 87 percent of the stops were of Blacks or Latinos and 9 percent were of whites), the policy has contributed to the continued criminalization and mass incarceration of Blacks and Latinos. See Owen Brown Jr., "The Legal Murder of Trayvon Martin and New York City Stop-and-Frisk Law: America's War Against Black Males Rages On," *Western Journal of Black Studies* 37, no. 4 (2013): 258–71. The "stand your ground" law sanctions deadly force in the service of self-defense. Looking at FBI homicide data from 2005–2010 submitted by twenty-three states that had such laws, John K. Roman found that "white-on-black homicides were most likely to be ruled justified (11.4 percent), and black-on-white homicides were least likely to be ruled justified (1.2 percent)." John K. Roman, "Race, Justifiable Homicide, and Stand Your Ground Laws: Analysis of FBI Supplementary Homicide Report Data," Urban Institute, last modified July 26, 2013, http://www.urban.org/research/publication/race-justifiable-homicide-and-stand-your-ground-laws. The Support Our Law Enforcement and Safe Neighborhoods Act, also known as the "show me your papers" law or SB1070, was a state Senate bill signed into law by Arizona governor Jan Brewer in 2010. It enables law enforcement to stop anyone suspected of being undocumented to ask for documents proving legal U.S. residency. See "SB 1070 at the Supreme Court: What's at

Stake," American Civil Liberties Union, accessed January 4, 2016, https://www.aclu.org/
infographic/infographic-whats-stake-sb-1070-supreme-court?redirect=immigrants-rights/
whats-stake-sb-1070-supreme-court-infographic.

12. Sonya Rastogi, Tallesse D. Johnson, Elizabeth M. Hoeffel, and Malcolm P. Drewery
Jr., "The Black Population: 2010," U.S. Census Bureau, last modified September 2011, http://
www.census.gov/prod/cen2010/briefs/c2010br-06.pdf; Sharon R. Ennis, Merarys Rios-Vargas,
and Nora G. Albert, "The Hispanic Population: 2010," U.S. Census Bureau, last modified
May 2011, http://www.census.gov/prod/cen2010/briefs/c2010br-04.pdf.

13. Philip J. Deloria, *Playing Indian* (New Haven: Yale University Press, 1998), 20. If
Native Americans assimilated and accepted individual parcels of land that helped weaken
communal land structures, they were given the chance to become citizens in 1887 through
the General Allotment Act. It was a policy that Alan Trachtenberg describes as seeking "the
making of Americans by the unmaking of Indians." Alan Trachtenberg, *Shades of Hiawatha:
Staging Indians, Making Americans, 1880–1930* (New York: Hill and Wang, 2004), 30. All
Native Americans received citizenship in 1924, but they continued to face voting rights ob-
structions from some states until the middle of the twentieth century.

14. Donald Bogle, *Toms, Coons, Mulattoes, Mammies, and Bucks: An Interpretive History of Blacks in American Films*, 3rd ed. (New York: Continuum, 1994). The Fourteenth
Amendment, ratified in 1868, granted African Americans citizenship, yet Jim Crow laws
continued to sanction discrimination and violence toward Black people and prevented the
accumulation of wealth on the same level as whites. Benjamin P. Bowser, *The Black Middle
Class: Social Mobility and Vulnerability* (Boulder, CO: Lynne Rienner, 2007).

15. Ronald T. Takaki, *Strangers from a Different Shore: A History of Asian Americans* (1989.
Boston: Little, Brown, 1998). Anti-Asian racism led to immigration restrictions such as the
1882 Chinese Exclusion Act; the 1907–8 Gentleman's Agreement between the United States
and Japan; and parts of the Immigration Act of 1924, more explicitly barring Japanese immigration and limiting East Asian and Indian immigration.

16. Natalia Molina, *How Race Is Made in America: Immigration, Citizenship, and the
Historical Power of Racial Scripts* (Berkeley: University of California Press, 2014).

17. Deloria, *Playing Indian*, 174. These images elide the outcomes of centuries of disenfranchisement: that a quarter of Native Americans live in poverty, and that health disparities
endure. Jens Manuel Krogstad, "One-in-Four Native Americans and Alaska Natives Are Living in Poverty," Pew Research Center, last modified June 13, 2014, http://www.pewresearch
.org/fact-tank/2014/06/13/1-in-4-native-americans-and-alaska-natives-are-living-in-poverty;
David S. Jones, "The Persistence of American Indian Health Disparities," *American Journal
of Public Health* 96, no. 12 (2006): 2122–34.

18. Robert G. Lee explicates how U.S. sentiments toward Asia and Asian Americans
began to change as a result of international and internal pressures stemming from the Cold
War and the civil rights movement. In countering the spread of communism and developing itself as a global economic power, the United States had an incentive to ally with Asian
countries as trading partners. Amid nationwide protests during the 1960s by people of color
demanding economic and social change, news outlets also started disseminating stories of
high academically achieving Asian Americans, shaping a discourse of "triumphant ethnic
assimilation," in contrast with underachieving and oppositional racial minorities (149).

Robert G. Lee, *Orientals: Asian Americans in Popular Culture* (Philadelphia: Temple University Press, 1999), 145–79. The Immigration Act of 1965 also contributed to the narrative of Asian American success; it opened up greater Asian immigration to the United States, but with certain stipulations, giving preference toward immediate family members and those with professional backgrounds and technical skills, which led to new generations of Asian immigrants with higher education and class backgrounds than previously. Ronald T. Takaki, *Strangers from a Different Shore: A History of Asian Americans* (1989; Boston: Little, Brown, 1998). While ostensibly a positive relabeling, the term *model minority* obscures the variation that exists in educational attainment and economic backgrounds, as well as experiences of social marginality within the Asian American population. Rosalind S. Chou and Joe R. Feagin, *The Myth of the Model Minority: Asian Americans Facing Racism* (Boulder, CO: Paradigm, 2008); Samuel D. Museus and Peter N. Kiang, "Deconstructing the Model Minority Myth and How It Contributes to the Invisible Minority Reality in Higher Education Research," *New Directions for Institutional Research* 142 (2009): 5–15.

19. After 9/11, Muslims also came to be perceived as threatening racial others.

20. Martin Gilens, "How the Poor Became Black: The Racialization of American Poverty in the Mass Media," in *Race and the Politics of Welfare Reform*, ed. Sanford F. Schram, Joe Soss, and Richard C. Fording (Ann Arbor: University of Michigan Press, 2003), 101–30.

21. Oscar Lewis, *Five Families: Mexican Case Studies in the Culture of Poverty* (New York: Basic, 1959); Daniel P. Moynihan, "The Negro Family: The Case for National Action (1965)" (Washington, DC: U.S. Government Printing Office).

22. Charles Murray is a famous scholarly example whose books, *Losing Ground* (1984) and *The Bell Curve* (1994), correlated poverty with culture, race, and genetics. Inspired by Murray's arguments about the Black/white IQ gap, Jason Richwine, a former senior policy analyst at the Heritage Foundation, argued in his Harvard dissertation, "IQ and Immigration Policy" (2009) that there existed a Latino/white IQ gap, explained by genetics. Amy Chua and Jed Rubenfeld argue in *Triple Package* (2014) that the success of certain ethnic groups over others is due to cultural traits. Bill Cosby reiterated culture of pathology sentiment in his 2004 NAACP address, known as the "Pound Cake Speech," in which he encouraged Black self-help and attributed poverty, incarceration, and school drop-out rates to Black people's bad parenting, use of vernacular speech, and dress and consumption habits (http://www.rci.rutgers.edu/~schochet/101/Cosby_Speech.htm). In contrast to these arguments, Darrick Hamilton and William Darity Jr. and their colleagues argue that academic and financial achievement gaps can better be explained by disparities in intergenerational wealth transfers: Darrick Hamilton, William Darity Jr., Anne E. Price, Vishnu Sridharan, and Rebecca Tippett, "Umbrellas Don't Make It Rain: Why Studying and Working Hard Isn't Enough for Black Americans," last modified April 2015, http://www.insightcced.org.

23. Peter B. Kraska has explained the rise in martial crime rhetoric since the 1960s by demonstrating how leaders have used it to rally support: "What is at stake for politicians and bureaucrats who frame the crime problem in martial terms is the legitimacy and security of the state itself . . . that we risk our 'national security' by *not* waging war." Peter B. Kraska, "Crime Control as Warfare: Language Matters" in *Militarizing the American Criminal Justice System: The Changing Roles of the Armed Forces and the Police*, ed. Peter B. Kraska (Lebanon, NH: Northeastern University Press, 2001), 20. For an overview of how the police became increasingly

militarized as a result of the War on Drugs and the War on Terror, see Matthew Harwood, "How Did America's Police Get So Militarized?" *Mother Jones*, August 14, 2014, http://www .motherjones.com/politics/2014/08/america-police-military-swat-ferguson-westcott-tampa.

24. Kraska, "Crime Control as Warfare: Language Matters," 22.

25. Data in the 2010 census report that Latinos compose 16 percent of the country's population and 19 percent of the prison population, while Blacks compose 13 percent of the country's population and 40 percent of the prison population. Leah Sakala, "Breaking Down Mass Incarceration in the 2010 Census: State-by-State Incarceration Rates by Race/ Ethnicity," Prison Policy, May 28, 2014, http://www.prisonpolicy.org/reports/rates.html. See also Michelle Alexander, *The New Jim Crow: Mass Incarceration in the Age of Colorblindness* (New York: New Press, 2010); David Manuel Hernández, "Pursuant to Deportation: Latinos and Immigrant Detention," *Latino Studies* 6, no. 1 (2008): 35–63; Suzanne Oboler, ed. *Behind Bars: Latino/as and Prison in the United States* (New York: Palgrave Macmillan, 2009); and Victor M. Rios, *Punished: Policing the Lives of Black and Latino Boys* (New York: New York University Press, 2011).

26. Leo R. Chavez, *The Latino Threat: Constructing Immigrants, Citizens, and the Nation* (Stanford, CA: Stanford University Press, 2008).

27. It is through representations of benefactors and patrons, Robbins argues, that early European and American novels imagined a relationship between a class aspirant and social force that would enable the protagonist's upward rise, the force serving "as a sort of catalyst inciting or supervising the passage from origin to destination without entering into the end product." The role of benefactor would later be played by welfare state institutions, which help individuals rise by distributing resources and giving employment, and through the latter also offer a way for individuals to contribute to the common good themselves. Bruce Robbins, *Upward Mobility and the Common Good: Toward a Literary History of the Welfare State*. (Princeton, NJ: Princeton University Press, 2007), 13.

28. W. E. B. Du Bois, "Talented Tenth," in *The Negro Problem: A Series of Articles by Representative American Negroes of To-day*, ed. Booker T. Washington (New York: James Pott, 1903) 33–75. Du Bois's views endorsing integration and liberal arts education contrasted with Booker T. Washington's vision for racial progress through segregation and vocational training as expressed in Washington's 1895 Atlanta Exposition Address. Even though Washington and Du Bois had distinct views on how to move forward, they contributed to the post-Reconstruction political ideology of "racial uplift," a morality-based discourse that emphasized internal class differentiations and respectability politics as a way to counter the negative status and treatment of Blacks. See Kevin K. Gaines, *Uplifting the Race: Black Leadership, Politics, and Culture in the Twentieth Century* (Chapel Hill: The University of North Carolina Press, 1996). For a literary analysis of fiction and criticism expressing uplift ideology, see Gene Andrew Jarrett, *Representing the Race: A New Political History of African American Literature* (New York: New York University Press, 2011): 73–99. For an overview of the scholarship on the Black middle class, see Bart Landry and Kris Marsh, "The Evolution of the New Black Middle Class," *Annual Review of Sociology* 37 (2011): 373–94. Landry and Marsh observe that Frazier was possibly the first to explicitly refer to a "Black middle class" (374–75).

29. E. Franklin Frazier, *Black Bourgeoisie* (New York: Free Press, 1957). In 1948, influenced by Marxism, Du Bois issued a revision to his "Talented Tenth" thesis that would be

more akin to Frazier's thinking. In "The Talented Tenth: Memorial Address," he critiqued his past views for promoting an aristocratic view of leadership and urged a more expansive and ethical leadership program, one that would be more than one-tenth of the population, would be committed to sacrifice on behalf of the Black masses, would work toward an economic redistribution of wealth, and would make alliances with global efforts for equality. W. E. B. Du Bois, "The Talented Tenth: Memorial Address," 1948, https://www.sigmapiphi .org/home/the-talented-tenth.php. Joy James traces the evolution of Du Bois's ideas about the Talented Tenth in *Transcending the Talented Tenth: Black Leaders and American Intellectuals* (New York: Routledge, 1997) 15–33.

30. Andreá N. Williams, *Dividing Lines: Class Anxiety and Postbellum Black Fiction* (Ann Arbor: University of Michigan Press), 24. Williams is referring to fears of downward economic mobility, of being grouped with the lower class, and of being estranged "from the people, places, or values often associated with the imagined black community" (19).

31. Frank J. Webb, *The Garies and Their Friends* (1857. New York: Arno, 1969).

32. In 1870, the Black population was 4,880,009. In 1970, the Mexican-origin population was 4,532,435. See Campbell Gibson and Kay Jung, "Historical Census Statistics on Population Totals by Race, 1790 to 1990, and by Hispanic Origin 1970 to 1990, for the United States, Regions, Divisions, and States," last modified September 2002, https://www .census.gov/content/dam/Census/library/working-papers/2002/demo/POP-twps0056.pdf.

33. Sharon R. Ennis et al, "The Hispanic Population: 2010"; Rastogi et al, "The Black Population: 2010."

34. Raymund A. Paredes, "Special Feature: The Evolution of Chicano Literature." *MELUS* 2 (1978): 88. Paredes observes that pre-1940 writers tended to avoid writing about the present in order to play up an idealized Spanish heritage uninfluenced by outside forces and surmises that this was an accomodationist response to the pejorative connotation of "Mexican" in the United States (87). Paredes also points out that most writers wrote in forms other than the novel, such as diaries, journals, poetry, and Spanish language newspapers (81). Rather than upward mobility narratives, the nineteenth and early twentieth centuries saw some downward mobility narratives in the form of novels about landed elites, such as María Amparo Ruiz de Burton's *The Squatter and the Don* (1885), or Jovita González and Eve Raleigh's *Caballero* (1930s/1996), which depicted the dispossession of land that occurred among upper-class *Californios* after the U.S.-Mexican War.

35. Before the 1960s, few from this group were able to get published, especially given the stigma against Mexican-origin people based in ideas about race and national inclusion. Also, most of this writing was written in Spanish. The Recovering the U.S. Hispanic Literary Heritage Project, founded in the 1990s, has enabled the translation and publication of pre-1960s Latina/o writing.

36. Joe Rodriguez, "San Jose's National Hispanic University Will Close by 2015," *San Jose Mercury News*, accessed March 19, 2014, http://www.mercurynews.com/breaking-news/ci_25379797/san-joses-national-hispanic-university-will-no-longer.

37. In the 1970s, there was a concerted effort to increase publishing opportunities for scholarship and literature by Mexican Americans. The political activism of the Chicano movement entailed a cultural component to combat the stereotypical images of Mexican Americans and empower a marginalized population of people around a collective conscious-

ness. Journals such as *El Grito*, founded in 1967, and *Aztlán*, in 1970, along with Quinto Sol Publications, which published four Chicana/o novels it also honored through its literary prize in the early 1970s, as well as the founding of the presses Bilingual Press in 1973 and Arte Público Press in 1979 played a crucial role in creating and disseminating an identity for Chicana/o literature and culture (Lomelí, 86–96; Tatum, 64–65). Francisco A. Lomelí, "Contemporary Chicano Literature, 1959–1990," *Handbook of Hispanic Cultures in the United States: Literature and Art* 1 (1993): 86–108. Charles M. Tatum, *Chicano and Chicana Literature: Otra voz del pueblo* (Tucson: University of Arizona Press, 2006).

38. Tomás R. Jiménez, *Replenished Ethnicity: Mexican Americans, Immigration, and Identity* (Berkeley: University of California Press, 2010); Jessica M. Vasquez, *Mexican Americans Across Generations: Immigrant Families, Racial Realities* (New York: NYU Press, 2011); Vallejo, *Barrio to Burbs*.

39. José E. Limón, "Transnational Triangulation: Mexico, the United States, and the Emergence of a Mexican American Middle Class," in *Mexico and Mexicans in the Making of the United States*, ed. John Tutino (Austin: University of Texas Press, 2012), 236–256; John Alba Cutler, *Ends of Assimilation: The Formation of Chicano Literature* (New York: Oxford University Press, 2015).

40. Ayana Mathis, *The Twelve Tribes of Hattie* (New York: Vintage, 2013).

41. The same principle underlies the idea of the "respectability tax," which "refers to the extra lengths that some African Americans, and other people of color go to, in order to telegraph that they are middle-class, successful, and respectable." Noel King, "Do Non-White Americans Pay a 'Respectability Tax'?" *Frost Illustrated*, last modified August 13, 2013, http://www.frostillustrated.com/2013/do-non-white-americans-pay-a-respectability-tax.

42. Imani Perry, *More Beautiful and More Terrible: The Embrace and Transcendence of Racial Inequality in the United States* (New York: New York University Press, 2011), 163.

43. W. E. B. Du Bois, *Black Reconstruction in America 1860–1880* (1935; New York: Free Press, 1998), 700–701; David Roediger, *The Wages of Whiteness: Race and the Makings of the American Working Class* (London: Verso: 1991); Cheryl I. Harris, "Whiteness as Property," *Harvard Law Review* 106, no. 8 (1993): 1707–91; George Lipsitz, *The Possessive Investment in Whiteness: How White People Profit from Identity Politics* (Philadelphia: Temple University Press, 1998).

44. I do not take *community*, as a given, and use this term to reference the group formation denoted by the text. In order to convey a sense of betrayal that is not just personal, a text imparts that the betrayal affects more than just an individual.

45. James Weldon Johnson, *The Autobiography of an Ex-Colored Man* (Boston: Sherman, French, 1912); Américo Paredes, *George Washington Gómez* (1930s; Houston: Arte Publico Press, 1990); Ralph Ellison, *Invisible Man* (1952; New York: Vintage, 1995).

46. Ethnic and racial identities are lucrative for commercial purposes as well. Arlene Davíla shows, for example, how companies and marketing firms profit from creating a homogenous pan-Latino identity in order to sell products. See her *Latinos Inc.: Marketing and the Making of a People* (Berkeley: University of California Press, 2001).

47. Limón, "Transnational Triangulation," 236.

48. Candice M. Jenkins, "A Kind of End to Blackness: Reginald McKnight's He Sleeps and the Body Politics of Race and Class," in *From Bourgeois to Boojie: Black Middle-Class*

*Performances*, ed. Vershawn Ashanti Young and Bridget Harris Tsemo (Detroit: Wayne State University Press, 2011), 262.

49. Trey Ellis, "The New Black Aesthetic," *Callaloo* 38 (Winter 1989): 234.

50. Touré, *Who's Afraid of Post-Blackness? What It Means to Be Black Now* (2011; New York: Atria, 2014).

51. Ibid., 12.

52. Ibid., 153.

53. Randall Kennedy, *Sellout: The Politics of Racial Betrayal* (New York: Pantheon, 2008); Brando Simeo Starkey, *In Defense of Uncle Tom* (New York: Cambridge University Press, 2015).

54. Starkey, *In Defense of Uncle Tom*, 3-4.

55. Ibid., 21.

56. Benavidez describes post-Chicano movement art as follows: "The Post-Chicano artists often work within an ethnically-mixed context. They seem willing to more than accept and tolerate cultural ambiguity and contradiction. They seem interested in promoting it. Where contemporary Chicano art typically avoids visual confusion in favor of political correctness, Post-Chicano art thrives at the complex and sometimes off-balanced intersection of Western European avant-garde, world culture and Chicano art." Max Benavidez, "The Post-Chicano Aesthetic: Making Sense of the World," in *Post-Chicano Generation in Art: Breaking Boundaries* (Phoenix: MARS Artspace, 1990), 4.

57. "Melanie Cervantes on Post Chicano Art," YouTube video, 4:52, July 6, 2009, https://www.youtube.com/watch?v=A3h2VOA26t4.

58. Greg Thomas, "African Diasporic Blackness Out of Line: Trouble for 'Post-Black' African *Americanism*," in *The Trouble with Post-Blackness*, ed. Houston A. Baker Jr. and K. Merinda Simmons (New York: Columbia University Press, 2015), 62.

59. While they share similarities, there are key distinctions between *post-Black* and *post-Chicano*, as well as between these terms and one sometimes used interchangeably with *post-Black*: *post-Soul*. *Post-Black* has received more critical appraisals than the term *post-Soul* because the former has the connotation of being sympathetic to the idea of "post-race," while the latter is used more often to refer to aesthetic strategies in a post–Civil Rights era. To use the label *post-Chicano*, one is not necessarily conveying that one is past a racial or ethnic identity since "Chicano" is a label used predominantly to describe a specific identity under the broader category of Mexican American, one that is politicized and used mostly in activism, academia, and artistic spaces. Arguably, to be *post-Chicano* or not-Chicano (not wanting to identify with Chicano ideology), one could identify as "Mexican American," "Mexican," "Hispanic," or "Latino." In this sense, *post-Chicano* would be more akin to *post-Soul* in signifying a relationship to a historicized set of aesthetic practices, in this case associated with the Chicano movement. For an overview of the post-Soul aesthetic, see Bertram D. Ashe, "Theorizing the Post-Soul Aesthetic: An Introduction," *African American Review* 41, no. 4 (2007): 609–23.

60. Alejandro A. Portes and Min Zhou, "The New Second Generation: Segmented Assimilation and Its Variants," The *Annals of the American Academy of Political and Social Science* 533 (1993): 74–96.

61. Kathryn M. Neckerman, Prudence Carter, and Jennifer Lee, "Segmented Assimilation and Minority Cultures of Mobility," *Ethnic and Racial Studies* 22, no. 6 (1999): 945–65.

62. Ibid., 946.

63. Ibid., 950–51.

64. H. Samy Alim and Geneva Smitherman, *Articulate While Black: Barack Obama, Language, and Race in the U.S.* (Oxford: Oxford University Press, 2012).

65. Vallejo, *Barrio to Burbs*.

66. Neckerman, Carter, and Lee, "Segmented Assimilation," 949.

67. Mark McGurl, *The Program Era: Postwar Fiction and the Rise of Creative Writing* (Cambridge: Harvard University Press, 2009), 336.

68. Kenneth W. Warren, *What Was African American Literature?* (Cambridge, MA: Harvard University Press, 2011), 18.

69. Ibid., 139.

70. Walter Benn Michaels, "Plots Against America: Neoliberalism and Antiracism," *American Literary History* 18, no. 2 (2006): 297.

71. William Darity Jr., "Stratification Economics: The Role of Intergroup Inequality," *Journal of Ecoomics and Finance* 29, no. 2 (2005): 144–53.

72. Daria Roithmayr, *Reproducing Racism: How Everyday Choices Lock in White Advantage* (New York, NYU Press, 2014), 6.

73. Lawrence Buell, *The Dream of the Great American Novel* (Cambridge: Harvard University Press, 2014), 214.

74. Max Weber, "Class, Party, Status," in *From Max Weber: Essays in Sociology*, ed. H. Gerth and C. Wright Mills (New York: Oxford University Press, 1946): 180–95.

75. Elizabeth McHenry, *Forgotten Readers: Recovering the Lost History of African American Literary Societies* (Durham, NC: Duke University Press, 2002), 16.

76. Ralph E. Rodriguez, "Chicano Studies and the Need to Not Know," *American Literary History* 22, no. 1 (2009): 180.

77. Viet Thanh Nguyen, *Race and Resistance: Literature and Politics in Asian America* (New York: Oxford University Press, 2002), 4.

78. All the character types are employed to depict contradictions, but since the other terms—status seeker, mediator, and gatekeeper—designate actions, my choice of calling the fourth type the "conflicted artist" is to draw attention to the often unresolved tensions that emerge because of the artist's symbolic and structural position between groups.

79. Dorothy West, *The Living Is Easy* (1948; New York: Feminist Press, 1982); Paule Marshall, *Brown Girl, Brownstones* (1959; New York: Feminist Press, 1996); Gloria Naylor, *Linden Hills* (1985; New York: Penguin, 1986).

80. Sam Greenlee, *The Spook Who Sat by the Door: A Novel* (1969; Detroit: Wayne State University Press, 1990); John A. Williams, *Sons of Darkness, Sons of Light: A Novel of Some Probability* (1969; Boston: Northeastern University Press, 1999); Oscar Zeta Acosta, *The Autobiography of a Brown Buffalo* (1972; New York: Vintage, 1989); and *The Revolt of the Cockroach People* (1973; New York: Vintage, 1989).

81. *My Family / Mi Familia*, directed by Gregory Nava (New Line, 1995; Helena María Viramontes, *Under the Feet of Jesus* (1995; New York: Plume, 1996).

82. The other texts in this chapter might be more evidently mass-market, but *Hunger of Memory* was first published by David R. Godine in 1982, with an edition by Bantam Books coming out in 1983 and is now published through Random House.

83. Richard Rodriguez, *Hunger of Memory: The Education of Richard Rodriguez* (1982; New York: Random House, 2004); *George Lopez*, first broadcast March 27, 2002, by ABC; Michele Serros, *Honey Blonde Chica* (New York: Simon Pulse, 2006); *black-ish*, first broadcast September 24, 2014, by ABC.

84. Percival Everett, *Erasure* (New York: Hyperion, 2001); Lynn Nottage, *Intimate Apparel / Fabulation, or the Re-Education of Undine* (New York: Theatre Communications Group, 2006; the latter first performed in 2004).

85. *Machete*, directed by Robert Rodriguez and Ethan Maniquis (Twentieth Century Fox, 2010); *Sleep Dealer*, directed by Alex Rivera (Maya Entertainment, 2008); *The Gatekeeper*, directed by John Carlos Frey (Screen Media, 2002).

CHAPTER I

A portion of this chapter was previously published as "Mortgaged Status: Literary Representations of Black Home Ownership and Social Mobility," *Contemporary Literature* 55.4 (2014): 726–59, © 2014 by the Board of Regents of the University of Wisconsin System. Reproduced courtesy of the University of Wisconsin Press.

1. Ralph Ellison, *Invisible Man* (1952; New York: Vintage, 1995) 510.

2. Sandra Cisneros, "Preface" to *My Wicked Wicked Ways* (1987; New York: Alfred A. Knopf, 1999), x.

3. Wilhelmina A. Leigh, "Civil Rights Legislation and the Housing Status of Black Americans: An Overview," in *The Housing Status of Black Americans*, ed. Wilhelmina A. Leigh and James B. Stewart (New Brunswick: Transaction, 1992), 20.

4. The 1968 Fair Housing Act was landmark legislation outlawing discrimination when it came to selling or renting housing, but the 1988 Fair Housing Amendments Act expanded its coverage and gave HUD authority and means to enforce it.

5. Bart Landry, *The New Black Middle Class* (Berkeley: University of California Press, 1988), 79. Landry explains the significance of the home in the context of Jim Crow violence: "While blacks of all classes kept to themselves during the 1930s, 1940s, and 1950s, middle-class blacks especially were diligent in avoiding situations that reminded them of the dilemma of their status . . . preferring parties and dinners at home. In this context, a home assumed greater importance among blacks than whites. It was the symbol of success in a society that allowed them precious few opportunities for conspicuous achievement, and it was an oasis in a hostile environment. Behind closed doors, middle-class blacks could act as though the outside world that rejected them did not exist or at least could feel a little sheltered from it" (79).

6. Amy Schrager Lang, *The Syntax of Class: Writing Inequality in Nineteenth-Century America* (Princeton, NJ: Princeton University Press), 2003.

7. Dorothy West, *The Living Is Easy* (1948; New York: Feminist Press, 1982).

8. Jeffrey Louis Decker, *Made in America: Self-Styled Success from Horatio Alger to Oprah Winfrey* (Minneapolis: University of Minnesota Press, 1997), 133.

9. Jacqueline Jones, *Labor of Love, Labor of Sorrow: Black Women, Work, and the Family from Slavery to the Present* (New York: Basic, 1985); Enobong Hannah Branch, *Opportunity Denied: Limiting Black Women to Devalued Work* (New Brunswick, NJ: Rutgers University Press, 2011).

10. See Meredith Goldsmith, "The Wages of Weight: Dorothy West's Corporeal Poli-

tics," *Mosaic: An Interdisciplinary Journal of Literature* 40, no. 4 (2007): 31–59; Lawrence Rodgers, "Dorothy West's *The Living Is Easy* and the Ideal of Southern Folk Community," in "Women Writers," special issue of *African American Review* 26 no. 1 (1992): 161–72; Pamela Peden Sanders, "The Feminism of Dorothy West's *The Living Is Easy:* A Critique of the Limitations of the Female Sphere Through Performative Gender Roles," *African American Review* 36, no. 3 (2002): 435–46; Cherene Sherrard-Johnson, *Dorothy West's Paradise: A Biography of Class and Color* (New Brunswick, NJ: Rutgers University Press, 2012); Jennifer M. Wilks, "New Women and New Negroes: Archetypal Womanhood in *The Living Is Easy*," *African American Review* 39, no. 4 (2005): 569–79.

11. Fred Hirsch, *Social Limits to Growth* (Cambridge, MA: Harvard University Press, 1976), 20.

12. Vilna Bashi Treitler, *The Ethnic Project: Transforming Racial Fiction into Ethnic Factions* (Stanford, CA: Stanford University Press, 2013), 4.

13. Benjamin P. Bowser, *The Black Middle Class: Social Mobility and Vulnerability* (Boulder: Lynne Rienner, 2007), 36.

14. Ibid., 55-56.

15. Landry, *The New Black Middle Class*, 39.

16. Sherrard-Johnson, *Dorothy West's Paradise*, 144.

17. Lewis Corey, *The Crisis of the Middle Class* (New York: Covici-Friede, 1935), 174.

18. Pierre Bourdieu, *Outline of a Theory of Practice*, trans. Richard Nice (Cambridge: Cambridge University Press, 1977), 83.

19. Cheryl Hardy, "Hysteresis," in *Pierre Bourdieu: Key Concepts*, ed. Michael Grenfell (Stocksfield, UK: Acumen, 2008), 135.

20. William D. Howells, *The Rise of Silas Lapham*, ed. Walter J. Meserve and David J. Nordloh (1885; Bloomington: Indiana University Press, 1971), 27.

21. Scholars demarcate West Indian immigration into the United States into three waves, the early 1900s to 1920s, 1930 to 1965, and 1966 to the present. Philip Kasinitz, *Caribbean New York: Black Immigrants and the Politics of Race* (Ithaca, NY: Cornell University Press, 1992).

22. Paule Marshall, *Brown Girl, Brownstones* (1959; New York: Feminist Press, 1996), 11.

23. Kimberly W. Benston, "Architectural Imagery and Unity in Paule Marshall's *Brown Girl, Brownstones*," *Negro American Literature Forum* 9, no. 3 (1975): 67–70.

24. Vanessa D. Dickerson, "The Property of Being in Paule Marshall's *Brown Girl, Brownstones*," *Obsidian II: Black Literature in Review* 6 (1991): 2.

25. Gavin Jones, "'The Sea Ain' Got No Back Door': The Problems of Black Consciousness in Paule Marshall's *Brown Girl, Brownstones*," *African American Review* 32, no. 4 (1998): 597–606.

26. Nina Baym, "Melodramas of Beset Manhood: How Theories of American Fiction Exclude Women Authors," *American Quarterly* 33, no. 2 (1981): 135.

27. Lora Romero, *Home Fronts: Domesticity and Its Critics in the Antebellum United States* (Durham, NC: Duke University Press, 1997), 17.

28. Her mother, however, thought it best to spend the money taking the children to Barbados but lost the money after trusting a crooked travel agent. Joyce Pettis and Paule Marshall, "A *MELUS* Interview: Paule Marshall," in "Black Modernism and Post-Modernism," special issue of *MELUS* 17, no. 4 (1991–1992): 117–29.

29. Ibid., 118.

30. Branch, *Opportunity Denied*, 20–21.

31. Jones, *Labor of Love, Labor of Sorrow*, 238.

32. Branch, *Opportunity Denied*, 76.

33. Tressie McMillan Cottom, "Why Do Poor People 'Waste' Money on Luxury Goods?" Talkingpointsmemo.com, November 1, 2013, http://talkingpointsmemo.com/cafe/why-do-poor-people-waste-money-on-luxury-goods.

34. Martin Japtok, "Paule Marshall's *Brown Girl, Brownstones*: Reconciling Ethnicity and Individualism," *African American Review* 32, no. 2 (1998): 305.

35. W. E. B. Du Bois, "Criteria of Negro Art," *The Crisis* 32 (1926): 290.

36. Andrew Hoberek, *The Twilight of the Middle Class: Post-World War II American Fiction and White Collar Work* (Princeton, NJ: Princeton University Press, 2005).

37. Japtok, "Paule Marshall's *Brown Girl, Brownstones*," 312.

38. Pettis and Marshall, "A *MELUS* Interview," 121.

39. Richard Florida, *The Rise of the Creative Class: And How It's Transforming Work, Leisure, Community, and Everyday Life* (New York: Basic, 2004), 68.

40. Ibid., 8.

41. See William H. Whyte, *The Organization Man* (1956; New York: Anchor, 1957); C. Wright Mills, *White Collar: The American Middle Classes* (1951; New York: Oxford University Press, 1956); Robert L. Heilbroner, *The Quest for Wealth: A Study of Acquisitive Man* (New York: Simon & Schuster, 1956).

42. Florida, *The Rise of the Creative Class*, 68.

43. Susan Jahoda, Blair Murphy, Vicky Virgin, and Caroline Woolard, "Artists Report Back: A National Study on the Lives of Arts Graduates and Working Artists," BFAMFAPhD.com, accessed January 18, 2015, http://bfamfaphd.com/#artists-report-back.

44. Quoctrung Bui, "Who Had Richer Parents, Doctors Or Artists?" Planet Money, March 18, 2014, http://www.npr.org/blogs/money/2014/03/18/289013884/who-had-richer-parents-doctors-or-arists.

45. Stephen Schryer, *Fantasies of the New Class: Ideologies of Professionalism in Post–World War II American Fiction* (New York: Columbia University Press, 2011), 65.

46. Ibid., 2.

47. Ibid., 81.

48. Donald Bogle, *Toms, Coons, Mulattoes, Mammies, and Bucks: An Interpretive History of Blacks in American Films*, 4th ed. (London: Blue Ridge Summit, 2001), 268.

49. Sut Jhally and Justin Lewis, *Enlightened Racism: The Cosby Show, Audiences, and the Myth of the American Dream* (Boulder, CO: Westview Press, 1992).

50. Leslie B. Inniss and Joe R. Feagin, "The Cosby Show: The View from the Black Middle Class," *Journal of Black Studies* 25, no. 6 (1995): 705–6.

51. Gloria Naylor, *Linden Hills* (1985. New York: Penguin, 1986), 8.

52. Catherine C. Ward, "Gloria Naylor's *Linden Hills*: A Modern *Inferno*," *Contemporary Literature* 28, no. 1 (1987): 68.

53. Esther Milner, *The Failure of Success: The Middle-Class Crisis*, 2nd ed. (St. Louis: W. H. Green, 1968), 15.

54. Lawrence Otis Graham, *Member of the Club: Reflections on Life in a Racially Polarized World* (New York: HarperPerennial, 1996), 79.

55. E. Franklin Frazier, *Black Bourgeoisie* (1957; New York: Free Press, 1997), 219.

56. T. Alexander Smith and Lenahan O'Connell, *Black Anxiety, White Guilt, and the Politics of Status Frustration* (Westport, CT: Praeger, 1997), ix.

57. Georg Lukács, *The Historical Novel*, trans. Hannah Mitchell and Stanley Mitchell (Lincoln: University of Nebraska Press, 1983), 60.

58. Mark McGurl, *The Program Era: Postwar Fiction and the Rise of Creative Writing* (Cambridge, MA: Harvard University Press, 2009), xi.

59. Ibid., 49.

60. Bruce Robbins, *Upward Mobility and the Common Good: Toward a Literary History of the Welfare State* (Princeton, NJ: Princeton University Press, 2007), 28.

61. Paula M. L. Moya, "Another Way to Be: Women of Color, Literature, and Myth," in *Doing Race: Twenty-One Essays for the 21st Century*, ed. Hazel Rose Markus and Paula M. L. Moya (New York: Norton, 2010), 504.

62. Dorothy West began her literary career at a young age, when literary contests sponsored by Black magazines such as *Opportunity* and *The Crisis* offered opportunities to aspiring Black writers. During the depression, those opportunities dwindled. Undaunted, West started her own literary magazines, serving as editor of *Challenge* (1934) and coeditor of *New Challenge* (1937). Both were short-lived. Sherrard-Johnson, *Dorothy West's Paradise*, 118.

63. For example, West's *The Living Is Easy* preceded E. Franklin Frazier's arguments about the Black middle class's status seeking behavior in *Black Bourgeoisie* (1957) and Pierre Bourdieu's theorization of hysteresis in *Outline of a Theory of Practice* (1977); Marshall's *Brown Girl, Brownstones* was published before Mary C. Waters's *Black Identities: West Indian Immigrant Dreams and American Realities* (1999), which discusses the identity negotiations that West Indians in New York undertook to gain social incorporation in the United States, including those of distancing themselves from or identifying with African Americans; and Naylor's *Linden Hills* appeared before Bart Landry's survey of a post-1960s expanded Black middle class in *The New Black Middle Class* (1988), as well as before Mary Patillo-McCoy's study of middle-class Black neighborhoods in *Black Picket Fences: Privilege and Peril Among the Black Middle Class* (1999).

64. They could have portrayed status seeking in more sympathetic terms, given the severe disparity between Black and white home ownership. It is a disparity that did not start to noticeably lessen until the mid-1990s. Tougher federal law enforcement against racial discrimination, combined with higher wages, historically low interest rates, and the increasing availability of subprime loans, made it possible for more African Americans to purchase homes. But African Americans, along with Latina/os, were also the hardest hit with foreclosures by the mid-2000s because of subprime mortgages, revealing the tenuousness of those record-making gains. The novels examined in this chapter depict how precarious the markers of success are, since they are subject to market and social forces and since Blacks and Latina/os have less intergenerational wealth than whites.

65. Sandra Cisneros, *The House on Mango Street* (1984: New York: Random House, 2009).

CHAPTER 2

1. Amílcar Cabral, "The Weapon of Theory," in *Revolution in Guinea: Selected Texts by Amílcar Cabral* (New York: Monthly Review Press, 1969), 90–111.

2. Ibid., 108.

3. Ibid., 110.

4. PAIGC stands for Partido Africano da Independência da Guiné e Cabo Verde/African Party for the Independence of Guiné and Cape Verde. For more on its formation, see Basil Davidson, "On Revolutionary Nationalism: The Legacy of Cabral," *Latin American Perspectives* 11, no. 2 (1984): 15–42.

5. Thomas Meisenhelder, "Amilcar Cabral's Theory of Class Suicide and Revolutionary Socialism," *Monthly Review, Nov.* 1993, p. 40ff., Academic OneFile, accessed March 25, 2017, go.galegroup.com%2Fps%2Fi.do%3Fp%3DAONE%26sw%3Dw%26u%3Dusocal_main%26v%3D2.1%26id%3DGALE%257CA14541128%26it%3Dr%26asid%3Da48a1b11c9e3c3eaffb3cafcd57f491d.

6. Charles D. Peavy, "Four Black Revolutionary Novels, 1899–1970," *Journal of Black Studies* 1, no. 2 (1970): 219–23; Kali Tal, "That Just Kills Me: Black Militant Near-Future Fiction," *Social Text* 20, no. 2 (2002): 65–91.

7. Peavy, "Four Black Revolutionary Novels," 223.

8. Tal, "That Just Kills Me," 75.

9. Mark Bould, "Come Alive by Saying No: An Introduction to Black Power SF," *Science Fiction Studies* 34, no. 2 (2007): 220–40; Julie A. Fiorelli, "Imagination Run Riot: Apocalyptic Race-War Novels of the Late 1960s," *Mediations* 28, no. 1 (2014): 127–52.

10. Adolf Reed Jr., "The 'Black Revolution' and the Reconstitution of Domination," *Race, Politics, and Culture: Critical Essays on the Radicalism of the 1960s*, ed. Adolph Reed Jr. (Westport, CT: Greenwood, 1986), 73.

11. Ibid.

12. Cornel West, "The Paradox of the Afro-American Rebellion," *Social Text* 9/10, (1984): 52.

13. Ibid., 56.

14. See, for example, Robin D. G. Kelley, *Race Rebels: Culture, Politics, and the Black Working Class* (New York: Free Press, 1994); Kevin K. Gaines, *Uplifting the Race: Black Leadership, Politics, and Culture in the Twentieth Century* (Chapel Hill: The University of North Carolina Press, 1996); Hazel V. Carby, "Policing the Black Woman's Body in an Urban Context," *Critical Inquiry* 18 (Summer 1992): 738–55; Joy James, *Transcending the Talented Tenth: Black Leaders and American Intellectuals* (New York: Routledge, 1997); and Erica R. Edwards, *Charisma and the Fictions of Black Leadership* (Minneapolis: University of Minnesota Press, 2012).

15. Cabral, "The Weapon of Theory," 110.

16. Peter M. Nichols, "NEW DVD'S; A Story of Black Insurrection Too Strong for 1973," *New York Times*, January 20, 2004, http://www.nytimes.com/2004/01/20/movies/new-dvd-s-a-story-of-black-insurrection-too-strong-for-1973.html.

17. Leah Samuel, "After 30 Years, 'Spook' Is Out," *Michigan Citizen* (Highland Park, MI), April 25, 2004.

18. The novel was adapted into a screenplay by Sam Greenlee and Melvin Clay that

was directed by Ivan Dixon. For the film's production and reception history, see Christine Acham, "Subverting the System: The Politics and Production of *The Spook Who Sat by the Door*," *Screening Noir* 1, no. 1 (2005): 13–125; Samantha N. Sheppard, "Persistently Displaced: Situated Knowledges and Interrelated Histories in *The Spook Who Sat by the Door*," *Cinema Journal* 52, no. 2 (2013): 71–92.

19. Leah Samuel, "After 30 Years, 'Spook' Is Out."

20. By examining data of World War II veterans whose service led to educational opportunities and to the development of skills transferable to other vocations, sociologists Irving Smith III, Kris Marsh, and David R. Segal identified a "veteran advantage" and concluded that "service in the armed forces can be a viable option to gain entry into the middle class, especially entry into the black middle class." "The World War II Veteran Advantage? A Lifetime Cross-Sectional Study of Social Status Attainment," *Armed Forces & Society* 38 (1): 24.

21. Drawing from Wilson Smith and Thomas Bender's research on the effect that the substantial funding from militarization efforts had on the expansion of higher education, which included monies from the GI Bill and the National Defense Education Act to universities and students ($3 billion in NDEA loans and fellowships by 1968), Roderick A. Ferguson observes that a "historical contradiction" emerged "in which the itineraries of war would—along with civil rights gains—help to produce the conditions for expanding student-body populations." Roderick A. Ferguson, *The Reorder of Things: The University and Its Pedagogies of Minority Difference* (Minneapolis: University of Minnesota Press, 2012), 49; Wilson Smith and Thomas Bender, introduction to *American Higher Education Transformed 1940–2005: Documenting the National Discourse*, ed. Wilson Smith and Thomas Bender (Baltimore: John Hopkins University Press, 2008), 2.

22. Acham, "Subverting the System: The Politics and Production of *The Spook Who Sat by the Door*," 115–16.

23. Ibid., 116.

24. Ibid., 116–17.

25. Ibid., 118.

26. Karl Marx and Friedrich Engels, *Manifesto of the Communist Party*, accessed April 22, 2017, https://www.marxists.org/archive/marx/works/1848/communist-manifesto/ch01.htm.

27. Katy Fletcher, "Evolution of the Modern American Spy Novel," *Journal of Contemporary History* 22, no. 2 (1987): 323.

28. Sandra Hollin Flowers, *African American Nationalist Literature of the 1960s: Pens of Fire* (New York: Garland, 1996), 139.

29. Ibid., 138.

30. Ibid., 139.

31. Ibid.

32. Robin D. G. Kelley, "House Negroes on the Loose: Malcolm X and the Black Bourgeoisie," *Callaloo* 21, no. 2 (1998): 420.

33. In a real-life parallel, Amílcar Cabral was betrayed and assassinated by a member of his political party, the PAIGC, who allied with the Portuguese, possibly in return for financial and political rewards. See Patrick Chabal, *Amílcar Cabral: Revolutionary Leadership and People's War* (Cambridge: Cambridge University Press, 1983), 132–35.

34. Quoted in Gilbert H. Muller, *John A. Williams* (Boston: Twayne, 1984), 90.

35. Richard Yarborough, foreword to *Sons of Darkness, Sons of Light: A Novel of Some Probability* (1969; Boston: Northeastern University Press, 1999).

36. Eric Sundquist reads Hod as the other protagonist in the novel, the means by which the novel explores links between Black liberation and Zionism but also engages with the critique over Israel's involvement in the 1967 Six Days War against Palestinians, complicating an easy parallel between African Americans and Jews, since the novel could also be comparing African Americans to the Arabs. Sundquist also explains the novel's title in relation to an apocalyptic war depicted in the Dead Sea Scrolls between the "Sons of Darkness" and the "Sons of Light." See Eric J. Sundquist, *Strangers in the Land: Blacks, Jews, Post-Holocaust America* (Cambridge, MA: Harvard University Press, 2005), 368–80, accessed March 7, 2015, ProQuest Ebrary.

37. Matthew Calihman, "Black Power Beyond Black Nationalism: John A. Williams, Cultural Pluralism, and the Popular Front," *MELUS* 34, no. 1 (Spring 2009): 155, 157.

38. Muller, *John A. Williams*, 87.

39. John O'Brien and John A. Williams, "The Art of John A. Williams," *The American Scholar* 42, no. 3 (1973): 494.

40. Ibid., 498.

41. For these insights into the periodization and institutional manifestations of the Black Power movement, I draw from Joyce M. Bell's book *The Black Power Movement and American Social Work* (New York: Columbia University Press, 2014). Published in 1969, *Sons of Darkness* is set in the near future in 1973, so the narrative's production and setting reference the latter years of the Black Power movement.

42. See Rodolfo F. Acuña, *The Making of Chicana/o Studies: In the Trenches of Academe* (New Brunswick: Rutgers University Press, 2011); Fabio Rojas, *From Black Power to Black Studies: How a Radical Social Movement Became an Academic Discipline* (Baltimore: Johns Hopkins University Press, 2007); and Michael Soldatenko, *Chicano Studies: The Genesis of a Discipline* (Tucson: University of Arizona Press, 2009).

43. Bell, *The Black Power Movement and American Social Work*.

44. Ibid., 11.

45. John Carlos Rowe, *Afterlives of Modernism: Liberalism, Transnationalism, and Political Critique* (Hanover, NH: Dartmouth College Press, 2011), 191.

46. Ibid., 12.

47. O'Brien and Williams, "The Art of John A. Williams," 491.

48. *Habla Men*, directed by Alberto Ferreras (Latino Media Works, 2014).

49. José E. Limón, "Transnational Triangulation: Mexico, the United States and the Emergence of a Mexican American Middle Class," in *Mexico and Mexicans in the Making of the United States*, ed. John Tutino (Austin: University of Texas Press, 2012), 238.

50. Gordon Hutner, *What America Read: Taste, Class, and the Novel, 1920–1960* (Chapel Hill: University of North Carolina Press, 2009), 14.

51. Philip Bracher, "Writing the Fragmented Self in Oscar Zeta Acosta's *Autobiography of a Brown Buffalo*," in *Ethnic Life Writing and Histories: Genres, Performances, and Culture* (Berlin: Lit Verlag, 2007), 169.

52. Jeanne Thwaites, "The Use of Irony in Oscar Zeta Acosta's *Autobiography of a Brown Buffalo*," *Americas Review* 20 (Spring 1992): 75.

53. Herant A. Katchadourian, *Guilt: The Bite of Conscience* (Stanford, CA: Stanford General Books, 2010), 15.

54. Ibid.

55. Héctor Calderón, "A Recorder of Events with a Sour Stomach: Oscar Zeta Acosta and *The Autobiography of a Brown Buffalo*," in *Narratives of Greater Mexico: Essays on Chicano Literary History, Genre, and Borders* (Austin: University of Texas Press, 2004), 85–110.

56. Michael Hames-García, "Dr. Gonzo's Carnival: The Testimonial Satires of Oscar Zeta Acosta," *American Literature* 72, no. 3 (2000): 471–72.

57. Ibid., 472.

58. James Smethurst, "The Figure of the *Vato Loco* and the Representation of Ethnicity in the Narratives of Oscar Z. Acosta," *MELUS* 20, no. 2 (1995): 126.

59. Stephen Schryer, "Cockroach Dreams: Oscar Zeta Acosta, Legal Services, and the Great Society Coalition," *Twentieth Century Literature* 60, no. 4 (2014): 461.

60. Ibid., 464.

61. Ibid., 467.

62. Ibid., 469.

63. Ernesto Chávez, "*¡Mi Raza Primero!: Nationalism, Identity, and Insurgency in the Chicano Movement in Los Angeles, 1966–1978* (Berkeley: University of California Press, 2002), 49.

64. Calderón, "A Recorder of Events with a Sour Stomach," 85–110.

65. Lawrence Buell, "Downwardly Mobile for Conscience's Sake: Voluntary Simplicity from Thoreau to Lily Bart," *American Literary History* 17, no. 4 (2005): 653.

66. Salvador Plascencia, *The People of Paper* (2005; Orlando: Harcourt, 2006), 53.

67. Another way to read Browning's outcome is that he does continue to enact class suicide in that his commitment to "teach down this system" (268) indicates he will continue to identify with the masses and not settle for material rewards. The novel offers us glimpses of the various ways Browning has been fighting the temptation to become more bourgeois, showing and gesturing to what a long-term commitment to class suicide might look like outside of an imperial context.

68. Women of color feminism has shown that in articulations of Chicano and Black nationalist radical politics, what was not radical was how women were treated and represented in these movements, a criticism that applies to these novels. In all three masculine fantasies, women are peripheral characters who provide support, information, and sex. Stephane Dunn's analysis of the gender politics in *The Spook* sums this up well: "While it is not a woman's place to lead or organize the core of the black revolution liberation movement or engage in the necessary violent actions of war, women serve the men who intellectually lead and wield the gun. Thus, the classed women in *The Spook* are primarily sexualized beings who are attracted to black phallic power." Stephane Dunn, *Baad Bitches and Sassy Supermamas: Black Power Action Films* (Urbana-Champaign: University of Illinois Press, 2008), 83. In the last statement, Dunn is referring to how the two female characters in the text occupy different class positions; Freeman has two girlfriends, Joy and a sex worker Freeman calls the "Dahomey Queen," who also has a relationship with a high-ranking official from whom she secures information to pass on to Freeman. While both women help support Freeman's playboy image, the latter is useful for the information she can obtain, and the former is treacherous for the information she passes on. An act of female betrayal

is also present in *Sons of Darkness*, through Browning's wife's affair that threatens to upend Browning's domestic sanctuary. Betrayal looms over *The Revolt*, but it is Brown Buffalo's potential betrayal to which the text alludes. Women still play a marginal role in service of bolstering Brown Buffalo's radicalness and hypermasculinity, however, from his sister whose suburban existence stands in for apolitical assimilation to the groupies who fawn over him.

69. Roderick A. Ferguson, *The Reorder of Things: The University and Its Pedagogies of Minority Difference* (Minneapolis: University of Minnesota Press, 2012), 144.

70. Ibid., 36.

71. Ibid., 8.

CHAPTER 3

A portion of this chapter was previously published in "'Jesus, When Did You Become So Bourgeois, Huh?': Status Panic in Chicana/o Cultural Production," *Aztlán: A Journal of Chicana/o Studies* 38.2 (2013): 11–40, © Regents of the University of California. Published by the UCLA Chicano Studies Research Center Press. Reprinted with permission.

1. Michael L. Schwalbe and Douglas Mason-Schrock, "Identity Work as Group Process," *Advances in Group Processes* 13 (1996): 113.

2. I discuss this more in Chapters 4 and 5. Some scholarly examples are Randall Kennedy, *Sellout: The Politics of Racial Betrayal* (New York: Pantheon, 2008); Brando Simeo Starkey, *In Defense of Uncle Tom* (New York: Cambridge University Press, 2015); and Vershawn Ashanti Young and Bridget Harris Tsemo, eds., *From Bourgeois to Boojie: Black Middle-Class Performances* (Detroit: Wayne State University Press, 2011).

3. *My Family / Mi Familia*, directed by Gregory Nava (New Line, 1995).

4. *Bourgeois* currently signals an ethical-political label more than it does a defined class, connoting values that range from positive (industriousness, sobriety, decorum, moderation and comfort) to negative (class superiority in relation to the proletariat or working-class, exemplified by preferences in taste or politics). Maria Ossowska, *Bourgeois Morality*, trans. G. L. Campbell (London: Routledge and Kegan Paul, 1986), 7. Furthermore, while there is a difference between the terms *bourgeois* and *middle class*, with the former more accurately characteristic of eighteenth- and nineteenth-century European social formations, the fact that it has become shorthand for a critique of values associated with the middle stratum in common parlance is worth taking into account.

5. Karen Pyke and Tran Dang, "'FOB' and 'Whitewashed': Identity and Internalized Racism Among Second Generation Asian Americans," *Qualitative Sociology* 26, no. 2 (2003): 152.

6. Randall Kennedy, *Sellout: The Politics of Racial Betrayal* (New York: Pantheon, 2008), 84.

7. Law professor Kevin R. Johnson discusses the various ways in which Latinoa/s try to assimilate by "whitening" themselves, which includes emphasizing their European ancestry, Anglicizing their names, marrying Anglos, and adopting society's racial attitudes. See Kevin R. Johnson, "'Melting Pot' or 'Ring of Fire'?: Assimilation and the Mexican-American Experience," *California Law Review* 85, no. 5 (1997): 1259–1313.

8. Richard T. Rodríguez, *Next of Kin: The Family in Chicano/a Cultural Politics* (Durham, NC: Duke University Press, 2009), 73.

9. Fregoso writes, "*My Family* is a Chicano family romance, an epic composed of

memory traces triggered by familiar historical tropes and desires: indigenous music and iconography, circular migrations, Californio territorial claims, service workers, repatriation during the thirties, state repression, pachuco resistance, political activism, and incarceration. These dominant tropes and desires provide the narrative threads for an alternative Chicano revisionist history and give voice to the film's veiled discourse on the nation. . . . Gregory Nava's 'familia Sánchez' is paradigmatic for a nation. The familia of José and María Sánchez are designed to stand for the familia of Chicanas and Chicanos." Rosa Linda Fregoso, *MeXicana Encounters: The Making of Social Identities on the Borderlands* (Berkeley: University of California Press, 2003), 71.

10. The older brother, Chucho (Esai Morales) is shown getting killed in the late 1950s, shot by the LAPD while attempting to hide out after a knife fight at a dancehall led to the accidental death of his rival in the fight.

11. José Antonio Villarreal, *Pocho* (1959; New York: Anchor Books, 1989); Tomás Rivera, *. . . y no se lo tragó la tierra / . . . And the Earth Did Not Devour Him* (1971; Houston: Arte Público Press, 1992); Sandra Cisneros, *The House on Mango Street* (1984; New York: Random House, 2009); Helena María Viramontes, *Under the Feet of Jesus* (1995; New York: Plume, 1996).

12. Américo Paredes, *George Washington Gómez* (1930s; Houston: Arte Publico Press, 1990).

13. Arthur H. Goldsmith, Darrick Hamilton, and William Darity Jr., "Shades of Discrimination: Skin Tone and Wages," *American Economic Review* 96, no. 2 (2006): 245.

14. George J. Sánchez, *Becoming Mexican American: Ethnicity, Culture, and Identity in Chicano Los Angeles, 1900–1945* (New York: Oxford University Press, 1993).

15. Richard A. Garcia, *Rise of the Mexican American Middle Class: San Antonio, 1929–1941* (College Station: Texas A & M University Press, 1991), 53.

16. Ibid., 264.

17. Ibid.

18. Scholars have also contested the argument that the League of United Latin American Citizens's (LULAC's) goals were assimilationist in the cultural and racial sense. María Josefina Saldaña-Portillo suggests that "even as LULACers sought to assimilate into white citizenship, they refused to 'give up [their] Mexican character,' to privatize their racial difference. Rather, one could argue that they tried to expand the notion of what it meant to be a white American so that it would approximate a *mestizo* consciousness." See María Josefina Saldaña-Portillo, "'How many Mexicans [is] a horse worth?' The League of United Latin American Citizens, Desegregation Cases, and Chicano Historiography," *South Atlantic Quarterly* 107, no. 4 (2008): 824. Along these lines, John Morán González argues that while LULAC wanted to assimilate into U.S. civic public life, it saw the domestic sphere as a vital space in which it preserved Mexican cultural values and beliefs. González also points out that while LULAC was conservative in its tactics, it tried to hold the United States accountable for its democratic promises. John Morán González, *Border Renaissance: The Texas Centennial and the Emergence of Mexican American Literature* (Austin: University of Texas Press, 2009), 95–126.

19. Rodolfo Acuña, *Occupied America: A History of Chicanos* 4th ed. (New York: Longman, 2000), 350.

20. Marcial González, *Chicano Novels and the Politics of Form: Race, Class, and Reification* (Ann Arbor: University of Michigan Press, 2009), 5.

21. Rosaura Sánchez, "The Chicana Labor Force," in *Essays on la mujer*, ed. Rosaura Sánchez and Rosa Martinez Cruz (Los Angeles: Chicano Studies Center Publications, UCLA, 1977), 14.

22. Most notable is the Chicano origin story: that Chicanos are the descendants of the Mexica people who once occupied Aztlán, the territory now demarcated as the U.S. Southwest. This posits that the migration of Mexicans to the United States was not really an occupation of a new land but a return to and reclamation of land once inhabited.

23. Fregoso, *MeXicana Encounters*, 72.

24. José E. Limón, "Transnational Triangulation: Mexico, the United States and the Emergence of a Mexican American Middle Class," in *Mexico and Mexicans in the Making of the United States*, ed. John Tutino (Austin: University of Texas Press, 2012), 238.

25. Luis Valdez, *Zoot Suit and Other Plays* (Houston: Arte Publico Press, 1992), 167.

26. Tomás R. Jiménez, *Replenished Ethnicity: Mexican Americans, Immigration, and Identity* (Berkeley: University of California Press, 2010).

27. Edward E. Telles and Vilma Ortiz, *Generations of Exclusion: Mexican Americans, Assimilation, and Race* (New York: Russell Sage Foundation, 2008), 140.

28. Rivera, *. . . y no se lo tragó la tierra / . . . And the Earth Did Not Devour Him*.

29. Ramón Saldívar, *Chicano Narrative: The Dialectics of Difference* (Madison: University of Wisconsin Press, 1990), 86.

30. Sandra Cisneros, *The House on Mango Street* (1984; New York: Random House, 2009).

31. Raymund A. Paredes, "Mexican American Authors and the American Dream," *MELUS* 8, no. 4 (1981): 76.

32. John Alba Cutler, *Ends of Assimilation: The Formation of Chicano Literature* (Oxford: Oxford University Press, 2015), 12.

33. Marcus Embry aptly observes, "Viramontes's text is clearly a retelling of Tomás Rivera's 1971 classic . . . From images of boys in trees, to constant travel, to learning to question authority, to a final scene in which the protagonist has climbed up off the ground in order to face the future, when these texts are paired the contrast and retelling is evident. In the retelling one can see the development of Chicana voices and perspectives since the days of Rivera." Quoted in Scott A. Beck and Dolores E. Rangel, "Representations of Mexican American Migrant Childhood in Rivera's *. . . y no se lo tragó la tierra* and Viramontes's *Under the Feet of Jesus*," *Bilingual Review Press* (2009): 14–15.

34. Beck and Rangel, "Representations of Mexican American Migrant Childhood," 18.

35. George Lakoff and Mark Johnson, *Metaphors We Live By*, 2nd ed. (1980; Chicago: University of Chicago Press, 2003).

36. Deborah Clarke, *Driving Women: Fiction and Automobile Culture in Twentieth-Century America* (Baltimore: Johns Hopkins University Press, 2007), 185.

37. Paula M. L. Moya, *Learning from Experience: Minority Identities, Multicultural Struggles* (Berkeley: University of California Press, 2002) 211.

38. Saldívar, *Chicano Narrative*, 87.

39. Moya, *Learning from Experience*, 200–206.

40. Moya explains, "It is embodied because Estrella's ability to read the world develops as a result of practical activity; it is intersubjective because what Estrella knows depends on her communicative interaction with others; and it is egalitarian because the knowledge Es-

trella gains is acquired through non-exploitive relations of human exchange." Moya, *Learning from Experience*, 184–85.

41. Jeehyun Lim, "Reimagining Citizenship Through Bilingualism: The Migrant Bilingual Child in Helena María Viramontes' *Under the Feet of Jesus*," *Women's Studies Quarterly* 38, nos. 1–2 (2010): 221–42.

42. Lydia R. Cooper, "'Bone, Flesh, Feather, Fire': Symbol as Freedom in Helena Maria Viramontes's *Under the Feet of Jesus*," *Critique* 51, no. 4 (2010): 376.

43. Moya, *Learning from Experience*, 210.

44. Lim, "Reimagining Citizenship Through Bilingualism," 233.

45. Jennifer Lee, "Cultural Brokers: Race-Based Hiring in Inner-City Neighborhoods," *American Behavioral Scientist* 41, no 7 (1998): 927–37; Jody Agius Vallejo, *Barrio to Burbs: The Making of the Mexican American Middle Class* (Stanford, CA: Stanford University Press, 2012), 83.

46. Cooper, "Bone, Flesh, Feather, Fire."

47. Dan Latimer, "The La Brea Tar Pits, Tongues of Fire: Helena María Viramontes's *Under the Feet of Jesus* and Its Background," *Soundings: An Interdisciplinary Journal* 85, no. 3–4 (2002): 323–46.

48. Helena María Viramontes and Carmen Flys-Junquera, "Helena María Viramontes: Social and Political Perspectives of a Chicana Writer," *Arizona Journal of Hispanic Cultural Studies* 5 (2001): 232.

49. Cherríe Moraga and Gloria Anzaldúa, eds., *This Bridge Called My Back: Writings by Radical Women of Color* (Watertown, MA: Persephone Press, 1981), 23.

50. Héctor Calderón, "The Novel and the Community of Readers: Rereading Tomás Rivera's *Y no se lo tragó la tierra*," in *Criticism in the Borderlands: Studies in Chicano Literature, Culture, and Ideology*, ed. Héctor Calderón and José David Saldívar (Durham, NC: Duke University Press, 1991), 107.

51. For example, Chicana artists have reconfigured the Virgin of Guadalupe into a feminist icon. See Ester Hernández, *La Virgen de Guadalupe Defendiendo los Derechos de los Xicanos* (The Virgin of Guadalupe Defending the Rights of the Xicanos), 1975; Yolanda M. López, *Portrait of the Artist as the Virgin of Guadalupe*, 1978; and Alma Lopez, *Our Lady*, 1999.

52. Isabel Dulfano, "Some Thoughts Shared with Helena Maria Viramontes," *Women's Studies* 30, no. 5 (2001): 658.

53. Rosaura Sánchez, "Ideological Discourses in Arturo Islas's *The Rain God*," in *Criticism in the Borderlands: Studies in Chicano Literature, Culture, and Ideology*, ed. Héctor Calderón and José David Saldívar (Durham, NC: Duke University Press, 1991), 116.

54. Calderón, "The Novel and the Community of Readers," 99.

CHAPTER 4

A portion of this chapter was previously published in "'Jesus, When Did You Become So Bourgeois, Huh?': Status Panic in Chicana/o Cultural Production," *Aztlán: A Journal of Chicana/o Studies* 38.2 (2013): 11–40, © Regents of the University of California. Published by the UCLA Chicano Studies Research Center Press. Reprinted with permission.

1. C. Wright Mills, *White Collar: The American Middle Classes* (1951; New York: Oxford University Press, 2002), 239–40.

2. *Brown Is the New Green: George Lopez and the American Dream*, directed by Phillip Rodriguez (PBS Home Video, 2007).

3. Richard Rodriguez, "Inside the Mexican-American Middle Class: Success Stories: Voices from an Emerging Elite," *Los Angeles Times*, November 6, 1988, http://articles.latimes.com/1988-11-06/magazine/tm-85_1_middle-class.

4. Gregory Rodriguez, "The Emerging Latino Middle Class," Pepperdine University for Public Policy AT&T Paper, October 1996, 7.

5. Mills, *White Collar*.

6. Ibid., first quote, 58; second quote, 34.

7. For example, the shows *The Jeffersons* (CBS, 1975–1985), *The Cosby Show* (NBC, 1984–1992), *Family Matters* (ABC, 1989–1997 and CBS, 1997–1998), *The Fresh Prince of Bel-Air* (NBC, 1990–1996), and *Girlfriends* (UPN, 2000–2006 and The CW 2006–2008).

8. Richard Rodriguez, *Hunger of Memory: The Education of Richard Rodriguez* (1982; New York: Random House, 2004); *Days of Obligation: An Argument with My Mexican Father* (New York: Viking, 1992); *Brown: The Last Discovery of America* (New York: Viking, 2002). Rodriguez produced a fourth collection of essays in 2013, *Darling: A Spiritual Autobiography*.

9. Tomás Rivera, "*Hunger of Memory* as Humanistic Antithesis," *MELUS* 11, no. 4 (1981): 9.

10. Norma Alarcón, "Tropology of Hunger: The 'Miseducation' of Richard Rodriguez" in *The Ethnic Canon: Histories, Institutions, and Interventions*, ed. David Palumbo-Liu (Minneapolis: University of Minnesota Press, 1995), 147.

11. Paula M. L. Moya, *Learning from Experience: Minority Identities, Multicultural Struggles* (Berkeley: University of California Press, 2002), 108.

12. Ramón Saldívar, *Chicano Narrative: The Dialectics of Difference* (Madison: University of Wisconsin Press, 1990), 159.

13. For how scholars have reassessed Rodriguez, see the special issue "Richard Rodriguez: Public Intellectual," ed. José E. Limón, *Texas Studies in Literature and Language* 40, no. 4 (1998). See also Teresa McKenna, *Migrant Song: Politics and Process in Contemporary Chicano Literature* (Austin: University of Texas Press, 1997), 50–70; Juan E. De Castro, "Richard Rodriguez in 'Borderland': The Ambiguity of Hybridity," *Aztlán* 26 (2001): 101–26; José David Saldívar, *Border Matters: Remapping American Cultural Studies* (Berkeley: University of California Press, 1997), 146–151; Rubén Martínez, "Rubén Martínez on *Darling: A Spiritual Autobiography*," *Los Angeles Review of Books*, October 24, 2013, http://lareviewofbooks.org/review/desert-pilgrimage.

14. Moya, *Learning from Experience*, 103.

15. Rodriguez, *Days of Obligation*, 66.

16. Moya, *Learning from Experience*, 117–18.

17. In their queer readings of Rodriguez's works, Randy Rodríguez and Sandra Soto have also brought attention to why Rodriguez would not want to identify as gay at this point in his career and why *Hunger of Memory* would express a desire for a separation between the private and public sphere. See Randy A. Rodríguez, "Richard Rodriguez Reconsidered: Queering the Sissy (Ethnic) Subject," in "Richard Rodriguez: Public Intellectual," special issue, *Texas Studies in Literature and Language* 40, no. 4 (1998): 396–423; Sandra K. Soto, *Reading Chican@ Like a Queer: The De-mastery of Desire* (Austin: University of Texas Press, 2010), 39–58, accessed July 15, 2015, ProQuest ebrary.

18. Like Rodriguez, Arturo Islas and Ruben Navarette also attempted to answer this question. Islas includes middle-class characters in his two semiautobiographical novels, *Rain God* (1984) and *Migrant Souls* (1990), in which, like Rodriguez, he describes experiences of self-loathing and generational disconnect. In the autobiography *A Darker Shade of Crimson: Odyssey of a Harvard Chicano* (1994), journalist Reuban Navarette also expresses ambivalence about upward mobility that arises in the course of trying to disprove Rodriguez's claims in *Hunger of Memory* that education necessitates cultural sacrifices.

19. Henry Staten, "Ethnic Authenticity, Class, and Autobiography: The Case of *Hunger of Memory*," *PMLA* 113, no. 1 (1988): 118.

20. Susan E. Keefe and Amado Padilla, *Chicano Ethnicity* (Albuquerque: University of New Mexico Press, 1987), 48.

21. Herman Gray, *Watching Race* (Minneapolis: University of Minnesota Press, 2004), 59.

22. Mark Sachs, "The Good, the Bad, the Funny," *Los Angeles Times*, January 12, 2003.

23. The show endured in popularity in its syndicated run on Nick-at-Nite.

24. "Profiles in Courage," *George Lopez*, ABC, aired on March 12, 2003. In this episode, George cannot prevent the Powers brothers from denying the Arab worker, Hosni, the head inspector job, but assures Hosni he will make sure he gets the same pay and benefits, and the episode wraps up with them still friends. On one hand, George's role in mediating this conflict could be read as him preserving the status quo—a power dynamic in which ethnics are read primarily through stereotypes and which informs the status panic he himself feels. On the other hand, George Lopez wrote this episode, and by featuring the clear misreading and mistreatment of the Arab character, the episode challenges the dominant portrayal of Arabs in the media as terrorists.

25. "George Thinks Max's Future Is on the Line" and "George Decides to Sta-Local Where It's Familia," *George Lopez*, ABC, aired on May 8, 2007.

26. "Token of Unappreciation," *George Lopez*, ABC, aired on October 9, 2002.

27. Rodriquez, *Hunger of Memory*, 173–74.

28. Another difference is that while both demonstrate status panic, George in the end finds resolution when he stops being an assembly line worker; Rodriguez, however, never stops being a minority.

29. *Bread and Roses*, directed by Ken Loach (Lions Gate, 2000).

30. David Román, *Performance in America: Contemporary U.S. Culture and the Performing Arts* (Durham, NC: Duke University Press, 2005), 36.

31. "Meet the Cuban Parents," *George Lopez*, ABC, aired on December 11, 2002.

32. Lopez's stand-up routines are notoriously more critical of family life, but this critique is relegated to his working-class upbringing, specifically how his grandmother's cruel teasing and lack of support affected his self-esteem, once again painting working-class family relationships as dysfunctional.

33. John Markert, "'The George Lopez Show': The Same Old Hispano?" *Bilingual Review / La Revista Bilingüe* 28, no. 2 (2007): 148–65.

34. Michele Serros, "Latino-Themed Writing 101," Fox News, January 27, 2012, http://latino.foxnews.com/latino/entertainment/2012/01/27/michele-serros-latino-themed-writing-101.

35. Dave Chapelle, "Chapelle's Story," Oprah.com, February 3, 2006, http://www.oprah.com/oprahshow/Chappelles-Story.

36. Serros, "Latino-Themed Writing 101."

37. George Lopez and Armen Keteyian, *Why You Crying? My Long, Hard Look at Life, Love, and Laughter* (New York: Simon and Schuster, 2004), 116.

38. Erica Scharrer, "From Wise to Foolish: The Portrayal of the Sitcom Father, 1950s–1990s," *Journal of Broadcasting and Electronic Media* 45 (2001): 23–40.

39. *Brown Is the New Green: George Lopez and the American Dream.*

40. Maria Elena Fernandez, "TV Just Got a Lot 'Whiter,' Says a Canceled George Lopez," *Los Angeles Times*, May 14, 2007, http://latimesblogs.latimes.com/showtracker/2007/05/post_1.html.

41. In *Hybrid Fictions*, Daniel Grassian calls Serros a "Generation X Latina" because she openly embraces ethnic hybridity and does not reject assimilation. Grassian, *Hybrid Fictions: American Literature and Generation X* (New York: McFarland, 2003).

42. Michele Serros, *Chicana Falsa: And Other Stories of Death, Identity, and Oxnard* (New York: Riverhead Books, 1998); *How to Be a Chicana Role Model* (New York: Riverhead Books, 2000).

43. Ernesto Galarza, *Barrio Boy: The Story of a Boy's Acculturation* (1971; Notre Dame, IN: Notre Dame University Press, 1980); José Antonio Villarreal, *Pocho* (1959; New York: Anchor Books, 1989); Sandra Cisneros, *The House on Mango Street* (1984; New York: Random House, 2009).

44. *Honey Blonde Chica* (New York: Simon Pulse, 2006). A sequel, *Scandalosa*, was published in 2007.

45. Interview with Debbie Elliot, *All Things Considered*, National Public Radio, May 28, 2006, http://www.npr.org/templates/story/story.php?storyId=5436106.

46. Amy Pattee, "Commodities in Literature, Literature as Commodity: A Close Look at the Gossip Girl Series," *Children's Literature Association* (2006): 168.

47. Barbara Ehrenreich, *Fear of Falling: The Inner Life of the Middle Class* (New York: Perennial, 1990).

48. Ralph E. Rodriguez, "Chicano Studies and the Need to Not Know," *American Literary History* 22, no. 1 (2009): 180–90.

49. Raphael Dalleo and Elena Machado Sáez, *The Latino/a Canon and the Emergence of Post-Sixties Literature* (New York: Palgrave Macmillan, 2007), 7.

50. Rafael Pérez-Torres, *Movements in Chicano Poetry: Against Myths, Against Margins* (New York: Cambridge University Press, 1995), 48.

51. A *Los Angeles Times* critic observed that "Many black Americans were immediately offended (what's with the '-ish'?), many white Americans were immediately outraged ('How is ABC Television allowed to have a show entitled "Blackish"?,' tweeted Donald Trump. 'Can you imagine the furor of a show, "Whiteish"! Racism at highest level?').'" Mary McNamara, "This Is the Season That Made 'black-ish' a Hit," *Los Angles Times*, May 18, 2016, http://www.latimes.com/entertainment/tv/la-et-st-blackish-finale-20160517-snap-story.html.

52. Brennan Williams, "'Black-ish' Creator Kenya Barris Defines New Show and Responds to Critics," *The Huffington Post*, last updated September 4, 2014, http://www.huffingtonpost.com/2014/08/29/black-ish-kenya-barris-critics-_n_5737966.html.

53. Quote from Tracee Ellis Ross's explanation of the term "black-ish" on *The Late Show with Stephen Colbert*, CBS, aired on September 15, 2016.

54. "Pilot," *black-ish*, ABC, aired on September 24, 2014.

55. Carrol Washington, Joseph Broussard, and Ralph Williams, "Mr. Big Stuff Lyrics," accessed March 26, 2017, http://www.lyrics.com/lyric/22810188.

56. For example, the opening episode to season three revolves around Dre's joy at being able to use and flaunt his family's VIP pass at Disney World. "VIP," *black-ish*, ABC, aired on September 21, 2016.

57. Emily Nussbaum, "In Living Color: With "black-ish" Kenya Barris Rethinks the Family Sitcom," *The New Yorker*, April 25, 2016, http://www.newyorker.com/magazine/2016/04/25/black-ish-transforms-the-family-sitcom.

58. "The Gift of Hunger," *black-ish*, ABC, aired on November 12, 2014.

59. "Martin Luther Skiing Day," *black-ish*, ABC, aired on January 14, 2015.

60. Relaying that concerns about racism are irrational, the show on other episodes conveys that classism is rational, depicting Dre's working-class extended family in the form of rough-around-the-edges cousins who make the family fearful because they lack propriety and inflict casual and needless violence.

61. "Mistaken Identity," *The Fresh Prince of Bel-Air*, NBC, aired on October 15, 1990.

62. Yesha Callahan, "Chris Rock Uses Selfies to Chronicle Times Police Pull Him Over," *The Root*, April 1, 2015, http://www.theroot.com/blog/the-grapevine/chris_rock_chronicles_his_police_pullovers_with_selfies.

63. Nussbaum, "In Living Color."

64. "Hope," *black-ish*, ABC, aired on February 24, 2016.

65. Debbie Emery, "'Black-ish' Episode on Police Brutality Hits Hard on Social Media: 'This Scene Was So Real,'" *The Wrap*, February 24, 2016, http://www.thewrap.com/black-ish-episode-on-police-brutality-hits-hard-on-social-media-this-scene-was-so-real.

66. Nussbaum, "In Living Color."

67. James Poniewozik, "With Police Brutality Episode, 'black-ish' Shows How Sitcoms Can Still Matter," *New York Times*, February 25, 2016, https://www.nytimes.com/2016/02/26/arts/television/blackish-police-brutality.html?_r=0.

68. Nussbaum, "In Living Color."

69. Williams, "'Black-ish' Creator Kenya Barris Defines New Show and Responds to Critics."

70. Nussbaum, "In Living Color."

CHAPTER 5

1. James Weldon Johnson, *The Autobiography of an Ex-Colored Man* (1912; New York: Random House, 1989: 197).

2. Noah Frankovitch, "Why Can't Anyone Tell I'm Wearing This Business Suit Ironically?" *The Onion*, November 30, 2005, http://www.theonion.com/content/node/43032.

3. Percival Everett, *Erasure* (New York: Hyperion Books, 2001).

4. Lynn Nottage, *Intimate Apparel / Fabulation, or the Re-Education of Undine* (New York: Theatre Communications Group, 2006; the latter first performed in 2004).

5. Herman Gray, *Watching Race* (Minneapolis: University of Minnesota Press, 2004), 148.

6. Thelma Golden, Introduction to *Freestyle* (New York: The Studio Museum in Harlem, 2001), 14–15; Mark Anthony Neale, *Soul Babies: Black Popular Culture and the Post-Soul Aesthetic* (New York: Routledge, 2002).

7. Bertram D. Ashe, "Theorizing the Post-Soul Aesthetic: An Introduction," *African American Review* 41, no. 4 (2007): 614.

8. Paul Beatty, *White Boy Shuffle* (New York: Houghton Mifflin, 1996), 52.

9. Colson Whitehead, *Sag Harbor* (New York: Doubleday, 2009), 57.

10. Vershawn Ashanti Young, "Introduction: Performing Citizenship," in *From Bourgeois to Boojie: Black Middle-Class Performances*, ed. Vershawn Ashanti Young and Bridget Harris (Detroit: Wayne State University Press, 2011), 16.

11. E. Franklin Frazier, *Black Bourgeoisie* (New York: Free Press, 1957); Dorothy West, *The Living Is Easy* (1948; New York: Feminist Press, 1982); Gloria Naylor, *Linden Hills* (1985; New York: Penguin, 1986).

12. Gayle Wald, "*Passing Strange* and Post-Civil Rights Blackness," *Humanities Research* 16, no. 1 (2010): 12.

13. Catherine Rottenberg, "Passing: Race, Identification, and Desire," *Criticism* 45, no. 4 (2003): 435.

14. A reference to Stagger Lee, a folk figure and trickster based on the life of Lee Shelton (1865–1912), a carriage driver and pimp who shot a friend during a spirited political discussion. His crime has been narrated in the often-recorded blues folk song "Stagger Lee." See Cecil Brown, *Stagolee Shot Billy* (Cambridge, MA: Harvard University Press, 2003).

15. M. Giulia Fabi, *Passing and the Rise of the African American Novel* (2001; Urbana: University of Illinois Press, 2004), 16.

16. Ramón Saldívar, "Speculative Realism and the Postrace Aesthetic in Contemporary American Fiction," *A Companion to American Literary Studies*, ed. Caroline F. Levander and Robert S. Levine (London: Blackwell, 2011), Blackwell Reference Online, August 22, 2014, http://www.blackwellreference.com/subscriber/tocnode.html?id=g9781405198813_chunk_g9781405198813‌33.

17. Brian Yost, "The Changing Same," *Callaloo* 31 no. 4 (2008): 1329.

18. John K. Young, *Black Writers, White Publishers: Marketplace Politics in Twentieth-Century African American Literature* (Jackson: University Press of Mississippi, 2006), 12.

19. Eddie Stone, *Donald Writes No More* (Los Angeles: Holloway House, 2001), 229–30.

20. Danielle Fuentes Morgan, "'It's a Black Thang Maybe': Satirical Blackness in Percival Everett's *Erasure* and Adam Mansbach's *Angry Black White Boy*," in *Post-Soul Satire: Black Identity After Civil Rights*, ed. Derek C. Maus and James J. Donahue (Jackson: University Press of Mississippi, 2014), 166.

21. Valerie Smith, foreword to *Sarah Phillips*, by Andrea Lee (1984; Boston: Northeastern University Press, 1993), x.

22. Michael Knight, "My Friend, Percival," *Callaloo* 28, no. 2 (2005): 293.

23. Gillian Johns, "Everett's *Erasure*: Black Satire Meets 'The Pleasure of the Text,'" in *Post-Soul Satire: Black Identity After Civil Rights*, ed. Derek C. Maus and James J. Donahue (Jackson: University Press of Mississippi, 2014), 96.

24. Margaret Russett, "Race Under Erasure: For Percival Everett, 'A Piece of Fiction,'" *Callaloo* 28, no. 2 (2005): 364.

25. Imani Perry, *More Beautiful and More Terrible: The Embrace and Transcendence of Racial Inequality in the United States* (New York: New York University Press, 2011), 173.

26. The novel assumes that an audience for Monk's work does not exist, as if Monk does not have a peer group who would be interested in his more experimental novels.

27. Glenda Carpio, *Laughing Fit to Kill: Black Humor in the Fictions of Slavery* (Oxford, UK: Oxford University Press, 2008), 14.

28. Linda Hutcheon, *Irony's Edge: The Theory and Politics of Irony* (New York: Routledge: 1995).

29. George Lipsitz, *The Possessive Investment in Whiteness: How White People Profit from Identity Politics* (Philadelphia: Temple University Press, 1998), vii.

30. Kennell Jackson, "Introduction: Traveling While Black," *Black Cultural Traffic: Crossroads in Global Performance and Popular Culture*, ed. Harry J. Elam and Kennell Jackson (Ann Arbor: University of Michigan Press, 2005), 5.

31. Ibid., 8.

32. Darryl Dickson-Carr, "From Pilloried to Post-Soul: The Future of African American Satire," in *Post-Soul Satire: Black Identity After Civil Rights*, ed. Derek C. Maus and James J. Donahue (Jackson: University Press of Mississippi, 2014), 278.

33. Søren Kierkegaard, *The Concept of Irony with Continual Reference to Socrates*, ed. and trans. Howard V. Hong and Edna H. Hong (Princeton: Princeton University Press, 1989), 261.

34. Ibid.

35. *Bamboozled*, directed by Spike Lee (New Line Cinema, 2001).

36. Richard T. Ford, *Racial Culture: A Critique* (Princeton, NJ: Princeton University Press, 2006), 41.

37. *8 Mile*, directed by Curtis Hanson (Imagine Entertainment, 2002).

38. Harry Elam, "Change Clothes and Go: A Postscript to Postblackness," in *Black Cultural Traffic: Crossroads in Global Performance and Popular Culture*, ed. Harry J. Elam and Kennell Jackson (Ann Arbor: University of Michigan Press, 2005), 384.

39. Aimee Zygmonksi, "Slaves? With Lines? Trickster Aesthetic and Satirical Strategies in Two Plays by Lynn Nottage," in *Post-Soul Satire: Black Identity After Civil Rights*, ed. Derek C. Maus and James J. Donahue (Jackson: University Press of Mississippi, 2014), 204.

40. Lisa B. Thompson, *Beyond the Black Lady: Sexuality and the New African American Middle Class* (Urbana: University of Illinois Press, 2009) 3.

41. Wahneema Lubiano, "Black Ladies, Welfare Queens, and State Minstrels: Ideological War by Narrative Means," in *Race-ing Justice, En-gendering Power: Essays on Anita Hill, Clarence Thomas, and the Construction of Social Reality*, ed. Toni Morrison (New York: Pantheon, 1992), 335–38.

42. Sanford Schram and Joe Joss, "America Demonizes Its Poor: Ronald Reagan, Sam Brownback and the Myth of the 'Welfare Queen,'" *Salon*, last modified September 8, 2015, http://www.salon.com/2015/09/08/how_welfare_restrictions_demonize_the_poor_partner.

43. Zygmonksi, "Slaves? With Lines?"

44. Nicole King, "'You Think Like You White': Questioning Racial Community Through the Lens of Middle-Class Desire(s)," *NOVEL: A Forum on Fiction* 35, nos. 2/3 (2002): 211–30; Rolland Murray, "The Time of Breach: Class Division and the Contemporary African American Novel," *NOVEL: A Forum on Fiction* 43, no. 1 (2010): 11–17; Kenneth W. Warren, *What Was African American Literature?* (Cambridge, MA: Harvard University Press, 2011).

CHAPTER 6

1. Randall Kennedy, *Sellout: The Politics of Racial Betrayal* (New York: Pantheon, 2008), 62.

2. Américo Paredes, *George Washington Gómez* (1930s; Houston: Arte Publico Press, 1990), 204.

3. Bruce Robbins, *Upward Mobility and the Common Good: Toward a Literary History of the Welfare State* (Princeton, NJ: Princeton University Press, 2007), 235.

4. Héctor Calderón and José Rósbel López-Morín, "Interview with Américo Paredes," *Nepantla: Views from South* 1, no. 1 (2000): 197–228.

5. *The Gatekeeper*, directed by John Carlos Frey (Screen Media, 2002); *Machete*, directed by Robert Rodriguez and Ethan Maniquis (Twentieth Century Fox, 2010).

6. *Sleep Dealer*, directed by Alex Rivera (Maya Entertainment, 2008).

7. Rosa Linda Fregoso, *The Bronze Screen: Chicana and Chicano Film Culture* (Minneapolis: University of Minnesota Press, 1993), xv.

8. Randy J. Ontiveros, *In the Spirit of a New People: The Cultural Politics of the Chicano Movement* (New York: New York University Press, 2013), 39.

9. Kelly Lytle Hernandez, *Migra! A History of the U.S. Border Patrol* (Berkeley: University of California Press, 2010), 21.

10. Ibid., 42.

11. Neil Foley, *The White Scourge: Mexicans, Blacks, and Poor Whites in Texas Cotton Culture* (Berkeley: University of California Press, 1997), 13.

12. Lytle Hernandez, *Migra!*, 43.

13. James Pinkerton, "Hispanics Hold 52 Percent of Border Patrol Jobs," *Houston Chronicle*, December 29, 2008.

14. "5-Year Estimates," *U.S. Census Bureau, 2005–2009 American Community Survey* (Washington, DC: U.S. Census Bureau, 2011).

15. U.S. Customs and Border Protection, *Fiscal Year 2010 Annual Report on Hispanic Employment* (Washington, DC: Department of Homeland Security, 2011).

16. "Border Patrol Agent Pay and Benefits," Department of Homeland Security, accessed March 24, 2017, https://www.cbp.gov/careers/frontline-careers/bpa/pay-benefits#CareerProg.

17. Pinkerton, "Hispanics Hold 52 Percent of Border Patrol Jobs."

18. Verne G. Kopytoff, "Hispanic Agents Face Hurdles on Border Patrol," *New York Times*, January 29, 1996.

19. Sebastian Rotella, "Latino Agents See Patrol as Ladder to Success Series: Crossing the Line: Turmoil in the U.S. Border Patrol," *Los Angeles Times*, April 23, 1993.

20. Kopytoff, "Hispanic Agents Face Hurdles on Border Patrol."

21. "How Does Mexico and Her People Feel About Mexicans Working for the Border Patrol Arresting Mexicans?" Yahoo! Answers, accessed March 17, 2017, https://answers.yahoo.com/question/index?qid=20110129175641AATcFyt; Gustavo Arellano, "Are Mexican-American Border Patrol Agents Traitors?" *Dallas Observer*, September 2, 2010.

22. Most immigration films center on the Mexican working class crossing the border. David R. Maciel and María Rosa García-Acevedo survey the tradition of immigration films to explain the differences between those produced in Mexico and those in the United States, with the latter tradition extended by Chicana/os. None of the films they mention, however, feature a Mexican American Border Patrol agent. David R. Maciel and María Rosa García-

Acevedo, "The Celluloid Immigrant," in *Culture Across Borders: Mexican Immigration and Popular Culture*, ed. David R. Maciel and María Herrera-Sobek (Tucson: University of Arizona Press, 1998), 149–202.

23. Douglas Massey, Jorge Durand, and Nolan J. Malone, *Beyond Smoke and Mirrors: Mexican Immigration in an Era of Economic Integration* (New York: Russell Sage Foundation, 2003).

24. Ibid., 94.

25. Ibid., 94.

26. Ramón Saldívar, *Borderlands of Culture: Américo Paredes and the Transnational Imaginary* (Durham, NC: Duke University Press, 2006), 173.

27. Paz writes, "If the Chingada is a representation of the violated Mother, it is appropriate to associate her with the Conquest, which was also a violation, not only in the historical sense but also in the very flesh of Indian women. The symbol of this violation is doña Malinche, the mistress of Cortés. It is true that she gave herself voluntarily to the conquistador, but he forgot her as soon as her usefulness was over. Doña Marina becomes a figure representing the Indian women who were fascinated, violated or seduced by the Spaniards. And as a small boy will not forgive his mother if she abandons him to search for his father, the Mexican people have not forgiven La Malinche for her betrayal." Octavio Paz, *The Labyrinth of Solitude* (1961; New York: Grove Press, 1985), 86.

28. Ibid., 86–87.

29. Norma Alarcón, "Traddutora, Traditora: A Paradigmatic Figure of Chicana Feminism," *Cultural Critique* 13 (1989): 66; Sandra Messinger Cypess, *La Malinche in Mexican Literature: From History to Myth* (Austin: University of Texas Press, 1991), 97.

30. Michael C. Dawson, *Behind the Mule: Race and Class in African-American Politics* (New Jersey: Princeton University Press, 1994), 76.

31. Ibid., 80.

32. Gabriel R. Sanchez and Natalie Masuoka, "Brown-Utility Heuristic? The Presence and Contributing Factors of Latino Linked Fate," *Hispanic Journal of Behavioral Science* 32, no. 4 (2010): 519–31. The authors also argue that "Latinos with higher educational levels are more likely to believe that their individual fate is tied to that of other Latinos" (524).

33. Ibid., 523.

34. Jules Brenner, "The Gatekeeper," *Cinema Signals*, accessed March 24, 2017, http://variagate.com/gatekeep.htm?MRQE; Dave Kehr, "The Gatekeeper," *New York Times*, April 2, 2004.

35. John Carlos Frey, "*The Gatekeeper*: Talking Points,'" Gatekeeper Productions, last modified March 20, 2011, http://www.gatekeeperfilm.com.

36. Alex Jones, "Leaked *Machete* Script Confirms Race War Plot," last modified May 13, 2010, http://www.infowars.com.

37. John Nolte, "*Machete* Review: Dull, Convoluted, Racist and Anti-American," *Breitbart*, last modified September 4, 2010, http://www.bighollywood.breitbart.com.

38. Ian Buckwalter, "Machete: Out of the 'Grindhouse,' Trailer First," *NPR*, September 2, 2010, http://www.npr.org/templates/story/story.php?storyId=129472808.

39. Kyle Smith, "Blades of Gory," *New York Post*, September 3, 2010; Stephen Holden, "Growl, and Let the Severed Heads Fall Where They May," *New York Times*, September 2, 2010; Ty Burr, "*Machete*," *The Boston Globe*, September 3, 2010.

40. The film is a full-length expansion on Machete, a character introduced in a trailer spoof sandwiched by the double feature *Grindhouse* (2007), directed by Robert Rodriguez and Quentin Tarantino.

41. An early, undated version of the script is available on the Internet and omits this scene: http://screenplayexplorer.com/?tag=machete-script. It can also be found on the Internet Movie Script Database: http://www.imsdb.com/scripts/Machete.html.

42. "Jessica Alba Uncomfortable with Sexy Script," *Contact Music*, last modified November 11, 2010, http://www.contactmusic.com/jessica-alba/news/jessica-alba-uncomfortable-with-sexy-script_1183028.

43. Mimi Valdés Ryan, "Lost in Translation," *Latina*, March 2008, 97–102.

44. Ibid., 102.

45. Michele Elam, *The Souls of Mixed Folk: Race, Politics, and Aesthetics in the New Millennium* (Stanford, CA: Stanford University Press, 2011).

46. Javier Duran, "Virtual Borders, Data Aliens, and Bare Bodies: Culture, Securitization, and the Biometric State," *Journal of Borderlands Studies* 25, nos. 3–4 (2010): 224.

47. Dennis Lim, "At the Border Between Politics and Thrills," *New York Times*, March 15, 2009.

48. Lysa Rivera, "Future Histories and Cyborg Labor: Borderlands Science Fiction After NAFTA," *Science Fiction Studies* 39 (2012): 425.

49. Eric Schocket, *Vanishing Moments: Class and American Literature* (Ann Arbor: University of Michigan Press, 2006), 108.

50. The characters all speak in Spanish, but the cited quotes are from the subtitles provided with the film.

51. Charles Ramírez Berg, *Latino Images in Film: Stereotypes, Subversion, and Resistance* (Austin: University of Texas Press, 2002). Examples of films he identifies as part of this genre include *Bordertown* (1935), *A Medal for Benny* (1945), *The Ring* (1952), *Salt of the Earth* (1954), *Trial* (1955), and *Giant* (1956).

52. Building on the definitions put forth by Peter Roffman and Jim Purdy in *The Hollywood Social Problem Film*, Berg explains that the genre's project "was to expose topical issues rather than conceal them," with "the genre's distinguishing feature being its didacticism." Berg, *Latino Images in Film*, 111.

53. Berg, *Latino Images in Film*, 115.

54. Ibid., 114.

55. W. Marvin Dulaney, *Black Police in America* (Bloomington: Indiana University Press, 1996), 9.

56. See Christine Byers, "Black and in Blue: A Ferguson Police Sergeant Reflects on a Tough Time," *St. Louis Post-Dispatch*, October 3, 2014, http://www.stltoday.com/news/local/crime-and-courts/black-and-in-blue-a-ferguson-police-sergeant-reflects-on/article_b71556de-68b1-566f-a6ce-cc02c01b8343.html; Jesse J. Holland and Kristin J. Bender, "Black Police Straddle a Line Between Race and Duty," *Columbus Telegram*, December 10, 2014, http://columbustelegram.com/news/national/black-police-straddle-a-line-between-race-and-duty/article_dfaa27d2-f9e7-52a1-8b75-2d5128971ce4.html.

57. Wesley Morris, "Let's Be Real: 'Let's Be Cops,' Cop Movies, and the Shooting in Ferguson," *Grantland*, August 15, 2014, http://grantland.com/features/lets-be-cops-review-michael-brown-shooting-ferguson.

58. Franklin T. Wilson and Howard Henderson, "The Criminological Cultivation of African American Municipal Police Officers: Sambo or Sellout," *Race and Justice* 4, no. 1 (2014): 51.

59. Ibid., 60.

60. *The Glass Shield*, directed by Charles Burnett (Lionsgate, 1995).

61. Jonathan Rosenbaum, *Movies as Politics* (Berkeley: University of California Press, 1997), 164.

62. Amy Abugo Ongiri, "Charles Burnett: A Reconsideration of Third Cinema," *Nka: Journal of Contemporary African Art* 21 (2007): 83.

63. Ed Guerrero, *Framing Blackness: The African American Image in Film* (Philadelphia: Temple University Press, 1993), 162–63.

64. Jared Sexton, "The Ruse of Engagement: Black Masculinity and the Cinema of Policing," *American Quarterly* 61, no. 1 (2009): 55.

65. Ibid., 47.

EPILOGUE

1. "Latino 101," *Cristela*, ABC, aired on March 27, 2015.

2. Sandra Cisneros, *A House of My Own: Stories from My Life* (New York: Vintage Books, 2015), 39–40.

3. Crystal Parikh, *An Ethics of Betrayal: The Politics of Otherness in Emergent U.S. Literatures and Culture* (New York: Fordham University Press, 2009), 1–2.

4. Arnold Rampersad, *Ralph Ellison: A Biography* (New York: Vintage Books, 2008).

5. Ibid., 297.

6. Ibid., 432.

7. Ibid., 513.

8. Ibid., 549.

9. *The Pursuit of Happyness*, directed by Gabriele Muccino (Sony Pictures Home Entertainment, 2006). I say this in jest, though the film clearly relies on proven popular templates for self-fashioning stories. Aside from the race of the protagonist, what is most different about the film from Franklin's *Autobiography* and Alger's most popular novel, *Ragged Dick*, is that the protagonists in both those narratives ascend financially with support from members in their communities and commit themselves to helping others. This dynamic is absent in the film but, as I discuss, is fully present in the book version.

10. Jeffrey Louis Decker, *Made in America: Self-Styled Success from Horatio Alger to Oprah Winfrey* (Minneapolis: University of Minnesota Press, 1997).

11. Chris Gardner and Quincy Troupe, *The Pursuit of Happyness* (New York: HarperCollins, 2006), Kindle edition.

12. Ibid, chapter 5.

13. Ibid, chapter 10.

14. Ibid, chapter 4.

15. Ibid, chapter 12.

16. Ibid.

17. Ibid, Epilogue.

# INDEX

*The Emotional Politics of Racism: How Feelings Trump Facts in an Era of Colorblindness*
Paula Ioanide
2015

*Beneath the Surface of White Supremacy: Denaturalizing U.S. Racisms Past and Present*
Moon-Kie Jung
2015

*Race on the Move: Brazilian Migrants and the Global Reconstruction of Race*
Tiffany D. Joseph
2015

*The Ethnic Project: Transforming Racial Fiction into Racial Factions*
Vilna Bashi Treitler
2013

*On Making Sense: Queer Race Narratives of Intelligibility*
Ernesto Javier Martínez
2012